Western Frontiersmen Series
XXXV

Detail of Valentine T. McGillycuddy
during the 1875 Black Hills Expedition. The sign on
the tent identifies it as McGillycuddy's office. Visible are
surveying equipment and a rifle, and McGillycuddy
holds a sextant. *Courtesy State Archives of the
South Dakota State Historical Society.*

VALENTINE T. McGILLYCUDDY

Army Surgeon, Agent to the Sioux

By
Candy Moulton

THE ARTHUR H. CLARK COMPANY
An imprint of the University of Oklahoma Press
Norman, Oklahoma
2011

ALSO BY CANDY MOULTON

(with Flossie Moulton) *Steamboat, Legendary Bucking Horse: His Life and Times, and the Cowboys Who Tried to Tame Him* (Glendo, Wyo., 1992)

Roadside History of Wyoming (Missoula, Mont., 1995)

(with Ben Kern) *Wagon Wheels: A Contemporary Journey on the Oregon Trail* (Glendo, Wyo., 1996)

The Grand Encampment: Settling the High Country (Glendo, Wyo., 1997)

Chief Joseph: Guardian of the People (New York, 2005)

Roadside History of Colorado (Missoula, Mont., 2006)

Legacy of the Tetons: Homesteading in Jackson Hole (Cheyenne, Wyo., 2007)

Forts, Fights, and Frontier Sites: Wyoming Historic Locations (Glendo, Wyo., 2010)

LIBRARY OF CONGRESS CATALOGING-IN-PUBLICATION DATA

Moulton, Candy Vyvey, 1955–

Valentine T. McGillycuddy : army surgeon, agent to the Sioux / by Candy Moulton.

p. cm. — (Western frontiersmen series ; v. 35)

Includes bibliographical references and index.

ISBN 978-0-87062-389-9 (hardcover : alk. paper)

1. McGillycuddy, Valentine, 1849–1939. 2. Indian agents—South Dakota—Biography. 3. Physicians—United States—Biography. 4. United States. Army—Surgeons—Biography. 5. Surveyors—Dakota Territory—Biography. 6. Dakota Indians—Wars, 1876. 7. Dakota Indians—Government relations. 8. United States. Office of Indian Affairs. Red Cloud Agency—History. 9. Pine Ridge Reservation (S.D.)—History. 10. South Dakota—History—19th century. I. Title.

E78.S63M68 2011

973.8—dc22

[B]

2010034099

Valentine T. McGillycuddy: Army Surgeon, Agent to the Sioux is Volume 35 in the Western Frontiersmen Series.

The paper in this book meets the guidelines for permanence and durability of the Committee on Production Guidelines for Book Longevity of the Council on Library Resources, Inc. ∞

1 2 3 4 5 6 7 8 9 10

Table of Contents

IV. Public Servant

Illustrations

Map

Preface

IN THE COURSE OF my writing career, I have sat in bars and back rooms of writing conferences and disparaged researchers who did not know when to stop investigating and begin writing. I have always understood that a writer is someone who gathers information, sits down in the chair, writes about the subject at hand, and then goes on to a new project. With Valentine T. McGillycuddy, I slipped into the research trap myself, feeling that I could not write the book, or at least could not finish it, until I knew every detail, had every scrap of information possible about my subject. Finally, after eleven years of gathering letters, telegrams, notes, articles, documents, and other sources about McGillycuddy, I told myself, "Quit. Just write the book." And so it is done, in this form, though never finished. For as in all stories of complex, interesting subject matter, another piece of the puzzle always exists. Undoubtedly there are archives I have not sat in and files I have not read that might be stored away in an attic or public facility that I could not visit on this leg of the adventure.

During the years I have spent with McGillycuddy, I've found that he was tall and lean, had blue eyes and a stupendous mustache, and eventually had a neatly trimmed beard and a bald pate. He was stubborn, honest, and meticulous. A child of Irish immigrants, he drank military officers under the table, loved theater and music, danced poorly, had a droopy left eyelid, and displayed a wry sense of humor. He married two women, loved them both intensely, had a daughter, and worked with native people throughout his life. Most of his career was spent at the edge of a frontier in his many roles: topographer and cartographer, doctor, Indian agent.

For the story of Valentine McGillycuddy that I tell here, I give my sincere appreciation for support and encouragement to many people. Dale L. Walker first introduced me to Valentine T. McGillycuddy in 1996, during a program he gave at a meeting of Wyoming Writers Inc. After a two-minute narrative of McGillycuddy's life, Dale turned to the roomful of writers and asked, "Who is going to write this book?" My hand went up almost involuntarily—and the journey began. Along the way I found references to my subject in virtually every history written about Crazy Horse, Red Cloud, and Calamity Jane, and more details in books about George Crook, Richard Dodge, the Northern Boundary Survey, and Wounded Knee. I read the biography McGillycuddy's second wife wrote and pored over hundreds of pages of documents from the period that are housed in institutions across the West.

I am deeply indebted to Bob Clark, the most patient editor in the Western history world, who worked this field of Valentine T. McGillycuddy decades before I even heard the name. Bob not only gave me a contract for this book before I had done the research—indeed, even before I had a decent proposal—but also gave me solid advice on research and writing and in the process became my friend. I also appreciate the efforts of the staff at the Arthur H. Clark Company/University of Oklahoma Press who helped shape the final manuscript.

Research assistance came from the Charles Redd Center for Western Studies, Brigham Young University, Provo, Utah, which provided me with an individual research grant. Paul Hutton, distinguished professor of history at the University of New Mexico, endorsed my request for that funding. I appreciate that from him, as well as his continued support of my work.

A number of other friends and writers, including Terry A. Del Bene, James A. Crutchfield, and Quackgrass Sally, have endured my stories of McGillycuddy over the years, as have my family, Steve, Shawn, Erin Marie, and now Luke. I particularly appreciate the men and women who plowed ground ahead of me in the study of the northern plains: Eli Paul, Jerry Greene, John D. McDermott, Paul Hedren, Jim Potter, Tom Buecker, Robert Larson, Susan Badger Doyle, Kingsley Bray, Joseph Marshall III, Tom Lindmier, Wayne Kime, John H. Monnett, Charles M. Robinson III, and Robert Utley. I am fortunate in that I consider most of them friends as well as professional associates. For assistance I also appreciate Fred Egloff, Kevin Reddy, Don Erickson, and Dr. Roger Blair, the last particularly for his assistance regarding frontier medicine. For their sharp pencils I thank Clark, Hedren, and Walker.

I am indebted to the archival and research staffs at the Harold B. Lee Library, Brigham Young University, Provo; the South Dakota State Historical Society, Pierre; the Fort Robinson Museum, Crawford, Nebraska; the Journey Museum, Rapid City, South Dakota; the Denver Public Library, Western Research Center; the University of Wyoming Coe Library, Laramie, particularly Tamsen Hert; the Great Plains Division of the National Archives, Kansas City, Missouri, particularly Barbara Larsen, Tim Rives, and Allen Perry; the Racine Heritage Museum, Racine, Wisconsin, Dick Ammann, archivist; the Lilly Library, Bloomingdale, Indiana; and the Devereaux Library, South Dakota School of Mines and Technology, Rapid City, South Dakota.

Especially valuable information was provided by Daniel Stanton, of Rapid City, South Dakota, who owned and lived in the house built by Valentine and Fanny McGillycuddy, and Delio Gianturco, Valentine T. McGillycuddy's grandson, of Falls Church, Virginia.

To them and many other people, unnamed here, who provided assistance, thank you!

Julia Blanchard McGillycuddy wrote the only book-length work about her husband, Valentine McGillycuddy. It was published as *McGillycuddy, Agent* by Stanford University Press in 1941 and reprinted under the title *Blood on the Moon* by the University of Nebraska Press in 1990. The initial hardcover volume sold for $3. An early review noted that the book was "written by Mrs. McGillycuddy in her words and style from material dictated to her by her husband."

Newspaper reviewer Roy L. Sharpe, in a lengthy article titled "Factual but Romantic Tale of Frontier Life," published on March 30, 1941, in the *Oakland Tribune*, noted, "Many of the factors, episodes, and incidents that went into the warp and woof of history on the American Frontier in the period beginning with the War Between the States and running through the '70s are introduced."

Initially, Julia wrote a fictionalized account of McGillycuddy's life. "In disgust he protested that if I wrote of his experiences, I must not deviate from the facts," she told Sharpe. In her preface she wrote, "His life was history, he said, and must be exact. He then began relating the story."

Candy Moulton
Encampment, Wyoming
June 2010

I

TOPOGRAPHER

White people should remember
that although an Indian may not learn
to love a white man, he may learn to respect him.

———•◆•———

VALENTINE T. MCGILLYCUDDY

I

An Irish Lad

B LOOD TRICKLING FROM the bayonet wound stained the ground in front of the guardhouse at Camp Robinson that September day in 1877 as men pressed around the downed Lakota fighter. Into the melee pushed a wiry, blue-eyed young doctor. Kneeling, he saw the victim "on his back, grinding his teeth and frothing at the mouth."[1] Already the man's pulse had weakened; his heart failed to strike every beat. Hundreds of Sioux Indians and soldiers surrounding the injured man reeled in shock. The doctor understood that a wrong move could set off full-scale bloodletting.

Valentine Trant McGillycuddy knew this patient well: he was Crazy Horse, war leader of the young Oglala Lakota fighters. The doctor moved back through the crowd, crossed the parade ground, and found the post's commanding officer, Lieutenant Colonel Luther Prentice Bradley. The commander ordered the doctor and the officer of the day, Captain James Kennington, to put Crazy Horse in the guardhouse and give him medical care. The doctor returned to the injured man and with help from Kennington and a nearby Sioux began lifting Crazy Horse. But before they could transfer the patient, it became clear that if they did so, more than one man's blood would be spilled on the grounds of Camp Robinson that day.

Undaunted, the doctor began walking back to Bradley's office to persuade him to change his order. On the way he met angry Indians. American Horse peered down from his mount as McGillycuddy explained that Crazy Horse was badly hurt but would be put in the guardhouse,

---

[1]Clark, *Killing of Crazy Horse*, 125.

where the doctor would care for him. The Indian curtly replied, "Crazy Horse is a Chief and cannot be put in the guard house."[2]

McGillycuddy continued across the parade ground and told Bradley that although his eight hundred men could force the issue and place Crazy Horse in the guardhouse, the consequence would be more violence. The doctor stated the obvious about the Lakotas' mood: "The Indians are ugly." Reluctantly, the colonel agreed to the doctor's plan of moving Crazy Horse into the adjutant's office instead.[3]

Red Shirt and Two Dogs, under direction from American Horse, helped McGillycuddy carry Crazy Horse to the office, where the doctor instructed the men to lay him on the table.[4] The Indians resisted, instead placing their injured leader on a blanket spread on the dirt floor. From his black satchel the doctor retrieved a syringe and a bottle of morphine. He knew the stab wound was fatal; he would keep his patient as comfortable as possible.

As the sun crossed the sky, Old Crazy Horse, also called Worm, father of the injured chief, arrived at the adjutant's office. So did the war leader's Miniconjou uncle, Touch The Clouds, who bent his nearly seven-foot frame to enter the small log building. With the young doctor, the two Indians sat beside Crazy Horse, the man who had been instrumental in the battle that had killed Lieutenant Colonel George Armstrong Custer and his Seventh Cavalry troopers the previous year. Outside, hundreds of Indians and soldiers hunched in denial, anger, disbelief, and fear as day turned to night and Crazy Horse's spirit fled. Kennington, other officers, and an interpreter came and went; guards paced outside.

The doctor who tried valiantly to save Crazy Horse and who insisted on affording him as much dignity and comfort as possible in his final hours already had a history with these Lakotas. Soon, he would become their federally appointed agent. With the change would come additional interaction—and further conflict—with the Indian people who claimed the Black Hills as their homeland. The Lakotas could not have known that McGillycuddy's circle with them had only begun.

———————— ⋅ ◂▸ ⋅ ————————

[2]Ibid.
[3]Ibid., 126.
[4]Ibid., 95.

The doctor had a full-bodied name reflecting both his birthday and his heritage. Valentine Trant O'Connell McGillycuddy had come into the world on February 14, 1849, the son of good Irish stock. The Irish ancestors of his father, Daniel McGillycuddy, originally Catholics, had converted to Protestantism in 1685 after James II ascended to the English throne in a coup that overthrew the Irish government and usurped Catholic-owned land. Although his family held onto its land, Daniel found life in Ireland oppressive under English rule, and in 1842 he boarded a ship bound for the United States.

On the vessel he met Johanna Trant, a Catholic Irishwoman who was traveling with her sister. The Trant sisters, "well educated, religious," and of "spotless purity and propriety of conduct," had watched their parents die and left their grief in Ireland. They were armed with an optimistic spirit and a letter of introduction to the archbishop of New York written by Daniel O'Connell, a relative and, more important, one of the most influential men in Ireland.[5] He was considered the uncrowned king of Ireland for his effort in passing the 1829 Catholic Relief Act. That act, for which O'Connell first campaigned in 1823, removed many of the restrictions placed on Catholics, giving them greater freedom than they had previously known.

Drawn together during the passage, the Protestant Daniel McGillycuddy and the Catholic Johanna Trant wed, passed through New York, and avoided the archbishop. Instead they traveled west to Detroit and eventually settled in Racine, Wisconsin, where in 1849 their second son was born on Valentine's Day. Their elder son, Francis Stewart McGillycuddy, then five, had been born on September 25, 1843.[6] The couple also had a daughter, who died in infancy.[7]

---

[5]Julia B. McGillycuddy, in *McGillycuddy, Agent,* 107–108, quotes a letter written by Daniel O'Connell, dated London, July 11, 1842. This prized letter remains in the McGillycuddy family.

[6]Census, City of Racine, Wisconsin, 1850. This census shows Daniel McGillycuddy, age thirty, working as a grocer. Johanna, thirty-three, was apparently raising the children. Francis, whose age is given as six, was reported as having been born in Ireland, although almost certainly his birth took place after the couple immigrated to the United States. At the time of the census Daniel was attending school in Wisconsin. Younger son "Valentine T.O.C." (Trant O'Connell), age one, had been born in Wisconsin on February 14, 1849. The 1860 census reported similar information, including a birthplace for Francis of Ireland, although at that time both Daniel and Johanna were listed as being thirty-eight years old. It is unclear why both census records give Francis's place of birth as Ireland. Other family data come from Brady, *McGillycuddy Papers,* provided by Delio (Dale) Gianturco, Valentine T. McGillycuddy's grandson.

[7]V. T. McGillycuddy affidavit, March 2, 1929, sworn in Alameda County, California; copy in private collection.

Once living in Racine, with a home on Chatham Street, Daniel McGillycuddy became a store clerk and later had his own business on Main Street.[8] As the *Racine Daily Journal* reported on September 4, 1858, Daniel had opened a confectionary establishment at the corner of Main and Fifth Streets, "where he intends keeping fruit and confectionery of every description."

A year earlier the *Daily Journal* had noted the accidental shooting of one of the boys. "We learn that a son of Daniel McGillicudy [*sic*] was badly wounded in his left thigh on Saturday, by the accidental discharge of a pistol. He, in company with another lad was hunting and when passing through a piece of underbrush, the lock of the pistol caught and went off."[9]

It is uncertain whether the gunshot was to Francis or to Valentine, but perhaps as a result of the child's treatment after this accident, Valentine soon began to take a vivid interest in medicine. As a boy, he treated cats and dogs that had real or perceived medical problems. He began reading medicine at age seventeen at the University of Michigan and ministered to sailors at the Marine Hospital of Detroit for six months after completing his first year of courses. At the hospital he learned to avoid diseases by washing his hands with strong disinfectant, a practice not necessarily common at the time. Meticulous and concerned for his health, he seldom touched a doorknob at the Marine Hospital unless he first covered his hand with the tail of his coat. His ministrations to the sailors, and his subsequent treatment of prostitutes who worked in Detroit's brothels, exposed him to the drudgery of the job.[10]

McGillycuddy became a full-fledged doctor in 1869, at the age of twenty, when he completed his medical school instruction at the Marine Hospital, where he interned and then joined the training faculty. He lectured men who were just beginning their own medical training about the use of splints and bandages. He administered anesthetics and worked with the Detroit city police and ambulance corps, again serving all classes of humanity. But it was his job as a physician at the Wayne County Insane Asylum that was the first step on a

---

[8]Daniel McGillycuddy's confectionery store was variously listed in the Racine business directory as being at 133 Main, 140 Main, and 233 Main.

[9]*Racine Daily Journal*, May 18, 1857.

[10]McGillycuddy, *McGillycuddy, Agent*, 14.

course that would change his life. There he treated patients suffering from a multitude of mental conditions.[11] The misery he confronted pulled the talented young doctor into a pit of his own. To forget what he saw each day, he began drinking—lightly at first, then heavily. His health spiraled downward like that of his patients. His mentor, Dr. T. A. McGraw, watched the young man become pale and scrawny. In 1870 McGraw ordered an examination, diagnosed McGillycuddy with a "weak heart," and told him to recuperate by spending a year working outdoors.[12]

---

[11]Ibid.
[12]Ibid., 15.

2

Into the Outdoors

WHILE STUDYING MEDICINE at the University of Michigan, McGillycuddy had also taken some engineering courses. In 1870, needing new direction after his mentor's diagnosis, he contacted General Cyrus B. Comstock, superintendent of the geodetic survey of the northern and northwestern Great Lakes. Comstock, who had served with the Union balloon corps during the Civil War as the engineering supervisor for all federal balloon operations, hired McGillycuddy—with his limited engineering background but the advantage of his medical training—as an assistant engineer and recorder. He told the young man to prepare for the expedition, which would begin a week later.[1]

The Great Lakes and St. Lawrence Seaway Survey had been established in 1841 under the U.S. Corps of Topographical Engineers, and by 1870 General Comstock had overall command of the effort. The survey involved systematic mapping of the Great Lakes, including shorelines, rivers, shoals, and other navigational hazards. By 1871 McGillycuddy was working as the expedition's surgeon and as an assistant surveying engineer, gaining valuable field experience in both professions and regaining his health. He surveyed the shores of Lake Michigan, spending weeks at the head of a sounding crew, riding an open boat on the choppy waters.[2]

Accustomed to city life, McGillycuddy adjusted to living in the outdoors and sleeping in a tent in all sorts of weather. His body toughened under the experience. But not all his work was done in remote

[1]Ibid.
[2]Shaefer, *Heroes without Glory*, 205.

regions. Highly competent, he attracted the attention of General Comstock, who sent him to Chicago when that city faced its greatest conflagration.

Around nine o'clock on the evening of Sunday, October 8, 1871, flames flicked straw in the cow barn behind Patrick O'Leary's cottage at 137 DeKoven Street on Chicago's West Side. The inferno spread quickly. Within three hours the fire had jumped the river's south branch, and by one-thirty the next morning the business district was ablaze. The inferno continued throughout Monday and was squelched only because it began to rain late that night. By Tuesday morning the devastation was clear: a four-mile-long, one-mile-wide stretch of downtown Chicago lay in ruins. Three hundred people had died, another ninety thousand were homeless, and the total property loss was estimated at between $200 million and $300 million. When it came time to rebuild, McGillycuddy worked with the team that resurveyed the devastated city.[3]

During this period McGillycuddy occasionally visited Detroit, where a twenty-five-year-old blonde, blue-eyed schoolteacher named Fanny Hoyt had caught his eye.[4] But after completing his work in Chicago, he packed his bags and struck into the outdoors again, serving for the next three years on Comstock's survey of the Great Lakes and with the United States Boundary Commission as it surveyed the British-American border. This survey, the final act of the British North American Boundary Commission, was completed in concert with the transfer of the British dominion to Canada.[5]

—— • ◆ • ——

The U.S. Boundary Commission was organized by the secretary of war under the direction of two former Union officers in the Civil War. One was Captain Francis Ulric Farquhar, a Pennsylvanian who

[3]Mansfield, *History of the Great Lakes.*

[4]McGillycuddy, *McGillycuddy, Agent,* 18. Information about Fanny G. Hoyt comes from 1870 census records for Ionia Township, Ionia, Michigan, in which she was listed as living with her parents, Benjamin, age fifty-three, and Risina Hoyt, age forty-nine, and younger brother, Henry, age twenty-one. Her father was listed as a carpenter, and her mother's occupation was "keeping house." Brother Henry was "at school." The census record shows that her father had been born in Connecticut, whereas she, her brother, and her mother were all born in New York. At some point before the 1870 census, McGillycuddy's parents relocated from Wisconsin to Detroit, so he likely met Fanny Hoyt while visiting his own family.

[5]Rees, *Arc of the Medicine Line,* 6.

had been recognized for gallantry and meritorious service during the battles of Williamsburg and Cold Harbor, Virginia. The other, Major William Johnson Twining, was similarly recognized for his service in the battle of Nashville and other engagements in Tennessee and Georgia in 1865. Both were now part of the United States Engineering Corps, and although Farquhar left the Boundary Commission at the end of the 1872 season, Twining remained throughout the project as chief astronomer. Working with them were Captain James Fingal Gregory, an 1861 West Point graduate from New York, who served as the assistant astronomer, and Second Lieutenant Francis Vinton Greene, of Illinois. Greene had completed training at West Point in 1866 and now worked as an assistant to both Farquhar and Twining, taking astronomical readings and directing topographical units. As a member of the topographic corps, McGillycuddy served under Greene's direction. This gave the doctor further field experience and, more important, his first exposure to the indigenous people with whom he would be entwined for the rest of his life.[6]

From 1872 through the summer of 1874, the Northern Boundary Survey team worked its way west, covering 860 miles from Lake of the Woods, where the northern edge of Minnesota meets the southeastern corner of Manitoba, to the Rocky Mountains. Again McGillycuddy took to the outdoor regimen, riding horseback or in a wagon or field ambulance, packing both medical and engineering equipment, enduring heat, cold, wind, rain, snow, and a diet based on wild game, beans, and hardtack. During these first two years with the Northern Boundary Survey, McGillycuddy honed his skills as a topographer, engineer, and surveyor.

Official reports do not mention him by name, but it is clear that he was with the topographical crews in 1873 led by F. Von Schrader, Charles L. Doolittle, and Alfred Downing, who also worked under the direction of First Lieutenant Greene. Von Schrader was in the field through the summer but departed in September, to be replaced by Doolittle, who would remain with the boundary survey until its conclusion in 1875.[7]

---

[6]Heitman, *Historical Register*, 414, 976; Rees, *Arc of the Medicine Line*, 10.

[7]Greene, "Report." In this report, chapter 3 of the official report of the Northern Boundary Survey (Campbell and Twining, *Reports upon the Survey . . .*), Greene cited McGillycuddy's "excellent" work, particularly as a survey crew leader in 1874, thus placing him on the topographical crews for the overall survey.

As part of its duties, the Boundary Commission team would sur-vey the international boundary between Lake of the Woods and the Rocky Mountains, marking it at one-mile intervals on the eastern end. Beyond Fort Pembina, on the Red River where the present states of Minnesota and North Dakota meet Manitoba, the survey-ors marked the line at points three miles apart. Where the boundary passed through timber, they cut a swath and erected monuments of earth or stone. Farther west, in country characterized by open plains, only the earth and stone markers were needed to identify the border. Once the entire route had been surveyed, the temporary stone and earth mound markers would be replaced with iron monuments.[8]

The survey party in 1873 consisted of about fifty men organized into a "tangent," or survey line, party and two topographical parties. They started work at Fort Pembina on June 9 and "continued it without interruption until the 3d of October," Greene reported. They had a twofold mission: to undertake a geodetic survey, which "was necessary to establish and mark the forty-ninth parallel between adjacent astro-nomical stations," and to engage in topographical work to "survey a belt not less than five miles in width."[9]

Their most difficult work in the summer of 1873 occurred during the two weeks it took the engineers to cut "a sight-line in Turtle Moun-tain," east of the Mouse River in present north-central North Dakota. Their surveys covered 384 miles west of Fort Pembina and concluded in western Dakota, just short of reaching the end point for the North-ern Boundary Survey's astronomers, organized under the leadership of Captain James Fingal Gregory.

"The lateness of the season and scantiness of supplies on hand pre-cluded the idea of finishing the topography of the twenty-four miles intervening between us and Captain Gregory's most westerly station," Greene wrote. So he turned east, caught up with a letter from Major William Twining on October 13, and proceeded to Fort Totten, which had been established in 1867 at a site just south of Devils Lake in pres-ent North Dakota.[10]

Earlier in the year the surveying parties had been unable to negotiate a swampy area between Lake of the Woods and the Red River. With

---

[8]Campbell and Twining, *Reports upon the Survey . . .* , 24, 25 (hereafter referred to as "Northern Boundary Survey, official report").
[9]Greene, "Report," 332.
[10]Ibid., 333–34.

colder weather closing in, Twining ordered Greene's party to complete that section, writing in the official report: "A work so difficult could only be justified by the fact that the ground was utterly impossible in the summer. The freezing of the swamps would enable the supply-train to move east as far as the Roseau Lake." In ordering Greene to do the work during winter, Twining knew the crew would face grave weather conditions. "The men, though they had a rather rough summer, most of them, readily volunteered for the winter," he wrote.[11]

Twining, Gregory, and other assistants retired from the field to Detroit, where they worked on the astronomical calculations that were part of the survey. Twining noted that "the topographers being in the field, no work could be done on the maps."[12]

During September and early October, Greene's topographers had been accompanied by an escort of "twenty-five cavalry-men under command of Lieut. R.H.L. Alexander, Seventh Cavalry."[13] As they began their late fall and winter work, they were unaccompanied by military escorts.

Again, no document specifically mentions McGillycuddy as having worked with the survey parties Greene kept in the field that winter, but he almost certainly was there, probably surveying, recording, and making field notes for the topographical maps he would later draw. As the only doctor known to have been with Greene, he likely also spent time ministering to the men's ailments as they endured excruciating cold, undeniably harsh weather, and isolation.[14]

On October 24, 1873, Greene's contingent left Fort Totten, traveling over "an open prairie from which the grass had been burned" and making the trip "in the face of a northerly snow-storm."[15] The group headed toward Fort Pembina under orders to "adopt, without examination, the intermediate astronomical stations observed by the British parties during the preceding winter." The stations, located at West Roseau and Pine Ridge, were twenty and fifty-six miles, respectively,

---

[11]Northern Boundary Survey, official report, 73.

[12]Ibid.

[13]Greene, "Report," 333.

[14]The evidence that McGillycuddy was with the winter survey teams comes from Northern Boundary Survey, official report, in which Twining noted that no maps were drawn during the winter because the topographical crews were still in the field, and from the subsequent reference by Greene that when his party returned to the office in Detroit and went to work in March 1874, McGillycuddy was "draughting."

[15]Greene, "Report," 371.

east of Fort Pembina. In all, the distance to be surveyed by Greene's winter teams covered eighty-nine miles across the northern border of present-day Minnesota.[16]

Once at Fort Pembina, the men repaired tents, tools, and instruments and obtained winter gear: snowshoes, forage, rations, and stoves to be used in their tents. Greene, after considerable discussion with the British Boundary Commission officers and civilians at Fort Pembina, learned that the common means of transportation in the region during the winter were either "wagon-beds mounted on runners or single ox-sleds." Also useful would be dogsleds. Accordingly, he obtained a combination of the forms, including "four government wagons (six mules each), an ambulance (four mules), and three hired teams, two of which were drawn by two mules each, and the other by a pair of oxen." Greene found "a sufficient number of second-hand sleigh-runners, known by the freighters as 'Maineite bobs,' for all the wagons." He hired additional men who would serve as laborers, teamsters, and dogsled drivers, swelling his party to forty-eight.[17]

Although the mules could easily pull loads of up to three tons on hard roads and in soft snow if the footing underneath was solid, Greene soon recognized that it took great skill for a driver to handle the six-mule teams when following crooked roads through the woods. Because trees were difficult to avoid, repairs to the bobs often became necessary after a trip. At least the men found an adequate supply of ash and white oak to do the job.[18]

Fed oats, barley, and wheat, along with about forty pounds of hay each day, the mules weathered the increasingly colder temperatures and long pulls. Greene had one ox team, used by Doolittle's party, but it was inefficient, traveling more slowly than the mules and covering far less distance in a day. Greene said the greatest daily travel for the oxen was eighteen miles, in comparison with forty-four miles for a mule team.

The men believed that once at the swampy area, they would easily be able to complete their surveying, because the ground would be frozen. At first, though, the ground was still soupy. Greene wrote that when he reached the "edge of the Great Roseau Swamp, about

[16]Ibid.
[17]Ibid., 372.
[18]Ibid.

midway between Red River and the Lake of the Woods," he put an "empty sleigh on this swamp, and, in so doing, mired the mules to their bellies, and lamed one quite badly." To his surprise, "it was found that the swamp was not frozen at all, in spite of the fact that we had already had the thermometer down to 35° below zero." The men observed that a heavy layer of tall, thick grass had been bent down by heavy snow, covering the swamp like an insulating blanket that kept the water from freezing.[19]

Knowing he could not use the mules and sleighs on the unstable swamp surface, Greene had his carpenters make toboggans, which in his official report he consistently referred to as "tobogans." But even with these lighter conveyances, more work had to be done to build a "road" over the marsh. Greene sent men on snowshoes out onto the swamp. They packed the snow and grass, pressing it into the water below, where it froze and became "hard enough to hold several tons." This made it possible for the toboggans, pulled by dogs, to cross and eventually, as it became firmer and wider, for the mule teams with their sleighs to cross as well. But there were issues. "It was a not a very safe road," Greene wrote, "for the drifting snow soon filled it up to the level of the surrounding country. It was not distinguishable by the eye, and had to be followed by feeling, the road being hard, and the rest very soft snow. If, by any carelessness, a sleigh got a runner off the road and in the soft snow, the whole was instantly upset, and it required several hours to right it again."[20]

In places where the swamp was heavily timbered, the presence of deadfalls made the large sleighs impractical. Consequently, Greene stockpiled supplies at the Pine Ridge astronomical station and used dogsleds to reach the areas farther east. The five- or six-dog teams, with their sleds, procured at Fort Pembina, cost about $80 each. The sleds were built of hickory or ash and constructed from a single board about half an inch thick, ten inches wide, and ten feet long. Using steam, builders curled the front of the board and attached five transverse cleats to keep the wood from splitting. Each sled was covered with a moose hide placed on the board and wrapped up and around the load before being secured with buffalo thong lashes.[21]

---

[19]Ibid., 373.
[20]Ibid., 374.
[21]Ibid.

A harness made of moose hide hooked the dogs together and to the sled and was adorned with "bells, fancily worked cloth covering the back, flags, &c." Although Greene eventually managed one of the teams himself, for the most part the sled drivers were "half-breeds from Pembina," whom he called "lazy and unreliable." Wielding short whips and flinging across the dogs' backs an "unbroken volley of oaths in bad French," they got a great deal of work out of the canines. These men were themselves "capable of great endurance in running, and possessed of enormous gastronomic powers."[22]

During the winter, Greene divided the teams much as he had during the previous summer and fall. Some, most likely including McGillycuddy, surveyed with Doolittle; others built the mounds necessary to mark the boundary. All had similar gear. They wore close-fitting skullcaps made from two thicknesses of wool blanket lined with flannel, with an attached Havelock, or shawl-like collar, that hung over their shoulders and buttoned beneath the nose, leaving only their eyes and nose exposed. Greene and his assistants wore pants made from moose hide, which cost twice as much as buffalo leather but was more effective, he said, at keeping out the cold and wind. Beneath these leather garments the men had on "a suit of woolen clothes and two or three suits of woolen underclothes." To keep snow out, they tied the bottoms of their pant legs tightly.[23] They donned buffalo-leather coats and moose-hide mittens lined with wool blanket material and featuring gauntlets reaching to their elbows.

Because they tramped through snow and on ice all winter, foot coverings were particularly important. Although Greene began the season with some "Fort Garry 'beef packs,'" he found that once the temperature dipped to twenty degrees below zero, they were "useless, as the leather froze stiff as iron." Then he and the men switched to Sioux-style moccasins, several sizes too large. Before putting on the moccasins, the men encased their feet in "one or two pairs of woolen socks, then a pair of 'neeps' (slippers made of blanket), then a square piece of blanket wrapped several times around the foot from heel to toe." Finally the men added their oversize moccasins, "more to keep the blanket and slipper in place than for any other purpose," Greene said.[24]

---

[22]Ibid., 375.

[23]Ibid., 378.

[24]Ibid., 377.

Working both in wooded areas and in the open, in all sorts of weather, the men suffered considerably, "with frozen ears, noses, and fingers, with icicles hanging from the beard, and with the eyelashes closed from time to time with ice."[25] The frigid temperatures were never more evident than when the men cooked or ate a meal. Using tin cups became a challenge as damp fingers or lips froze to the metal and could be removed only by tearing the skin.

Similar hardships arose from the survey work itself. Equipment such as chronometers had metal parts that absorbed the cold. "If a tangent screw was touched with the bare fingers," Greene wrote, "the instantaneous result was a 'burn,' and not a temporary sensation, but one like that from a hot iron, lasting several minutes."[26] When taking azimuth readings at night, Greene and the man assisting him "found [it] necessary to pitch a tent within a few feet of the instrument, and to keep a bright fire in it. If the wind blew the smoke in the direction of the instrument the observations had to cease, for the fire was essential to thaw out the lamps, keep the observer's fingers flexible, and occasionally unfasten his eye lashes stuck together with frost. The pain in the eyes, from the proximity of the cold eye-piece, was at times very severe, and occasionally brought tears, which congealed in little icicles depending from the eyelashes, and gave the face a comical look, somewhat like that in the children's pictures of Jack Frost."[27]

Possibly, McGillycuddy, with his medical training, treated these forms of frostbite and more serious situations of frozen extremities. In one case a man froze his foot after breaking through ice on an unknown creek.[28] The topographical parties, with which McGillycuddy worked, had less difficulty with their instruments than the astronomical crew, partly because they did their work during the day, when temperatures were twenty to thirty degrees warmer than at night, when the azimuth readings had to be recorded.[29] Even so, the mercury often remained below zero for days at a time. "One night," Greene wrote, "just before going to bed, I looked at the two spirit-thermometers fastened to a tree, and they read 46° and 47° below. In

---

[25]Ibid., 378.
[26]Ibid., 381.
[27]Ibid., 382.
[28]Ibid., 387, 388.
[29]Ibid., 382.

the morning they recorded the astounding temperature of 50° and 51° below zero. Every one had slept soundly, however, inside of skin and blanket bags."[30]

Greene and his assistants each slept in "a bag of buffalo-leather, eight feet long, and about the same in circumference," which was "surrounded, above and below, by several thicknesses of blanket, and the whole was strapped in the canvass bed-cover." The other men bunked four to a bed made of eight layers of Hudson Bay wool blankets as a "mattress," with "four thickness of blanket and a buffalo-robe over them, the whole well tucked in on the sides and ends."[31] These beds were placed in tents that often had three feet of snow piled up around them to form a barricade against wind and cold. Each tent or group of two tents attached end to end had a small stove for heating, which could also be used to warm metal cups and plates or cook basic meals. The food often consisted of bad bread, indigestible "flippers," strong tea, and rich, fat pork.[32]

Greene's party completed the difficult survey of the swampy land between Lake of the Woods and Red River by early February. Using the mule-drawn sleighs, the men then undertook a 180-mile, five-and-a-half-day crossing to Fort Abercrombie, situated on the high west bank of the Red River south of the present city of Fargo, North Dakota. They suffered "greatly on the open prairie from the cold and the driving snow."[33] While the wagon master took the sleighs across country to Saint Cloud, Minnesota, Greene and his other men, including McGillycuddy, finally got out of the cold when they boarded a train that would take them to Saint Paul. On February 20 Greene reported to Major Twining in Detroit "with my assistants and records." There the men settled in to a warm atmosphere, which might have seemed stifling after nearly a year in the field. "From March 1 to June 1, 1874, Mr. Doolittle and Mr. Wilson were engaged in adjusting the stadia-lines; Mr. E. Mahlo and Mr. V. T. McGillycuddy in plotting and draughting."[34]

---

[30]Ibid., 391. Greene also included in his report the official temperature and weather readings taken at Fort Pembina, which were similar to his own recorded temperatures. See Northern Boundary Survey, official report, 394, for those records.

[31]Ibid., 379.

[32]Ibid., 386. "Flippers" was a name for a food we would today consider a pancake, bread dough, or a piece of hard bread (hardtack) fried in hot grease.

[33]Ibid., 392.

[34]Ibid., 334.

3
Mapping the Border

By 1874 McGillycuddy had toughened up physically and mentally and gained significant experience in topographical engineering. As a result, when the Boundary Commission resumed its work in the spring, he joined Wilson and Doolittle as a leader of one of the topographical parties, taking charge of a crew supported by an army sergeant, ten privates, and an orderly. These topographical teams, working under the direction of Lieutenant Greene, also had with them "a party of mound-builders—in all, counting scouts and teamsters, about seventy men."[1]

The topographers, along with the astronomy parties and Major Twining, organized themselves at Fort Buford, beside the Missouri River in western Dakota Territory. Some supplies and workers reached Fort Buford by steamboat. Because they were now entering Northern Plains Indian territory, the Northern Boundary Survey parties would have military escorts, including Companies E and I of the Sixth Infantry, commanded by Captain E. R. Ames. There were also "twelve Indian scouts," according to Greene's report, but he did not identify them by tribe.[2] The previous year, several skirmishes and battles had taken place between the military commands stationed on the northern plains and Indians who considered the region their territory. Among the fighters were Hunkpapas in bands led by Sitting Bull, a man who would become an important tribal medicine man, and his lieutenant-in-training, Gall, who later distinguished himself in fighting the frontier military at Little Bighorn. The conflicts had erupted

---

[1]Ibid., 335.
[2]Ibid.

when surveyors intent on identifying a route for the Northern Pacific Railroad pushed west along the Yellowstone River into the northern tribes' prime buffalo country.[3]

Members of the Seventh Cavalry, commanded by Major Marcus Reno, had been among the units involved in the 1873 battles in the Yellowstone River country. Reno was an Illinois native and West Point graduate who had performed meritorious service for the Union during the Civil War battles at Kelly's Ford and Cedar Creek in Virginia. In 1874, members of the Seventh Cavalry, too, joined the engineering party at Fort Buford.[4]

The Northern Boundary Commission topographers had experienced no problems with Indians during the previous two years. Now, farther west, boundary commissioner and attorney Archibald Campbell, in the official report presented to President Ulysses S. Grant and ultimately to Congress, wrote, "As the commissioners were moving through a country far from civilization, occupied by Blackfeet and other warlike Indians, this large escort was considered necessary to its safety and exemption from molestation."[5]

The combined parties set off from Fort Buford with supplies adequate for six weeks in the field and assurance that "arrangements had been made to have further supplies sent up from Fort Benton."[6] When they reached the "Quaking Ash or Poplar River" on June 25, the parties separated. At the fork of the Poplar River, Greene turned up the east branch and sent teams led by McGillycuddy and Doolittle "to follow and reconnoiter the west fork."[7] This put McGillycuddy in position to run survey lines for what would be the northern border of Montana, sometimes finding the way blocked by massive herds of buffalo.[8]

In his report of February 14, 1877, Major Twining wrote of the area known as Three Buttes or the Sweet Grass Hills of present Montana, saying that it was "the center of the feeding-ground of the great northern herd of buffaloes." He added, "This herd, which ranges from the Missouri River north to the Saskatchewan, made its appearance, going

---

[3]For details see Larson, *Gall;* Utley, *The Lance and the Shield;* Lubetkin, *Jay Cooke's Gamble;* and Frost, *Observations on the Yellowstone Expedition.*
[4]Heitman, *Historical Register,* 824; Northern Boundary Survey, official report, 75.
[5]Northern Boundary Survey, official report, 26.
[6]Ibid., 75.
[7]Greene, "Report," 335.
[8]Shaefer, *Heroes without Glory,* 207.

south, about the last of August. The number of animals is beyond all estimation. Looking at the front of the herd from an elevation of 1,800 feet above the plains, I was unable to see the end in either direction."[9]

Traveling on the fringes of the immense herd were "the half-breeds, Sioux, Assiniboines, Gros Ventres of the prairie, and Blackfeet," Twining wrote. Still, "with all their wasteful slaughter, they made but little impression on [the herd]. It is even said by the traders at Fort Benton that the number of buffaloes is increasing owing to the destruction of wolves in late years."[10]

McGillycuddy himself later recalled, "Buffalo dotted the plains as far as the eye could see. Often we had to suspend astronomical observations at our stations located at 20 mile intervals because the vibrations from the drumming hoofs of herds nearby shook the instruments."[11]

The "large parties of Indians" the surveyors encountered were most often Assiniboines. The Indians "were all friendly, except a few Unkapapas [Hunkpapa Sioux] of Long Dog's band, who threatened a small detachment of troops," the *New York Times* reported, adding that "a little 'moral suasion' induced them to leave."[12]

At times that summer, McGillycuddy's crew traveled with Reno's command. The two men became well acquainted while McGillycuddy located the boundary west from the Marias River in northeastern Montana Territory, where Captain Meriwether Lewis had had his run-in with some Blood Indians in 1806 while returning with members of the Corps of Discovery from their explorations to the Pacific. In 1874, a party of Hunkpapa Sioux led by Sitting Bull rode into the survey camp to inquire whether the government men had seen any buffalo. Major Reno told the Indians where some of the beasts had been spotted, and the hunting party departed.[13]

An astute observer, McGillycuddy no doubt watched the interplay between Reno and Sitting Bull. Those two had not met directly on a field of war, although that was coming. But certainly, animosity had flared between soldiers and Indians on the northern plains in recent years, as in the events of the previous year along the Yellowstone, and particularly after the development of the Bozeman Road through the

---

[9] Northern Boundary Survey, official report, 63.
[10] Ibid.
[11] "Indian Wars Veteran Never Ill in 70 Years," *Oakland Tribune,* February 15, 1934, p. 9.
[12] "The Northern Boundary Survey," *New York Times,* September 21, 1874, p. 4.
[13] McGillycuddy, *McGillycuddy, Agent,* 19–20.

Powder River Basin. Snaking its way from the North Platte River east of Platte Bridge Station, along the front range of the Bighorn Mountains in north-central Wyoming, and then west across Crow country to Bozeman and Virginia City, Montana, this road for gold-hungry emigrants had led to Red Cloud's War, a two-year conflict running from 1866 to 1868. Red Cloud was the primary Lakota war chief at the time, but the fighting gave war experience to others, including Crazy Horse and American Horse, of the Oglala Lakotas, and Dull Knife and Little Wolf, of the Cheyennes. Sitting Bull, meantime, established himself as a war chief and spiritual leader of the Hunkpapas, as did Gall.[14]

Later in the season the surveying teams came across an area believed to have been a battlefield between Blackfeet and Crow warriors. In it lay the bodies of some twenty Crows who had been scalped, their corpses "completely sun-dried and well-preserved." McGillycuddy left his surveying responsibilities long enough to visit the place, later recording that he "got three pairs of femurs, one head [skull]," and one other bone.[15]

———— •‑◆‑• ————

The battles of the first Indian war in the Powder River country had ended when Red Cloud signed a treaty in 1868 at Fort Laramie. Its terms established the Great Sioux Reservation, covering the western half of Dakota Territory and encompassing all of the Black Hills. Hunting privileges, under the terms of the treaty, extended to the tribes in the area north of the Platte River in Wyoming Territory and along the Republican River in Kansas and Nebraska. The agreement noted that the land east of the Bighorn Mountains and north of the North Platte River in Wyoming was "unceded" and therefore reserved for the Sioux. The Bozeman Road was closed, and the military abandoned three forts it had established there—Reno, Philip Kearny, and C. F. Smith.

The treaty conditions provided for clothing for tribal members, to be distributed annually; the establishment of an agency managed by a government-appointed agent; and the construction of buildings

[14]Larson, *Gall;* Larson, *Red Cloud;* Bray, *Crazy Horse.* For the most complete details about the Bozeman Road, see Doyle, *Journeys to the Land of Gold.*

[15]Rees, *Medicine Line,* 291.

including a sawmill, a gristmill, a shingle mill, a schoolhouse, homes for the Indian agent and the agency physician, and buildings for use by the agency blacksmith, carpenter, farmer, miller, and engineer. The land set aside was believed sufficient to allow at least 160 acres for every Indian affected by the treaty. Tribesmen could continue to hunt off the reservation "on any lands north of North Platte, and on the Republican Fork of the Smoky Hill River, so long as the buffalo may range thereon in such numbers as to justify the chase."[16]

In exchange, the Indians agreed not to oppose railroads or roads passing through their land, not to attack or capture travelers or people from nearby settlements, and to withdraw their opposition to military posts—existing or to be built later—south of the North Platte River.[17]

By 1874, however, Indians' hostility toward the railroad survey work had escalated, and new provocations were about to arise. Just as gold discoveries in Grasshopper Creek and Alder Gulch had set off the flood of prospectors to Montana's gold fields and sparked the earlier Sioux conflict, so events were shaping up that would soon launch the Great Sioux War.

As Valentine McGillycuddy slept on the ground, ministered to ailments, surveyed, and kept meticulous notes about topographical features along the United States–British boundary in preparation for drawing maps, to his south Lieutenant Colonel George Armstrong Custer of the Seventh Cavalry led his own party into the Black Hills. Eventually he confirmed what until then had been speculation and rumor: There was gold in the region. Custer's command "consisted of ten companies of the Seventh Cavalry, one each of the Twentieth and Seventeenth Infantry, a detachment of Indian scouts, together with the necessary guides, interpreters, and teamsters, in all about one thousand men. The wagon-train consisted of about one hundred and ten wagons and ambulances, while the artillery was represented by three Gatlings and a 3-inch rifle."[18]

The Northern Boundary Survey teams reconnoitered along the border, surveying and mapping five miles south of the international line. They also mapped rivers and streams in the area that is now

---

[16]Treaty, 1868, Fort Laramie, Wyoming Territory, Article II.

[17]Ibid.

[18]Ludlow, *Report of a Reconnaissance,* 8. A detailed account is contained in "Orders and Circulars of the Black Hills Expedition," RG 393, National Archives and Records Service (NARS), Washington, D.C.

northwestern North Dakota and northeastern Montana. The *New York Times*, in reporting on the Northern Boundary Survey as work concluded that fall, said that "the country operated in this Summer has been of the usual uninteresting and uninviting nature characteristic of Northern Dakota. The marches have been hot, and one's thirst was only to be assuaged with alkali water."[19]

When working, the topographers maintained communication "between front and rear targets and the transit instrument . . . by means of large flags, and the United States Army signal code of three elements." The men carried a card with the alphabet, to ensure accuracy, and developed some additional "special signals." Major Twining wrote, "By this means, and by transporting the targets and men in light wagons, as much as eighteen miles of line has been traced in one day." He added, "The greatest length of chaining in one day was fifteen miles."[20]

The survey lines, called tangents, were identified using stadia rods and a six-inch theodolite, a type of chronometer made by the Würdeman Company of New York. The theodolites had fixed cross-hairs, and the rods could be accurate to fifteen hundred feet. They were more accurate than chains in rough and broken country, and always "more expeditious," Twining noted in his report.[21] As the men worked, they kept angles "by the method of traversing, or 'keeping the azimuths'; each recorded angle being the angle of the line of sight with the true meridian, and were counted from 0° to 360°."[22] To determine the line, the men started from a stake on the tangent where they had determined the azimuth and continued to the next point. They determined vertical angles in order to approximate vertical height in the field, and once they returned to the office, they converted their stadia readings to horizontal and vertical distances by using a set of tables established for such calculations.[23]

The chronometers they used were delicate instruments and so "were habitually transported from station to station in a four-spring wagon, generally, in 1873, incased [*sic*] in a cotton-padded box, but in 1874, under the care of an assistant, on the cushioned seat of the wagon." When in camp, the chronometers were placed in the observatory

[19]*New York Times*, "Northern Boundary Survey."
[20]Northern Boundary Survey, official report, 93.
[21]Ibid., 94.
[22]Ibid.
[23]Ibid.

tent.[24] While Greene's party was in the field during the winter of 1873–74, he often transported the instruments by dogsled. On one particularly harrowing night-time trip in frigid weather, Greene found it necessary to abandon the sled and the dogs, which had played out, and proceed on foot. Before doing so, he wrote, "by the aid of some matches I wound the chronometers (2.15 A.M.); and covered them and the records with the sleigh-wrapper."[25] This last act of protecting the chronometers, in a situation that was dangerous if not life threatening, shows the care necessary to maintain the instruments in order to obtain accurate readings.

By August 20, 1874, the work was complete to the Rocky Mountains. The military escorts, with some of the surveyors, then struck southeast toward Fort Benton, situated on a crook in the Missouri River at the point where the Whoop-up Trail to Canada had been established in 1869 to serve traders hauling goods across the border. By September 3 these men had reached the confluence of the Yellowstone River with the Missouri, "en route to their respective stations for the Winter."[26]

Some of the surveyors, including McGillycuddy's party, which had joined with Greene at the Sweet Grass Hills, remained in the field, "working on the line, so as to complete the work this year if possible," the *New York Times* reported.[27] In his official report, Greene said the combined force of about thirty men turned due south on September 4, "through the Piegan and Blackfoot country, for Fort Shaw, arriving there September 8. The object of taking this route was to reconnoiter the country, and, principally, to run a meridian-line to Fort Shaw for longitude purposes."[28] Once this work was completed, they struck out for Fort Benton. There they found awaiting them eight twenty-five-foot-long Mackinaw boats, made of rough-sawn lumber, which they pushed into the Missouri River for an eighteen-day journey to Fort Abraham Lincoln, near Bismarck, North Dakota.[29]

---

[24]Greene, "Report," 318.

[25]Ibid., 389.

[26]*New York Times*, "Northern Boundary Survey."

[27]Ibid.

[28]Greene, "Report," 336.

[29]Ibid.; also see McGillycuddy, *McGillycuddy, Agent*, 23–24. The *New York Times* reported on September 21, 1874, that "navigation on the Upper Missouri to Fort Benton has ceased for the season, and contracts have been made at Benton, Montana Territory, for the construction of 'Mackinaws'—huge flat-bottomed boats—to be ready by Sept. 10, for transportation of the engineers down the river."

The riverbanks, lined with ashes, oaks, cottonwoods, and other trees, provided cover for elk and buffalo that became meat for the party. On the river, Greene "had charge of the survey of the river, making the astronomical observations myself. Messrs. Doolittle and McGilly-cuddy relieved each other in taking compass-bearings and sketches."[30]

At Fort Lincoln, McGillycuddy met Custer, just back from the Black Hills survey.[31] Although Custer was known for his long hair, at the time his locks were "clipped short at his wife's request as his old rig of long hair and red shirt made him [too] conspicuous a mark for a stray bullet in a fight," McGillycuddy wrote years later.[32] At Bismarck, McGillycuddy settled into a car on a Northern Pacific train headed east, no doubt eager to see Fanny, who had written to him occasionally while he was on the work party in the West.[33] He already knew the big news of the year: Custer's discovery of gold.[34]

The *New York Times,* in an article titled "The Black Hills Expedition," published on August 23, 1874, quoted a dispatch Custer had sent from St. Paul, Minnesota, the previous day, in which he said, "Almost every earth produced gold in small yet paying quantities. . . . It has needed no expert to find gold in the Black Hills, as men without former experience in mining have discovered it at an expense of but little time and labor." Although the region was off limits to prospectors and miners under the terms of the 1868 Fort Laramie Treaty, that did not stop the buzz of excitement, particularly when people heard Custer's account that "gold and silver are found in numerous places, and in quantities so great that with pick and pan a single miner may take out $100 per day."[35]

The engineers passed through Detroit, and there McGillycuddy called on Fanny, whom he asked to marry him. To his delight, she said yes. McGillycuddy then departed for Washington, D.C., where he joined his field companions, including seven other "draughtsmen,"

[30]Greene, "Report," 336.
[31]Valentine T. McGillycuddy to Walter Mason Camp, January 14, 1913, Walter M. Camp Papers, Roll 1, Brigham Young University (BYU).
[32]McGillycuddy to Camp, December 22, 1919, Camp Papers, Mss 57, Roll 2, BYU.
[33]Shaefer, *Heroes without Glory,* 206.
[34]McGillycuddy, *McGillycuddy, Agent,* 23–24.
[35]Ibid.

on November 1 to begin converting his field notes into maps of the northern boundary—a tedious process not nearly as stimulating as gathering the data in the hinterlands.[36]

While McGillycuddy had been resurveying Chicago, traveling the northern latitudes, and recording field notes in preparation for eventually rendering maps of the boundary, another explorer, John Wesley Powell, had launched three boats into the Green River in 1869, beginning a survey of the Colorado River drainage. His first trip nearly ended in disaster: boats overturned, equipment sank into the roiling current of the river, expedition members broke ranks and were subsequently killed by Indians. But Powell fought the terrain and succeeded in traversing the Grand Canyon.[37] He returned to the region for a second expedition in 1871 but was in Washington, D.C., by 1875, directing the Geographical and Geological Survey of the Rocky Mountain Region for the Department of Interior. In the department's offices he found McGillycuddy perched on a high stool, meticulously, laboriously drawing maps.[38]

Would the doctor, with his engineering and cartography skills, accompany another expedition into the West, Powell wanted to know. This time, the area to be explored was on the northern plains: the Black Hills. Although Custer's party had confirmed the presence of gold, the question remained whether it was a substantial reserve or a piddling amount. Ferdinand V. Hayden, in his early survey of the West, had claimed that little gold existed in the Black Hills, but the Custer report suggested otherwise.[39] A new survey to resolve the difference in opinion would be carried out under the direction of Walter P. Jenney, of New York's Columbia School of Mines.

---

[36]Ibid., 24. In the official report of the Northern Boundary Survey, Greene wrote, "The office-work was resumed on the 1st of November, at Washington, and has been carried on, uninterruptedly, to this date. Messrs. Doolittle and Wilson reduced the stadia-readings and adjusted the co-ordinates of the topographical surveys between November 1, 1874 and April 1, 1875. The series of preliminary maps was finished October 1, 1875; photo-lithographic copies were made of each sheet as soon as it was finished. The series of final maps was commenced August 1, 1875, and finished April 15, 1876. The series of reconnaissance maps was begun November 1, 1874; and finished February 1, 1876. Special tracings of various sheets have been made from time to time. The office-force has usually comprised eight draughtsmen." Greene, "Report," 336.

[37]Worster, *A River Running West.*

[38]Ibid., 341.

[39]McGillycuddy to Camp, January 14, 1913. A portion of Custer's report is also included in "The Black Hills Expedition," *New York Times,* August 23, 1874, p. 1.

Although McGillycuddy planned a wedding with Fanny and had maps to draw, it was growing hot and humid in Washington, and he longed for the open spaces and cooler summer conditions he knew he would find in the West. Powell capitalized on the doctor's enthusiasm for returning to the field and found a cartographer who could render McGillycuddy's remaining notes into maps. The beanpole doctor with the steely blue eyes notified Fanny of his new assignment and packed his bags.[40]

---

[40]McGillycuddy, *McGillycuddy, Agent*, 24.

4

Into the Black Hills

THE DOCTOR-TURNED-ENGINEER rode the rails west, arriving in mid-May 1875 at Cheyenne, Wyoming Territory, the former Hell-on-Wheels railroad camp that was metamorphosing into a gold rush launch point. After a short reprieve to "outfit," McGillycuddy bounced and rattled in a stagecoach across ninety miles of dusty prairie to Fort Laramie, where he reported on May 20 at the quarters of Lieutenant Colonel Richard Irving Dodge, of the Twenty-third Infantry. McGillycuddy and the other young men eventually called Dodge "Richard the First."[1]

Once the principals had gathered at Fort Laramie, planning and organization for the expedition picked up steam as a constant stream of soldiers, civilians, and hangers-on found their way to and from the oldest permanent settled area in Wyoming Territory. Begun as a fur trade post in 1834, Fort Laramie became a military post in 1849. Situated beside the Laramie River at its confluence with the North Platte, the fort had been a primary way-station and provisioning point for overland emigrants since 1843. It was near the site of an 1851 treaty made with the Northern Plains Indians and was the place where the 1868 agreement with the tribes had been concluded.

Lieutenant Colonel Luther P. Bradley, commander of the Ninth Infantry at Fort Laramie, who also served as commander of the District of the Black Hills, ordered Dodge to escort the scientific expedition to the Black Hills. Bradley was a Connecticut native who had served with the Illinois infantry during the Civil War and been cited

---

[1]*Oakland Daily Evening Tribune,* April 30, 1875; McGillycuddy, "First Survey of the Black Hills."

for gallantry and meritorious service at the battles of Chickamauga and Resaca, Georgia. Dodge himself, fifty-eight, big-boned, and heavily bearded, had graduated from West Point in 1844, five years before McGillycuddy was born. Besides being considerably older, Dodge had long experience with the infantry, having served in the Twelfth, Thirtieth, and Third Infantries before assuming the position of second in command of the Twenty-third in 1873.[2]

Over a glass of wine with Dodge, McGillycuddy met the leaders of the survey party: geologists Walter P. Jenney and Henry Newton, both from the Columbia School of Mines in New York, and astronomer Horace P. Tuttle, of the Cambridge Observatory in Massachusetts.[3]

The men were an interesting mix of personalities. Twenty-five-year-old Jenney, characterized by his short, curly hair, clipped mustache, thin nose, and prominent chin, served as chief geologist and was de facto leader of the expedition. He previously had spent more than a year in New Mexico and Texas conducting survey work for the proposed Texas and Southwest Railroad.[4] Though "in charge" by most accounts, Jenney was not an effective leader. McGillycuddy called him a "queer chap," and Dodge butted heads with him on more than one occasion. "I think Jenney is an aspiring man—ready to do anything for his own advancement," Dodge wrote in his journal on May 31, adding his impression that Jenney was "very weak, very jealous, and very much disappointed that he has not Military Comd of the Expedition. I think he is a small man & that he will not only try to arrogate to himself every particle of the credit of the Expedition, but will cast slurs on every other member of it who he thinks can in any way come in competition with him."[5]

McGillycuddy, the primary topographer, would eventually spend most of his time in company with chief astronomer Tuttle, whom he called "Old Tuttle." Dodge described Tuttle as a "gentleman of culture refinement & sense," who was "modest, unassuming, quiet devoted to his work & a most agreeable gentleman."[6]

---

[2]Kime, *Black Hills Journals of Richard Irving Dodge*, 7, nn. 10, 11; Heitman, *Historical Register*, 377.

[3]McGillycuddy, in *McGillycuddy, Agent*, 25, reported that Tuttle was with the Naval Observatory in Washington, D.C., but Kime, in *Black Hills Journals*, 55, correctly noted that Tuttle worked for the Cambridge Observatory before serving on the Black Hills Expedition.

[4]Kime, *Black Hills Journals*, 6, n. 8.

[5]Ibid., 55.

[6]Ibid., 55, 56.

By Dodge's account, McGillycuddy ranked third in the engineering party command. "He is smart and bright, well up in his business as a professional map maker, but runs too much to fancy & pretty."[7] In fact McGillycuddy was meticulous in his notes and eventually rendered a striking relief map of the region that was published with the official report, although he said it was "a rather rough and rush production."[8]

Newton, sporting a sweeping mustache that set off his square chin, served as assistant geologist and earned respect from both McGillycuddy and Dodge for his solid knowledge and quiet manner.[9] Although officially called the Black Hills Expedition, the project also became known familiarly as the Newton-Jenney Expedition, making it semantically clear at least who had the greater experience. Initially, Cleveland Newberry was hired as the party's naturalist, but when he became ill after inhaling the arsenic he used to preserve some bird skins, he resigned from the expedition.[10]

The Black Hills Expedition had already contracted with José Merrivale to serve as its official guide and scout when a red-headed, red-whiskered, blue-eyed fellow called California Joe showed up at Fort Laramie with his hound dog, seeking the job. The six-foot, three-inch scout had been born Moses Embree Milner in 1829, near Stanford, Kentucky. He drifted west during the California gold rush, homesteaded in Oregon, and then filled a number of army scout positions. California Joe had scouted for Custer on the southern plains in 1868 and rejoined Custer for the 1874 survey of the Black Hills.[11] Custer once said that "a huge sombrero, or black slouch hat[,] A soldier's overcoat, with a large circular cape, a pair of trousers, with the legs tucked in the top of his long boots, usually constituted the make-up of the man whom I selected as my chief scout. He was known by the euphonious title of California Joe. No other name seemed ever to have been given him, and no other name appeared to be necessary."[12]

When the Newton-Jenney Expedition was organized, California Joe was an obvious choice for frontier scout. McGillycuddy would

[7]Ibid., 56.

[8]McGillycuddy, "First Survey."

[9]McGillycuddy to Camp, January 14, 1913; Kime, *Black Hills Journals*, 231, 240.

[10]Walter P. Jenney to E. P. Smith, commissioner of Indian affairs, May 22, 1875, quoted in Turchen and McLaird, *Black Hills Expedition of 1875*, 13.

[11]Thrapp, *Encyclopedia of Frontier Biography*, vol. 2, vol. 4: 993–94; Elmo Scott Watson, "California Joe, a Great Frontiersman," *The News*, Fredericksburg, Iowa (no date).

[12]DeBarthe, *Life and Adventures of Frank Grouard*, 335.

come to know Milner–California Joe well, later calling him "one of our most reliable scouts, good natured, kind and not quarrelsome."[13] Dodge would eventually say that Merrivale knew nothing more about the Black Hills than a "New York Dandy," although he admitted the man could be useful as an Indian interpreter.[14]

The seventeen-member expedition also had a naturalist, a photographer, a head miner, and ten laborers, all under the auspices of the Office of Indian Affairs. It became a joint expedition with the Department of War by virtue of its military escort, which consisted of six companies of the Second and Third Cavalries, which had a Gatling gun and a twelve-pounder howitzer, and additional companies of the Ninth and Fourteenth Infantries, all commanded by Colonel Dodge.[15] At times the older commander butted heads with the young scientists. Both Jenney and McGillycuddy were only twenty-six, but they were firm in demanding support from Dodge and his military contingent. For the most part he complied, granting McGillycuddy the use of pack mules and bowing to Jenney's requests regarding campsites. On occasion, though, Dodge could not be buffaloed, as when Jenney wanted to follow a line along the 104th latitude in order to establish a camp at the western edge of the Great Sioux Reservation. Because McGillycuddy and Tuttle could not determine accurate readings, Dodge eventually demanded that they abandon their efforts to remain precisely on that line, and Jenney relented.[16]

The purpose of the expedition, McGillycuddy later confirmed, was to conduct "an independent survey or exploration ordered by Gen. [Ulysses S.] Grant to settle the disputed point as to whether gold existed in the Black Hills in paying quantities. Gen. Custer in his expedition of 1874 having claimed to have so found it while F. V. Hayden in charge of our U.S. Geological Surveys at Washington claimed that he had thoroughly examined this country many years before and that the 'geological formation' was such that gold could not exist in paying quantities."[17]

---

[13]McGillycuddy to Camp, October 9, 1912, Camp Papers, Roll 1, BYU.

[14]Kime, *Black Hills Journals*, 82.

[15]Bourke, *On the Border with Crook*, 160, 164; Kime, *Black Hills Journals*, 6. The artillery is referenced in Bourke, 160, and also in Dodge's December 22, 1875, report to the assistant adjutant general, Department of the Platte, Omaha, quoted in Turchen and McLaird, *Black Hills Expedition*, 31.

[16]Kime, *Black Hills Journals*, 16, 59. The line Jenney sought to follow was the boundary between Wyoming and South Dakota.

[17]McGillycuddy to Camp, January 14, 1913. At this time, Grant was in office as president of the United States.

The *New York Times* reported that the expedition "is to determine whether gold exists there or not. As we understand it, the Government not only desired to settle that disputed point for the benefit of gold-hunting mankind, but in order to find the real value of the territory." The paper editorialized in the news column, "If we are to pay the Sioux for the extinguishment of their title to the reservation, we do not want 'to buy a pig in a poke,' to use the rustic figure. The Indians are reported to be favorable to the objects of the expedition, and will aid it. We must suppose the Sioux are an honest people. If they were as unscrupulous as some of our own 'superior race,' they could easily put a fictitious value on their hunting-grounds by a little judicious 'salting' of the land."[18]

On May 25, 1875, twenty miles north of Fort Laramie, the Black Hills Expedition set its first field camp, with the officers sandwiched between the soldiers' quarters and a sutler's store holding supplies such as ammunition, tobacco, patent medicines, and groceries. There were 452 men, 71 wagons, 376 horses, and a beef herd of more than 130 head.[19] Five newspapers had made arrangements for regular reports from correspondents traveling with the party, each publication wanting to be the first to publish confirmation that the Black Hills had gold in them. The news dispatches would come from Second Lieutenant John G. Bourke, Third Cavalry, who would report to both the *Cincinnati Gazette* and the *San Francisco Alta California;* from Captain Andrew S. Burt, of the Ninth Infantry, sending messages to the *New York Tribune;* J. R. Lane, acting assistant surgeon with the scientific party, writing for the *Chicago Tribune;* Reuben B. Davenport reporting to the *New York Herald;* and Thomas C. MacMillan, whose work went to the *Chicago Inter-Ocean.*[20] Bourke had begun his military service with the Pennsylvania Cavalry during the Civil War, entered West Point in 1865, and was attached to the Third Cavalry as a second lieutenant in 1869. He traveled extensively with General George Crook, maintained official journals, and left a sweeping record of the Indian wars on both the northern and southern Great Plains.

During the summer and fall, these men vied for first placement of news from the Black Hills, often to the consternation of Dodge,

---

[18]*New York Times*, March 29, 1875, p. 4.
[19]Kime, *Black Hills Journals*, 13. In his official report, Dodge said there were 363 men, 376 horses, 4 ambulances, 61 wagons, 397 mules, and 134 head of beef cattle. Henry Newton and Walter P. Jenney, in their *Report on the Geology and Resources of the Black Hills of Dakota*, 20, reported a contingent of 400 men and 75 wagons.
[20]Kime, *Black Hills Journals*, 8.

who considered most of them pests and Burt downright despicable. Because they were interested in news about gold fields, the writers attached themselves to Jenney and Dodge. McGillycuddy, Tuttle, and Newton "fitted in well together, but we lacked the publicity reporters, who stuck to headquarters," McGillycuddy said.[21]

Among the "privates" with the troops was a woman—a lanky civilian named Martha Jane Dalton, also known as Martha Jane Canary. Although told to leave the camp, she would depart in the morning, only to worm her way back into the troop ranks by nightfall, adding her capable hands to theirs in handling the teams and managing the wagon train accompanying the party.[22] She was soon to become better known as Calamity Jane, a sobriquet she may have earned during the Black Hills Expedition.

When McGillycuddy first spied Jane Dalton strolling across the parade ground at Fort Laramie on May 20, 1875, she had on spurs, chaps, and a sombrero.[23] At the time, he was sharing a bottle of wine with Colonel Dodge, Henry Newton, and Horace Tuttle. When the doctor asked about the young woman, Dodge identified her as a "regimental mascot" who "didn't know the meaning" of the word *morals*.[24]

Post trader John Hunton and Sergeant John Q. Ward both said that Jane had worked at the road ranch—an establishment that offered supplies and often the services of a prostitute—six miles west of Fort Laramie operated by Adolph Cuny and Julius "Jules" Ecoffey. She had also worked at a road ranch near Fort Fetterman, and she had been with other military expeditions, Hunton and Ward said.[25]

McGillycuddy became acquainted with the woman following an incident at Fort Laramie not long after he arrived there. The troops considered McGillycuddy, coming as he did from Washington, D.C., a dandy and set out to prove his ineptitude when they assigned him a spirited black horse to use for the expedition. Before the journey

---

[21]McGillycuddy, "First Survey"; McLaird, *Calamity Jane.*
[22]McGillycuddy, *McGillycuddy, Agent,* 32–33.
[23]Ibid., 25–27.
[24]McLaird, *Calamity Jane,* 36.
[25]Ibid., 35; Brown, *Hog Ranches of Wyoming,* 30. McLaird incorrectly identified the Six Mile Hog Ranch as being near Fort Fetterman; in fact it was west of Fort Laramie. There was a road ranch near Fort Fetterman, and it is possible that Calamity Jane spent time there, as well as at other establishments nearer Fort Laramie. "Hog ranches," or road ranches, operated at sites from three to six miles from the fort. They dispensed liquor, some food, and the services of women.

began, the twenty-six-year-old topographer, pale and pasty after his winter of map drawing, decided to test the animal. He mounted, trotted up the hill away from the post, casually placed the reins over one arm, and started to remove his coat when the horse bolted, took the bit in his teeth, and rocketed across the prairie. McGillycuddy grabbed the reins and pulled back hard even as he leaned forward over the horse's streaming mane. His hat flew off as he sawed the bit, eventually bringing the horse under control some distance from the fort. Returning for his hat, McGillycuddy found that it had been knocked from his head by a low-hanging telegraph wire. Had he not been bent low over the horse's neck, he might have been garroted.

Back at the fort, flushed but in full control of the black horse, he returned the animal to the stable and went to his tent. There, Jane found him and inquired about his ride. He began telling her of the incident, and she nodded knowingly. The quartermaster had given him the unruly black horse, she said, "jest because he thought you was a city guy who didn't know how to ride."[26] It was the kind of prank the soldiers would pull on a rookie, Jane said, but they hadn't seen the low wire.

Although Jane pressed McGillycuddy to put in a word on her behalf with Colonel Dodge to be allowed to accompany the expedition, the doctor-topographer declined. Yet when the march north began, an "unaccounted for young private" trailed in the expedition's wake. It didn't take long for the "private" to be identified as Calamity Jane.[27]

When the Black Hills Expedition wound its way away from the bottoms along the Laramie River at Fort Laramie, McGillycuddy was astride the black horse, having shown both the animal and the troops he could control the fiery steed. Soldiers and scientists marched steadily north into the Black Hills, where a permanent camp was established on June 23 on the east fork of French Creek.[28] From that point, "Prof Jenney would go off somewhere hunting for gold."[29] McGillycuddy, accompanied by "Old Tuttle," rode the black beast from the French Creek camp on daily surveying excursions, recording his observations in pencil in a small brown notebook.[30] In the course of his work, he named many of the streams and other physical features throughout

---

[26]McLaird, *Calamity Jane*, 28–29.

[27]Ibid., 36; McGillycuddy, *McGillycuddy, Agent*, 25–29.

[28]McGillycuddy, *McGillycuddy, Agent*, 28.

[29]McGillycuddy, "First Survey."

[30]One of McGillycuddy's Black Hills Expedition field notebooks is held in the Valentine T. McGillycuddy Collection at the Devereaux Library, South Dakota School of Mines and Technology, Rapid City. Another is at the Journey Museum in Rapid City.

the Black Hills, adding to the information provided on a map of the region prepared by Captain William Ludlow of the Corps of Engineers for the Custer expedition of the previous year.

Although McGillycuddy had beaten the soldiers at their own game when they tested his horsemanship, they weren't through challenging him yet. The young doctor, who described himself as being on the "long, hollow" order at six feet and 125 pounds, with a twenty-eight-inch waistline, nevertheless showed the military escort that he could match them drink for drink when they concocted a scheme to force him under the proverbial table.

"The game commenced" once the expedition reached a camp beside Beaver Creek. McGillycuddy said it started "with toddies two parts water and one part whiskey, then two even parts, and finally two of whiskey and one water." Drink after drink, McGillycuddy proved that an Irishman could keep up with the boys in uniform. "I kept on while one by one they hung up in their hammocks or flopped upon the ground." When the drinking bout ended, McGillycuddy returned to the engineers' camp, where, he later wrote, Colonel Dodge found that "the long, thin doctor . . . had stood the ordeal better than any of his officers! From that time on my standing was thoroughly established."[31]

McGillycuddy and his assistants were all "well mounted" as they made what he called "meander surveys" in the valleys, sometimes traveling upward of twenty miles in a day. Initially his survey party, at the insistence of Colonel Dodge, who knew of the potential for Indian attacks, traveled with a wagon train for support. But often the surveyors and the wagons didn't meet up with each other before nightfall, "with the result that old Capt. Tuttle, myself and assistants, had to go without supper, bed or breakfast."[32] Showing his force of will, McGillycuddy convinced Dodge to allow his party to travel with only a small escort and supplies hauled on eight pack mules.

"That expedition was credited with being the most rapid and accurate survey ever made by the Government, considering the amount of ground covered and the facilities afforded us; I was young then—and ambitious," McGillycuddy wrote in 1928. "It ought to have been made into a moving picture, with its admixture of the flotsam and jetsam of civilization."

Different lieutenants assisted McGillycuddy, which gave them experience with the field surveys. Before each departure, the officers asked

---

[31]McGillycuddy, "First Survey."
[32]Ibid.

a routine question: Would this be a one-jug or a two-jug trip? They were wondering how much whiskey they should take along. Once, on a "one-jug" trip, the party rode toward base camp only to halt at Custer Peak. "I suggested to Mr. Newton and Capt. Tuttle," wrote McGillycuddy, "that being so near, we had better make the summit; while Newton worked up the geology, Tuttle could observe the stars for latitude, and I would shoot the distant peaks and close up the triangles. However, this overstayed our time two days and ran the lieutenant short of whiskey." During the night the lieutenant filled the empty whiskey keg with a small amount of water from his canteen, "shook the keg around to soak some flavor out of the wooden staves, and drank it with a sigh of relief." The following night the party was back in base camp, "where there was a reserve against such contingencies."[33]

During McGillycuddy's early years in the West, drinking was common practice, and he'd had his own experiences with alcohol as a young doctor. "A man who could not or would not drink on the frontier was usually not considered fit company," he wrote years later. "In marching with the cavalry it was our custom to halt wherever the end of the hour overtook us, dismount, loosen up the saddle [girths], unbridle and let the horses rest and graze for about ten minutes, while all officers gathered at the 'ambulance' and passed the bottle." This hourly routine meant that a man consumed "considerable liquor during a 25-mile march."[34]

———— • ◆ • ————

During the expedition, Calamity Jane stuck close to one of the men, variously identified as Sergeant Shaw, of Company E, Third Cavalry, or Sergeant Frank Siechrist.[35] Once found with the soldiers, Calamity was expelled from camp. Undaunted, she began working with the civilian teamsters and retained her tenuous position with the expedition, having made quite an impression on most of the men. One of them was acting assistant surgeon J. R. Lane, who had a contract to send articles from the expedition for publication in the *Chicago Tribune*. Accordingly, in his dispatch published on June 19, 1875, he wrote of the female teamster. "Calam is dressed in a suit of soldier's blue, and straddles a mule equal to any professional blacksnake swinger in the army," he reported. "Calamity also jumps upon a trooper's horse and

[33]Ibid.
[34]Ibid.
[35]McLaird, *Calamity Jane*, 37.

rides along in the ranks, and gives an officer a military [salute] with as much style as the First corporal in a crack company."[36]

Thomas C. MacMillan, writing for the rival *Chicago Inter-Ocean,* offered similar observations. He noted Jane's "reputation of being a better horse-back rider, mule and bull-whacker and a more unctuous coiner of English, and not the Queen's pure either, than any man in the command."[37]

McGillycuddy himself said she was "the only woman in the party, dressed in soldiers clothes, rode a horse astraddle, [and] could drink and swear 'like a trooper.'"[38] Years later he wrote a version of what he believed to be Jane's early history, saying that she was the "daughter of an enlisted soldier named Dalton" who resettled on La Bonte Creek west of Fort Laramie after being released from his duties. There, Dalton was killed and his wife was "shot in the eye with an arrow, destroying the sight, removing the arrow with her own hand, she placed her one [year] old daughter on her back and escaped." Several days later she arrived at Fort Laramie, "a mere skeleton of former self, her clothing in shreds, and in a short time expired."[39]

Then, McGillycuddy wrote, Jane was adopted by a soldier and his wife, who "prefixed to her name Jane Dalton, the word 'Calamity' so hence forth she was known as Calamity Jane."[40] The child spent her days at Fort Laramie, and by the time McGillycuddy met her in 1875, when she was about fifteen, she had become the "pet of the fort," he said. "She was something like Topsy in *Uncle Toms Cabin,* she was not exactly 'raised she growed.'"[41]

As she had been known to do at the road ranches and would later undertake on other military expeditions, Calamity Jane spent time tending wounds and ailments and mending clothes for the men. But as McGillycuddy noted, she wasn't one to restrict herself to domestic duties and would also leave camp, hunt down a deer or antelope, and haul the meat back to the cook fires. "She staid [*sic*] with us all summer and returned with us to Laramie in the Fall. She was a typical frontier camp follower, a type by herself, loud and rough in her ways, but kind

[36]*Chicago Tribune,* June 19, 1875.

[37]*Yankton Daily Press and Dakotan,* July 6, 1875.

[38]McGillycuddy to Camp, March 12, 1913, Camp Papers, BYU, Roll 1.

[39]McGillycuddy to editor, *Rapid City (South Dakota) Journal,* October 1, 1924; copy in South Dakota State Historical Society Archives.

[40]Ibid.

[41]Ibid.

hearted, always ready to help or nurse a sick soldier or miner, and ready to go on a spree when necessity required or opportunity offered."[42]

"She had no particular use for a citizen," McGillycuddy wrote, "but anybody with a blue coat and brass buttons could catch Calamity."[43]

Jane gave assistance, aid, and comfort on several levels, and McGillycuddy would name Calamity Peak for the intrepid young woman who wormed her way into the Black Hills Expedition and into some of the men's hearts.

Colonel Dodge remained in the base camps—Camp Jenney, on Beaver Creek in the western Black Hills; Camp Harney and Custer City, both along French Creek; and later Camp Crook, south of Rapid Creek. While he spent most of his time hunting and writing a book manuscript, the scientists were constantly roaming.[44]

Jenney most often worked with a crew of laborers. Tuttle, Newton, and McGillycuddy usually traveled in tandem, escorted by a troop of cavalry with wagons initially and eventually using McGillycuddy's hard-won pack mules to negotiate the difficult terrain of the Black Hills. They worked along various drainages and on July 25 set out to explore the highest point in the hills, Harney Peak. To their knowledge, no one had preceded them to the top of the rocky outcrop. Custer had tried the previous year but failed to summit when faced with "a mass of granite 40 feet in height, with perpendicular sides," and Dodge had made an attempt earlier that summer. The party found cartridges at the base of the peak, but no evidence of any trail up its face.[45] After

---

[42]McGillycuddy, *McGillycuddy Agent*, 38.

[43]McGillycuddy to editor, *Rapid City Journal*.

[44]Dodge's subsequently published book was *The Plains of North America and Their Inhabitants*. He also used his writings in preparing his official report of the expedition and for a second book, *The Black Hills*.

[45]Turchen and McLaird, *Black Hills Expedition*, 5. W. R. Wood, who was with Custer in the Black Hills, wrote on July 31, 1874: "Leaving the horses at the foot of the clear granite, the ascent was made on foot. Halting to rest and lunch, another summit, two or three miles west, was seen, rising higher than the one we were on." At the first summit Custer "fired a salute of three shots and the party drank to General Harney's health from canteens of cold coffee." The party then proceeded to the higher peak and ascended it. "While on the highest point we drank to the health of the veteran, out of compliment to whom the peak was named." Yet once there, they again spied an even higher peak, a mile or more to the west. They attempted an ascent but the sheer-sided granite "forbade an attempt to scale [it] without the aid of ropes and ladders." Custer's order and dispatch book, August 2, 1874, 38–39, quoted in Turchen and McLaird, *Black Hills Expedition*, 303–304.

reconnoitering the final ascent, McGillycuddy had a tree cut and wedged in a crevice leading to the peak. Leaning his back against the tree and placing his feet against the solid granite opposite, he began inching toward the top of the mountain. Twenty feet later he emerged at the summit, to be followed by Newton and Tuttle.[46]

The view from the peak astounded McGillycuddy and gave him an appreciation for the Black Hills that would stick with him the remainder of his life. He and his companions took in the sweeping vista and then signed their names on a card, which they placed in an "empty pickle jar" with a note inviting subsequent climbers to contact them.[47]

The topographer and his companions spent the afternoon assembling a pyre of firewood on the peak, hauling it hand over hand from a readily available source at the base of the peak. "After dark we touched it off, alarming the troops, miners, scouts, and probably also the Indians outside of the Hills. It was reported for several days afterward that the supposed 'signal fire,' seen for many miles over the surrounding hills and plains country, gave the general impression that the Indians were again on the warpath—easily believed because of the state of unrest at the time throughout that region."[48]

"We made only one ascent of Harney Peak, the key of the Black Hills for astronomical, altitude and triangulation purposes," McGillycuddy wrote. "The Sioux named it *Wakan Tonka Wakinyan Tipi* (Lodge of the Thunder God)—*Wakan*, Mystery; *Tonka*, Great; *Wakinyan*, Thunder; and *Tipi*, Lodge. Thunder storms are very frequent through all that region."[49]

Tuttle wrote that the "observations on Harney were all made on the *highest* point, which gave us much trouble and risk of life and limb to reach."[50] On July 29, John Gregory Bourke, aide-de-camp to General George Crook, camped five or six miles from Harney Peak. He noted that it was "a comparative insignificant and decidedly pugnosed butte, of granite rock, barren of timber, which looks ashamed of its own pretensions in presence of people who have traversed the loftier ridges beyond it."[51]

---

[46]"Final Resting Place," *Oakland Tribune*, October 3, 1939.

[47]McGillycuddy, *McGillycuddy, Agent*, 39; "On Height He Pioneered," *Oakland Tribune*, October 19, 1940.

[48]McGillycuddy, "First Survey."

[49]Ibid.

[50]Jenney, *Geological and Geographical Survey*, 548.

[51]Robinson, *Diaries of John Gregory Bourke*, 190.

To conduct their work, the men had an array of instruments. As he had done on the Northern Boundary Survey, McGillycuddy worked as topographer, mapping and recording with the use of a transit theodolite, an astronomical sextant, a lunar sextant, and two artificial horizons (stadia rods), all purchased from Stackpole and Brother in New York City. Once in the "rough country," he found that the "great weight" of the theodolite was a hindrance to the work. This had been expected, but as Tuttle noted in the official report of the expedition, "a lighter one could not be procured."[52]

Tuttle had purchased a marine chronometer, model number 1572, from the New York store of T. S. and J. D. Negus, where he also bought a Sidereal pocket chronometer and arranged a loan of a Parkinson and Frodsham marine chronometer, model 3192.[53] For barometric work the team also had "two mountain barometers (mercurial), five aneroid barometers, and a number of thermometers." Regular readings were taken in camp, and the mercury barometers were even transported to "the highest points of all, Harney and Terry Peaks."[54]

Tuttle intended to determine latitudes by observing occultations, or the eclipsing of light from the moon or stars, but as he noted, "unfortunately the only two good occultations which occurred during our presence in the Hills, vis *Scorpii,* on June 16, and *Virginis,* on August 6, were both lost." In June Tuttle was prepared for the event when he "had the mortification to see the moon sink behind the western slope of Lookout Mountain *five* minutes before the occultation took place." Two months later he lost the opportunity to view the stars "by the failure of our ambulance containing my telescope to meet us at our appointed rendezvous." The inability to make these observances deeply affected Tuttle, a true scientist, and he called them "disheartening to me in the extreme."[55]

On July 2, 1875, McGillycuddy, lean, tanned, and sporting a long, dark, shaggy beard and full mustache, came into camp from one of his surveying forays into the hills. Back among the soldiers, he visited with Colonel Dodge, who noted in his journal on July 3 that

[52]Jenney, *Geological and Geographical Survey,* 544.
[53]Ibid., 543.
[54]Ibid., 547.
[55]Ibid., 545 (emphasis in original).

McGillycuddy "has ten times the sense that Jenney has."[56] Following
a short respite in camp, McGillycuddy, wearing a slouch hat, set out
on his black horse, carbine in a sling on his saddle, for another ten-day
mapping venture. He took with him two of the four wagons available
to the Newton-Jenney party, no doubt having been able to comman-
deer these conveyances because of the favorable impression he made
on Colonel Dodge.[57]

By July 10, Dodge had reports that the men in the field had observed
evidence that Indians, too, were roaming the Black Hills. The country
near the Cheyenne River had burned, the blaze reportedly started by
Indians. Just as likely, this was a natural fire caused by a lightning
strike, as is common in the Black Hills when summer grasses begin to
cure and lightning storms sweep the region. In a letter to Edward P.
Smith, commissioner of Indian affairs, written on June 22 at the camp
on French Creek, Newton said the party had seen little Indian sign
and few trails, indicating that the tribesmen "rarely visit the interior
Park Country except to cut lodge poles, the game being most abundant along the foot hills."[58] Even so, when Colonel Dodge rode into
the area he had along a "howitzer and a gatling gun" as "protection
against the Indians."[59]

Newton and McGillycuddy, whom Dodge called "The Scientifics,"
again returned to base camp by July 15. They reported that their field
time had been difficult, because of the rugged terrain they had traversed. "McG says he has a good map," Dodge reported.[60] The readings had been made using "stadia, odometer, or timing as the nature
of the ground would permit," McGillycuddy wrote to the commissioner of Indian affairs on July 31, 1875.[61]

Using Harney Peak, Custer Peak, Bear Butte, and Terry's Peak for
triangulation, McGillycuddy determined distances and locations. He
verified the distances using astronomical observations taken at night
by Tuttle.[62] "So accurate were the courses run by the topographer,"
Tuttle wrote, "that the differences of latitude found by observation,

[56]Kime, *Black Hills Journals*, 116.

[57]Ibid., 117.

[58]Turchen and McLaird, *Black Hills Expedition*, 14–17.

[59]Ibid., 12.

[60]Kime, *Black Hills Journals*, 128.

[61]McGillycuddy, report of July 31, 1875, quoted in Turchen and McLaird, *Black Hills Expedi-
    tion*, 20–22; also Newton and Jenney, "Report on the Geology," 546.

[62]Ibid.

and that platted from course and distances, seldom varied by more than a few hundred yards in a run of twenty-five miles."[63]

It was raining on Saturday, July 17, when the explorers set out to investigate and map French Creek, and there would be more rain throughout July and August. The summer passed with McGillycuddy making regular five- to ten-day excursions into the Black Hills, taking readings, writing notes in his brown pocket notebook, and sketching the basic topographical features. In camp he visited frequently with Dodge, reporting on conditions, the terrain, and occasionally the loss of pack animals. On August 7, Dodge noted that McGillycuddy and Second Lieutenant James E. H. Foster, a Pennsylvanian with the Second Cavalry, had "lost their outfit entirely."[64] As a result, they had gone without provisions for a full day. Dodge sent troops out to find the missing wagons and "hunt up & bring in all the lost of that party."[65]

This "loss" of the outfit came about partly because of rough terrain and partly because Jenney failed to adequately support the explorers. Dodge noted, "The Scientists are all mad as March hares at Jenney, & loud are the swares 'swored' at him today—By his tom fool arrangemts 3 of his party went without food for 24 hours & slept without bedding last night."[66] McGillycuddy later wrote of the incident that "after a good deal of argument with the Colonel, I managed to secure eight pack mules, and a small escort which always kept along with me."[67]

The exasperation of working with the disorganized Jenney shows up in Dodge's journal: "He races over the country like one possessed, breaking down mules & if I don't put a stop to it he will cripple me seriously."[68] The colonel had no such concerns about Newton or McGillycuddy, and in taking command of the situation, he placed McGillycuddy in charge of a pack train while taking "every pack mule away from Jenney himself."[69] Just a week later, the tension had returned among the scientific party—so much so that McGillycuddy was ready to depart the camp once and for all. But before turning his back on the expedition, he went to the military leaders, who stripped Jenney

---

[63]Jenney, *Geological and Geographical Survey,* 546.
[64]Kime, *Black Hills Journals,* 160; Heitman, *Historical Register,* 431.
[65]Kime, *Black Hills Journals,* 160.
[66]Ibid., 161.
[67]McGillycuddy, "First Survey."
[68]Kime, *Black Hills Journals,* 162.
[69]Ibid.

of further responsibility and thus encouraged the doctor-topographer to remain on the job.[70]

As summer turned into fall, the mapping parties continued their work. The first gold had been reported on June 12 at a place later named Gold Creek, and by July 19 "the whole valley [was] filled with miners," Dodge wrote in his journal. (This account was submitted on December 22, 1875, as a report to the assistant adjutant general, Department of the Platte.) While some of the miners camped near their claims, others traveled continually throughout the region, "in wagons, on horseback and on foot, going and coming in all directions," Dodge wrote. "They seem to have suddenly sprung from the earth."[71]

Because his primary mission was to escort the scientific expedition, Dodge routinely discoursed about the members of that party in his journal. McGillycuddy's competence impressed the military commander, who often visited with the mapmaker when he returned to camp. He noted that McGillycuddy was a "really nice intelligent fellow."[72] Later he added that the difficulties of the summer might have been allayed "if Mr. Newton or Dr. McG. Were the head of the Scientific Expn."[73]

Continuing waves of rain swept over the region. "Scarcely a day passes without a shower," Jenney wrote, adding that thunderstorms were "very prevalent."[74] All the moisture resulted in verdant vegetation, including trees such as aspens, box elders, and white birches and plants such as tiger lilies, poison ivy, flax, and even hops and oats (perhaps the latter came from grain spilled by Custer's troops the previous year). Additionally, there was abundant wild fruit: raspberries, gooseberries, strawberries, red and black currants, elderberries, chokecherries, and even plums.[75]

---

[70]Ibid., 170.
[71]Dodge, report, December 22, 1875, quoted in Turchen and McLaird, *Black Hills Expedition*, 47.
[72]Kime, *Black Hills Journals*, 219.
[73]Ibid., 231.
[74]Turchen and McLaird, *Black Hills Expedition*, 24.
[75]Ibid.

5

Negotiating for the Hills

I
N MAY 1875, a delegation including Spotted Tail, Red Cloud, Iron Nation, and other headmen from the Sioux Nation, together with John L. Pennington, governor of Dakota Territory, met with President Ulysses S. Grant in Washington, D.C., to discuss the future of the Black Hills.[1] The men returned home in June having failed to reach agreement, partly because the Indian leaders said they could not make such a decision without consulting among their people, who had a say in matters of such importance. Further, under the terms of Article 12 of the 1868 treaty, any change required the affirmation of three-fourths of the men in the tribe.

The negotiations stalled but did not end. A second attempt at accord took place in the Black Hills in July. Red Dog, one of the Lakota leaders, "insisted Indian like on having a 'talk,'" but according to Dodge's report, the speech Red Dog gave became "a tirade against the Government for not keeping the miners out of the hills, and a demand that I immediately arrest them."[2] In response, Dodge told Red Dog that he "had nothing to do with the miners, and should not arrest any one of them; the 'talk' broke up soon, and Red Dog went off in a bad humor."[3]

A week later General George Crook arrived in the Black Hills, bringing troops to dislodge the encroaching miners and take back the region for the Indians. Crook found "two or three hundred miners collected" on French Creek.[4]

---

[1]Schell, *History of South Dakota*, 131.
[2]Dodge, report, December 22, 1875.
[3]Ibid.
[4]Ibid.

The escalating presence of miners in the Black Hills led to increased concern among Indian leaders. The Fort Wayne *Daily Sentinel* told readers, "A courier from the Black Hills reports that Red Cloud, Spotted Tail and other Indians are near Harney's peak demanding compensation for the damage done to their country, and that [Captain Edwin] Pollock [commander of Company E, Ninth Cavalry] wishes to know if Gen. Crook has any orders for him in case he meets the chiefs."[5]

The summer slid into fall as Crook's troops pushed the miners out of the hills and a new negotiating effort began with the Indians. In September, Senator W. B. Allison of Iowa, chairman of a commission appointed to resolve issues over ownership and use of the Black Hills, again launched talks about control of the area. Ill prepared for Indian consultation, Allison was joined by more adept men, including Brigadier General Alfred Terry, military commander of the Department of the Platte, and Reverend Samuel D. Hinman, an Episcopal priest who had experience with Santee and Dakota Sioux bands. Hinman spoke their dialects fluently but was limited in his knowledge of the Lakotas. To compensate, trader G. P. Beauvois, who had worked with some Lakota bands, joined the negotiators.

When all the Indian bands protested holding the new council near the Missouri River, Reverend Hinman suggested that it take place at the Red Cloud Agency, near Camp Robinson. Spotted Tail objected to that location, and in compromise the talks were moved to a site south of the White River.[6] The government representatives, appointed in mid-July, arrived at the council site in northwestern Nebraska in September. One hundred twenty members of Irish-born Second Lieutenant James "Teddy" Egan's gray troop of Second Cavalry, from Camp Robinson, acted as escort.[7] This military bodyguard angered the Indians, but the inexperienced federal negotiators—Brigadier General Terry aside—refused to proceed to the area without them. Allison's mission, according to Dodge, was to "negotiate for the sale of the black hills to the United States."[8]

On September 20, 1875, beside the White River some eight miles northeast of the Red Cloud Agency, the Allison Commission first

[5]*Fort Wayne Daily Sentinel,* August 13, 1875, p. 1.
[6]Larson, *Red Cloud.*
[7]McGillycuddy, *McGillycuddy, Agent,* 37.
[8]Dodge, report, December 22, 1875. On September 10 and 22, 1875, the *New York Times* reported on the intent of the commission as well as the location for the council.

met with tribal representatives. It was an inauspicious beginning. Red Cloud, who disliked the place chosen for the negotiations, was absent. Likewise, the Hunkpapa chief Sitting Bull and the Lakota headmen Crazy Horse and Black Twin did not show. Although Crazy Horse and Black Twin had not ruled out participation in the council, Sitting Bull "refused to treat with any commission as long as there was still game to hunt."[9]

Spotted Tail, able leader of the Brulé Sioux, having successfully moved the treaty negotiations away from Red Cloud's base at the agency near Camp Robinson, took the lead during the first session. But the discussion broke off quickly when Red Dog arrived bringing a message from Red Cloud urging a week's delay to allow incoming tribesmen to participate. Although the commissioners did not accede to the lengthy delay and insisted on resuming talks in three days, the opening meeting concluded with no real progress.[10]

Upon resumption of the talks, tension ran high. Thousands of Indians had arrived at the council ground and were in a "quarrelsome mood," according to Herbert S. Schell in his *History of South Dakota*.[11] They made menacing charges toward the commissioners and their military escort, brandishing weapons and wearing war paint. Threats by Little Big Man, from Crazy Horse's Oglala band, to "kill all white men trying to take his land" were forestalled by Young Man Afraid Of His Horses and other agency Indians, who took positions between Little Big Man and the federal negotiators. The second session also ended on a note of animosity. Three days later the Indians and the commissioners finally made some headway when talks resumed inside the stockade at the Red Cloud Agency. This time the negotiations involved only twenty Sioux headmen and the members of Allison Commission.[12]

Red Cloud and Spotted Tail seldom agreed on anything, but they did concur on one point: Any cession of land or rights to the Black Hills must come with the promise of support "for seven generations." The *New York Times* reported that they wanted cattle, flour and other food, horses, oxen, sheep, hogs, fowl, and wagons. They sought "ammunition, and moreover, . . . a hundred articles of food and clothing, which they wished sent them as annuity goods. They wanted

[9]Larson, *Red Cloud*, 188.
[10]Ibid., 190–91.
[11]Schell, *History of South Dakota*, 132.
[12]Larson, *Red Cloud*, 191–92.

houses, schools, sawmills and civilized furniture."[13] Red Cloud further demanded removal of Episcopal missionaries, to be replaced by Catholics.[14] He asked "that the bringing of whisky on the reservation by Mexicans be stopped."[15] Moreover, the tribal bands would allow only one road through the Black Hills: Custer's trail from Bismarck.

Although the Lakota bands were the primary negotiators for the Black Hills, other tribal groups were present, including the Arapahos, whose position was presented by Black Crow, and the Cheyennes, represented by Little Wolf and Living Bear.[16]

The intent of the Allison Commission was to negotiate a cession of the Black Hills, but in the end the commission proposed a purchase of mining rights only, offering either $400,000 in an "annual rental" or an outright purchase by paying $6 million. Allison also proposed that the Indians cede the hunting grounds in Wyoming's Powder River Basin, extending west to the Bighorn Mountain range.[17] The Indians refused all offers, setting the stage for violent encounters between themselves and frontier troops. Yet as the commission left the council, "the closing hand-shaking was most friendly," reported the *New York Times*. The article added that "the Indians betrayed no disappointment," implying that it had been the tribesmen who instigated the discussion, a fact far from the truth.[18]

Before the council, Valentine McGillycuddy and the surveying parties briefly met groups of Indians en route to the conclave, though always nonviolently. But once Allison withdrew from the region, the cavalry, which had been mildly effective in thwarting miners in their efforts to overrun the Black Hills, departed, too. Tacitly, the army's withdrawal opened the region to uncontrolled mining.

Valentine T. McGillycuddy first saw the Red Cloud Agency on October 9, 1875, a day when it was a beehive of activity associated with the distribution of treaty annuities. This camp, on the White River in extreme western Nebraska Territory, served Lakota Indians under the

---

[13]"The Indian Council," *New York Times*, October 1, 1875, p. 5.
[14]Larson, *Red Cloud*, 192.
[15]*New York Times*, "Indian Council."
[16]Ibid.
[17]Larson, *Red Cloud*, 193.
[18]*New York Times*, "Indian Council."

The Red Cloud Agency, about a mile from Camp Robinson in
northwestern Nebraska, 1876. The agency was eventually
relocated to Pine Ridge in South Dakota.
Nebraska State Historical Society, RG2095 PH O 80.

treaty terms set forth in 1868 at Fort Laramie. The spectacle of ration
day, when thousands of Indians rode horses, drove wagons, or walked
to the agency to get food, clothing, tools, and other products, riv-
eted the attention of the joint military-scientific party under Colonel
Dodge's command. Many Lakotas, Arapahos, and Cheyennes, along
with a few Sans Arcs, Hunkpapas, and Miniconjous, lined up at the
corner storage room to receive their annuities. Families gathered to
visit as children raced and played on the grass-covered hill where the
agency stood above the confluence of Soldier Creek and the White
River.[19]

By shortly after noon, however, McGillycuddy and the rest of the
road-weary scientific team had moved on to Camp Robinson, a scant
half mile to the west. The military camp had been established in 1874
to provide protection for the Red Cloud Agency.[20] Once there, the

[19]Buecker, *Fort Robinson*, 4.
[20]Ibid., 19, 20.

party found that "the grass is everywhere eaten off by the thousands of ponies possessed by the Indians."[21] Although the post had plenty of good water for men and animals, the lack of hay and grass convinced Dodge to spend only a single night before resuming the march toward Fort Laramie.

Over the next several days the company found plenty of grass and water at nightly campsites.[22] As the expedition wound its way back to Fort Laramie, the explorers visited often at Colonel Dodge's tent. Newton agreed to read and revise a section on geology that Dodge had prepared for the book he was writing.[23] They shared a bottle, swapped stories, and enjoyed each other's company before arriving at Fort Laramie on October 14. The following night the scout California Joe found himself a bottle of whiskey, became "desperately drunk," and made the night "hideous."[24]

Thus the Black Hills Expedition concluded its work and returned to Washington. Jenney's report would not be final for weeks, but on October 18, 1875, the *New York Times* said, "He reports gold-fields extending forty miles north from Harney's Peak and twenty miles wide that contain gold in quantities that will pay from $3 to $5 per day to the man, and that there are bars on numbers of streams that will pay much more than that." The paper added, "Prof. Jenney corroborates Gen. Custer's report of the Hills, and says that they will support thousands of miners when the Government opens them to settlement."[25]

A month later the *Times* ran an initial report from Jenney, who wrote of gold deposits in the "Harney's Peak gold field" as well as the "Bear Lodge gold field," again pointing to the opportunity for miners who would "push in to the region to work the gravel bars."[26]

On December 6, 1875, Indian agents in the region learned from Commissioner of Indian Affairs Edward P. Smith that Secretary of the

[21]Dodge, report, December 22, 1875.

[22]Ibid.

[23]After completing the 1875 expedition, Newton returned to the Black Hills, where he died of typhoid fever in Deadwood on August 5, 1877. Turchen and McLaird, *Black Hills Expedition*, 9.

[24]Kime, *Black Hills Journals*, 245.

[25]"The Black Hills Gold-Fields," *New York Times*, October 18, 1875, p. 1.

[26]"The Black Hills Country. Prof. Jenney's Final Report," *New York Times*, November 12, 1875, p. 1.

Interior Zachariah Chandler had ordered them to require all Indians to report to the reservations by January 31, 1876. The notification was ill timed. The Indians were scattered in their winter camps, making it nearly impossible to notify them of the order, let alone practical for them to relocate. Then, on February 1, 1876, the government transferred authority over the Plains Indians from the Department of the Interior to the War Department, which henceforth would be in control of the Sioux bands that had not yet reported to the agencies. Among the thousands of Lakotas still out were Sitting Bull, Crazy Horse, and Gall.

Assigned the task of herding the tribesmen onto their reservations was Lieutenant General Philip H. Sheridan, commander of the Military Division of the Missouri, headquartered in Chicago. Having conducted a winter campaign in 1874–75, the Red River war, which forced Southern Plains Indian tribes to relocate to reservations, Sheridan outlined a similar plan for the northern plains. He would send out three columns of soldiers. Brigadier General George Crook would advance into the region from the south, and Colonel John Gibbon would come from the west, where he had been based in western Montana. Brigadier General Alfred Terry, with Lieutenant Colonel George Armstrong Custer and the Seventh Cavalry, would approach from the east and their home base at Fort Abraham Lincoln, beside the Missouri River at Bismarck.

Sheridan laid plans for this coordinated campaign against the Sioux just as McGillycuddy became reacquainted with Fanny and began converting his field notes into topographical maps that could be used by the troops even then preparing to engage the tribal bands that remained off the reservation. Although no major violent confrontation had taken place with those Indians recently, they had nevertheless become classified as "hostiles."

For the Northern Plains tribes, the dominoes had begun to tumble.

II

DOCTOR

Detail of General George Crook, about 1860–1865.
National Archives, image 526407.

6

The Big Horn and Yellowstone Expedition

A STOOL BEFORE A drawing table became Valentine T. McGillycuddy's ritual seat once he washed off the dirt of the Black Hills, married Fanny Hoyt in Ionia, Michigan, on December 19, 1875, and began drafting maps in Washington. He was there in the spring of 1876 when the telegraph from General George Crook arrived. Would McGillycuddy turn over his notes from the Black Hills Expedition to another cartographer, pack his doctor's valise, and come west to serve in the medical corps with the Second Cavalry?[1]

The thin, cultured doctor must have known such a request could come. He certainly knew of the tension rising on the northern plains between civilian miners, emigrants, townspeople, the frontier military, and the native people when he left Fort Laramie in the fall of 1875. Now he would have an opportunity to return to his medical roots and hone his field skills. Little did he realize that he was about to be thrust into the middle of a Northern Plains Indian war. Fanny, too, must have recognized by this time that her husband would answer the call to serve his country any time it came. Like other wives of frontier soldiers, explorers, and contractors, she dutifully helped him pack his bags, placed her own possessions in trunks, and returned to Michigan, where she would stay while he joined Crook. McGillycuddy would serve with the Second and Third Cavalries for the next three years, and Fanny would eventually join him on the frontier.

[1]McGillycuddy, *McGillycuddy, Agent,* 24.

The 1876 Big Horn and Yellowstone Expedition began in March when Brigadier General George Crook, commander of the Department of the Platte since the previous summer, ordered cavalry into the field under the command of Colonel Joseph Jones Reynolds. A Kentucky native and West Point graduate, Reynolds had served with the Tenth Infantry and been cited for meritorious service at Chickamauga and again at Missionary Ridge, Tennessee.[2] He had assumed command of the Third Cavalry in 1870. Six years later he would set off a chain of events that would escalate during the spring and summer, leading to the deaths of hundreds of United States cavalrymen and Indians and the destruction of hundreds of horses and tons of personal possessions.

The initial planning for the winter offensive and subsequent action in the summer of 1876 came from Lieutenant General Philip H. Sheridan. General Crook took to the field first, with troops, a civilian pack train like the one he had used during his earlier expeditions in the Southwest, and a contingent of civilian scouts. Brigadier General Alfred H. Terry also entered the field that spring. He commanded the Dakota column, which included Lieutenant Colonel George Armstrong Custer and the Seventh Cavalry, three infantry companies, and a 150-wagon supply train. The Dakota column would reconnoiter along the Yellowstone River with the Montana column, commanded by Colonel John Gibbon. The Montana column included six companies of the Seventh Infantry and four companies of the Second Cavalry, totaling about 450 men.

Crook left Cheyenne on February 22 for Fort Laramie, where he assembled troops and met Dr. Curtis Emerson Munn, a Vermont native assigned as surgeon.[3] By February 27 Crook's enlarged command had traversed the well-beaten road to Fort Fetterman. That post, on a plateau overlooking the North Platte River at its confluence with LaPrele Creek, had been constructed in 1867–68 from materials dismantled at the Platte Bridge Station, which had lain farther west. Fort Fetterman became the staging base for Crook's marches into the Powder River country.[4]

---

[2]Heitman, *Historical Register*, 825.
[3]Ibid., 736.
[4]Lindmier, *Drybone*, 23–31, 31–32, 46.

General Crook's camp beside the North Platte River at
Fort Fetterman, 1876. *Wyoming State Archives, Department of
State Parks and Cultural Resources, image 19545.*

Located north of the Oregon Trail, the fort had two sets of kitch-
ens and mess rooms, a commissary, an adjutant's office, a school room,
a hospital, and a post library. There were quarters for officers, enlisted
men, laundresses, and quartermaster employees, cells in a guardhouse,
and shops for wheelwrights, blacksmiths, and saddlers.[5]

Additional troops joined Crook's Big Horn and Yellowstone Expedition at Fort Fetterman, including five companies each from the
Second and Third Cavalries and companies C and I of the Fourth
Infantry. Thomas Moore served as master of transportation, managing the eight hundred mules that made up the pack train and pulled
the eighty wagons used to haul supplies and forage.

The command lumbered north from Fort Fetterman on March 1
under a clear blue sky and over a layer of fresh snow that had fallen
the previous day. Crook and his aide-de-camp, John Gregory Bourke,
lagged at the fort, awaiting mail from Medicine Bow Station on the

[5]Ibid.

Union Pacific Railroad. They joined the expedition at its second camp, some thirty-three miles north of Fetterman.[6]

The Big Horn and Yellowstone Expedition's first engagement ensued on March 17, 1876, when Reynolds, acting on intelligence provided by scout Frank Grouard, struck a Northern Cheyenne winter camp on the Powder River in southern Montana. The assault became known to the military as the Powder River Fight, the Reynolds Fight, and the Crazy Horse Fight, although the Lakota warrior was nowhere near the camp at the time. For the Northern Cheyenne people whose peaceful village became a site of terror and carnage, it was the attack on Old Bear's camp. Reynolds and his subordinates destroyed the Indians' lodges and goods and secured eight hundred Indian horses, but the Northern Cheyennes under Two Moons counterattacked. They forced Reynolds to withdraw, leaving behind his dead and losing 376 of the Indian horses the troops had captured.[7]

The attack on Old Bear's camp was a fateful mistake. Not only did it come before Terry, Custer, and Gibbon were in position to aid Crook's column, but also it had been precipitated against a band of Northern Cheyennes who until then had been neutral in engagements involving the frontier army and the Sioux bands. Now punished severely and without provocation, the Northern Cheyennes fled north, where they sought refuge with Sitting Bull and with Crazy Horse's band of Oglalas.

Crook ordered a court-martial for Reynolds, but the damage had been done. The formerly peaceful Northern Cheyennes were now joined with the Lakota bands, creating a stronger force to resist the military incursion. Chiefs previously known as moderates, such as Two Moons, raised the clarion call to arms.[8]

In the wake of the attack on Old Bear's village, General Crook

---

[6]Robinson, *Bourke Diaries*, 219.

[7]Joseph Marshall, in *Journey of Crazy Horse*, 214–15, wrote that the Cheyennes were sleeping when the attack began, and most of the men had only bows and arrows for defense. He said that the women and children escaped, the camp was burned, and most of the horses were stolen, but that only two Cheyennes were killed. After this attack the Cheyennes took refuge in the Lakota camps, including that of Crazy Horse's band. Kingsley Bray, in *Crazy Horse*, 199–200, said the Indians killed ten soldiers but had their camp goods destroyed. In a counterattack they recovered 376 of their horses from Reynolds's command. For military accounts, see Robinson, *General Crook and the Western Frontier*, and Robinson, *Bourke Diaries*, 245–62.

[8]Bray, *Crazy Horse*, 200.

withdrew to Fort Fetterman. He preferred charges against Reynolds before reorganizing. Trying to emulate his previous successful campaign against the Southwestern tribes, Crook rode to northwestern Nebraska, visiting the Red Cloud and Spotted Tail Indian Agencies (the latter associated with Fort Sheridan), where he conferred with tribal headmen Red Cloud, Old Man Afraid Of His Horses, Blue Horse, Little Wound, and American Horse. He hoped to find support for a new field expedition from the tribesmen who had been on the reservation.

When meeting with Crook, the Indian leaders wore dark blue pantaloons, dark woolen shirts, and dark blue or black Mackinaw blankets. Around their necks hung strings of beads, shells, and brass rings. Although they had smeared red vermillion in the parts of their hair, they wore no paint on their faces and readily passed a pipe among themselves and the military men. The Indian men, probably influenced by the Red Cloud agent, James S. Hastings, would not support Crook's mission to take the field against the Lakotas and Cheyennes who remained in camps across the Powder River Basin. Without Sioux scouts, Crook tracked west from the Red Cloud Agency on May 16, headed unknowingly toward a fateful encounter on the Rosebud.[9]

Still in Washington drawing maps, Valentine McGillycuddy received orders from the surgeon general on May 25, 1876, to report to the frontier. The following day he and Fanny boarded the 5:15 Baltimore and Ohio train bound for Detroit, where his family then lived. After a three-day sojourn there, they continued on to Ionia, Michigan, where Fanny would spend the next several months with her family while her new husband answered the call of country. McGillycuddy was in Chicago on June 3 and soon en route to Omaha, where he overnighted on June 4 in the Grand Central Hotel, sitting up until the wee hours of the morning writing letters to his wife and his mother.

Orders that he report to Fort Fetterman, in Wyoming Territory, arrived in Omaha on June 5, and at noon the next day he boarded a Union Pacific train for Cheyenne. Upon reaching Sidney Barracks in western Nebraska on June 6, McGillycuddy found a message waiting: "Adj. Gen says I will have to fight." He spent the night at Sidney and

---

[9]Robinson, *Bourke Diaries*, 202–203, 260, 262, 264, 268, 274, 284.

on June 7 detrained in Cheyenne, where he checked into the Railroad House Hotel.[10]

The first stage bound for the Black Hills had departed from Cheyenne's InterOcean Hotel on February 3, 1876, and the city quickly became a launch point for a constant stream of miners hell-bent for the gold fields. This activity might have surprised McGillycuddy, but he had other people to draw his attention. By his own account, in Cheyenne on June 9 McGillycuddy met William F. "Buffalo Bill" Cody, who had established his reputation as a frontier army scout, buffalo hunter for the Kansas Pacific Railroad, and Indian fighter. He also met James Butler "Wild Bill" Hickok, a former military scout who had already spent some time acting out his exploits on the stage with Cody. Although McGillycuddy likely had not known Hickok previously, they had at least one acquaintance in common: Calamity Jane, whom the doctor had befriended the previous year.[11]

Hickok had initially come to Cheyenne to wed Agnes Lake Thatcher, a circus performer adept on both the high wire and horseback. The two had met in Abilene in 1871 and, following their marriage on March 5, 1876, traveled to Ohio, where Hickok left his new bride with her family. He had now returned to Cheyenne and would later join Charlie Utter on a venture into the Black Hills, even though the area was still officially Indian land and not open to white encroachments. It is plausible to assume that he queried McGillycuddy about resources in the region, although the doctor made no mention of such a conversation in his diary. Nor did McGillycuddy give any impression in his diary of Buffalo Bill, who, during the summer, joined Lieutenant Colonel Wesley Merritt, commander of the Fifth Cavalry, and proceeded into the field as a scout for that command.[12]

---

[10]McGillycuddy, "Diary Kept While a Member of the Yellowstone and Big Horn Expedition" (hereafter referred to as "McGillycuddy Diary, 1876–77"). This diary was first published by Agnes Wright Spring as "Dr. McGillycuddy's Diary" in *Westerner's Brand Book* 9 (1953): 277–307. A transcript is held by the Nebraska State Historical Society, Fort Robinson, Nebraska. The original notebook is in the Special Library Collections, Lee Library, Brigham Young University, Provo, Utah. All quotations are from the original. The notebook measures 3.74 inches wide by 6.5 inches high. It has a brown cardboard cover and lined pages. McGillycuddy made his entries on the fronts and backs of all pages, in pencil. On December 14, 1876, the handwriting in the diary changes, and thereafter it is clear from the tone and text that Fanny McGillycuddy kept the diary until its conclusion on April 11, 1877.

[11]McGillycuddy's diary refers to his meeting with Buffalo Bill on June 9, 1876, the same day he visited nearby Camp Carlin and General Eugene Carr's command.

[12]Robinson, *General Crook*, 187.

While in Cheyenne, McGillycuddy learned that the best route for him to take in joining General Crook was to continue by rail 120 miles west to Medicine Bow Station and then travel overland another 84 miles along the Fetterman Road to Fort Fetterman. From there he could await a military escort to Crook's command, which weeks before had broached the Powder River Basin.[13]

Accordingly, on June 11, at 1:40 P.M., McGillycuddy departed Cheyenne on a Union Pacific passenger train headed to Medicine Bow, arriving at 8:45 P.M. He "put up" in Medicine Bow for the night and rode out the next morning with the mail carrier bound for Fort Fetterman. By his account, the two-day trip took them over the Laramie Mountain Range, across snowbanks on the high peaks, and eventually to the North Platte River, which they forded to reach the fort.[14]

————— ·◆· —————

While McGillycuddy was making his way from Washington toward Fort Fetterman, Crook had moved north into the Powder River Basin, taking to the field again on May 29.[15] The expedition reached Prairie Dog Creek, which Crook's aide-de-camp, John Bourke, incorrectly identified as Goose Creek, on June 6. That day, as the men toiled over the broken country under a hot sun, they killed their first buffalo of the season.[16] Over the next two days they harvested other game, including "Sage cocks and Sickle-bill curlew," according to Bourke, as well as elk, buffalo, and deer. On the night of June 8 they camped at the confluence of Prairie Dog Creek and the Tongue River, awaiting the return of their Crow scouts. An indication of the tedium at the camp appears in Bourke's journal entry: "The monotony of camp life was agreeably broken in upon the evening of June 9th by an attack upon our camp by a mounted party of Sioux warriors." Two men were wounded, though not seriously, before the troops drove the Indians away. The skirmish led Bourke, an experienced campaigner, to opine, "It is to be hoped the Indians may make attacks of this kind every night: no greater advantage can accrue to young troops than to keep them constantly under fire; they learn the importance of implicit

---

[13]McGillycuddy, Diary, 1879, Pine Ridge Agency; McGillycuddy, *McGillycuddy, Agent*, 41–43.

[14]McGillycuddy Diary, 1876–77.

[15]Robinson, *Bourke Diaries*, 290.

[16]Ibid., 301.

obedience to authority, of keeping constantly in readiness for instant attack or defense and above all things of saving their ammunition."[17]

Valentine McGillycuddy reached Fort Fetterman in early June and met army surgeon Joseph Ruff Gibson, with whom he would stay and whom he would assist during the next few weeks. Gibson was a Pennsylvanian who had been cited for meritorious and distinguished service following a cholera outbreak at Harts Island, in New York harbor, in 1866. For McGillycuddy, the newly recruited army physician, the time at Fort Fetterman passed quickly as he wrote letters home and mounted maps made from his previous year's work with the Black Hills Expedition. One day he rode the fifteen miles south to the natural rock bridge on LaPrele Creek that had become a landmark south of the Oregon Trail.

While McGillycuddy held ground at Fort Fetterman, Crook pushed into the Powder River Basin, engaging in a minor fracas on Prairie Dog Creek. Meantime, the Lakotas organized a Sun Dance at a mile-long camp along Rosebud Creek in Montana Territory. The Sun Dance was, and remains, "the most holy of Lakota ceremonies." The one held in June 1876, wrote Joseph Marshall III in *The Journey of Crazy Horse,* was "the right thing at the right time," for the Indian people, both spiritually and psychologically. After selecting an appropriate location, the people were prepared to begin the Sun Dance activities with the Hunkpapa headman Sitting Bull, known both for his bravery in battle and as a spiritual leader. He himself offered "one hundred bits of flesh, fifty from each arm—a real and symbolic sacrifice" that served as inspiration to those gathered.[18]

At this Sun Dance, Sitting Bull dreamed that soldiers would be falling into the Indian camp. The Lakotas took this as a prophecy of a great battle from which they would emerge the victors.[19]

As the Sun Dance concluded, the Oglala war leader Crazy Horse, a man who had already distinguished himself as a fighter in earlier encounters, kept scouts on the lookout, particularly toward the south. When word reached his camp that soldiers had been spotted riding in their direction, the Indian warriors prepared for an offensive that they would launch when Crook—whom they called Three Stars—reached the Rosebud.[20]

---

[17]Ibid., 305.
[18]Marshall, *Journey of Crazy Horse,* 216, 217.
[19]Bray, *Crazy Horse,* 203–204; Marshall, *Journey of Crazy Horse,* 217–18.
[20]Bray, *Crazy Horse,* 204–207; Marshall, *Journey of Crazy Horse,* 217–20.

On June 16 Crook forded the Tongue River under a cloudy sky and turned northwest, riding over broken land where grass gave way to cacti, sagebrush, and wormwood. Buffalo had recently grazed the country, clipping the grass short, and the shaggy beasts could be seen "in droves" some distance from the troops. That evening Crook's command dined on the humps, tenderloins, hearts, and tongues of thirty buffalo that had been killed during the day, roasted over campfires, and sprinkled with salt—a welcome addition to an otherwise bland diet.[21]

Crook's march resumed the following morning but had covered a scant four miles when Crow scouts raced back toward the soldiers crying, "Sioux! Sioux!"[22]

Crazy Horse led the Indian combatants. This warrior had fought in two earlier engagements: a battle at Platte Bridge in 1865 and a clash with Captain William J. Fetterman in 1866. The skirmish at Platte Bridge and a subsequent attack on a military supply wagon train led by Sergeant Amos Custard in 1865 had been only moderately successful for the Indians; Lieutenant Caspar Collins and twenty-one other soldiers were killed, but the Indians failed to fully entice the soldiers at Platte Bridge away from the cover of the fortification. The Fetterman encounter the following year, however, became a complete rout, leading to the deaths of all eighty-one men with the captain.[23]

Now, ten years later, Crook's troops faced the same Indian combatants on a field of war some five miles long. The engagement at the Rosebud ended when the Indians withdrew and Crook, too, retreated, with his column nearly intact.[24] Even so, the six-hour battle left ten of his men dead, along with some thirty-nine Indians, and many more were wounded on both sides. Initially treated in the field, the casualties were soon transported south along the Bozeman Trail to Fort Fetterman, where they would receive additional care.[25]

• ◆ •

Back at Fort Fetterman, McGillycuddy heard on June 15 that "Indians were attacking [Crook's] camp," an apparent reference to the minor

---

[21]Robinson, *Bourke Diaries*, 323, 325.
[22]Ibid.
[23]Moulton, *Roadside History of Wyoming*, 169–73, 313–14; Marshall, *Journey of Crazy Horse*, 136, 151. The Lakotas called the Fetterman fight "Battle of the Hundred in the Hand."
[24]Hedren, *Traveler's Guide to the Great Sioux War*, 52–53.
[25]Robinson, *Bourke Diaries*, 328–29.

fracas the troops had engaged in on Prairie Dog Creek on June 9. On June 16 the doctor wrote in his diary that "180 Shoshones were joining Gen. Crook." Over the next three days McGillycuddy wrote letters home, made maps, and moved into new quarters. On June 20 he penciled a note that courier Ben Arnold had arrived from the north—riding 170 miles in four days—with a report that the troops were making "extensive preparations for a fight."[26] This diary entry makes it abundantly clear that it took time for information to be conveyed in frontier Wyoming Territory. The message of "extensive preparations" had no doubt been written before the fight on the Rosebud, but it reached Fort Fetterman three days after the battle.

As he baked in the hot sun of early summer—he logged a temperature of 98 degrees on June 21—McGillycuddy began to hear additional details of Crook's engagement at the confluence of Prairie Dog Creek and the Tongue River on June 9 and of the more serious battle on the Rosebud on June 17. "Courier Ben Arnold came from the Front, bringing news of fight with the Sioux," he wrote on June 22, adding that "we had 9 killed and 20 wounded." These men were even then being brought to Fort Fetterman for treatment.[27]

During the next few days, doctors McGillycuddy and Gibson prepared for the incoming wounded, who reached the fort in the afternoon of June 27. They suffered gashes from arrows, gaping holes left by bullets, bruises, strains, and other wounds. In the log hospital, situated on the northeastern side of the fort near the cavalry stables and hay corral, the doctors labored over the next few days, removing bullets and performing other surgeries. McGillycuddy wrote in his diary, "Wounded arrived at 4 P.M. train of 100 wagons came in at 1 P.M. 19 wounded. 5 legs. Rest arms, heads & bodies."

McGillycuddy focused on caring for the men wounded in the Rosebud fight over the next several days. With orders to join Crook in the field, he also made preparations to head north. Having received $150 in salary, the doctor sent a treasury check to Fanny for $100 and with

---

[26]McGillycuddy Diary, 1876–77.

[27]Ibid. In identifying the courier, McGillycuddy initially wrote "Louis Richard [Richaud]" but crossed through that name and inserted "Ben Arnold." It is unknown whether Arnold departed Fort Fetterman after delivering his message on June 20 only to intercept another scout, perhaps Richaud, and then return to the fort with the new report on June 22, or whether he remained at the fort and took receipt of the message before McGillycuddy saw it. McGillycuddy's reference to nine deaths among Crook's command is erroneous; there were ten.

money he had on hand paid another $62.50 in traveling expenses. He was ready to embark for Crook's camp on July 4.[28]

As he had done the previous year in the Black Hills, McGillycuddy rode a good horse from Fort Fetterman. Traveling with the supply wagon train gave him other amenities in the field, including a stretcher that he used for a bed.[29] Following the Bozeman Trail, freshly marked by the recent crossings of army couriers and the wounded soldiers, the campaigners had poor campsites, alkaline water, and rough trail conditions. They set camp on July 8 at the site of Fort Reno, a defunct military post built in 1866 when the Bozeman Trail first opened but razed by Indians after the military withdrew in 1868. This had also been Crook's base of operations before he pushed deeper into the Powder River Basin and eventually to the Rosebud. While the party was in camp at the Fort Reno site, Louis Richaud, another scout for Crook, rode in with the stunning news that George Armstrong Custer (whom McGillycuddy referred to as Custar) had been killed at the Little Bighorn.[30]

McGillycuddy met the first units from Crook's command on July 11 when his relief party reached the site of Fort Phil Kearny, another of the Bozeman Trail forts constructed in 1866 but abandoned by the military and burned by Indians in 1868. There, two companies of cavalry informed the doctor about the location of Crook's camp. With the reinforcements, McGillycuddy rode fourteen miles on July 12 and another four on July 13 to Crook's camp on Goose Creek. There he joined messmates First Lieutenant Frank Taylor, of Ohio, and Second Lieutenant Richard Thompson Yeatman, of Iowa, both of the Fourteenth Infantry, and reported to Albert Hartsuff, Crook's medical director. Hartsuff had served as an army surgeon since 1861 and had recently received a promotion to major.[31]

From the soldiers who were with Crook on June 17 at the Rosebud, McGillycuddy learned that they had been "taken by surprise" when Lakota and Northern Cheyenne warriors rode pell-mell into the soldiers' camp, launching the six-hour battle at the Rosebud.[32] After that

---

[28]Ibid.

[29]The use of the stretcher continued until after he joined Crook's contingent. One night, shots fired at the camp struck close to his pallet and caused him to roll onto the ground, where he felt less vulnerable to a stray bullet.

[30]McGillycuddy Diary, 1876–77.

[31]Ibid.; Heitman, *Historical Register,* 507.

[32]McGillycuddy to William Garnett, March 15, 1926, quoted in Clark, *Killing of Crazy Horse,* 112–13; Hedren, *Traveler's Guide,* 52.

fight, Crook withdrew his detachment to Goose Creek. He stayed there through June and into July, waiting for reinforcements for his expedition. These were the troops McGillycuddy accompanied into the Powder River Basin. Crook later garnered harsh criticism for not moving aggressively against the Indians.

A week before the Rosebud battle, Brigadier General Alfred Terry had ordered Major Marcus A. Reno, whom McGillycuddy had first met on the International Boundary Survey in 1874, with six companies of the Seventh Cavalry to advance along the Powder and Tongue Rivers. Reno went farther than he had been ordered to after his scout, Mitch Boyer, observed signs of an Indian village in the Rosebud Valley.[33] Unlike Crook's men, Reno's troops did not engage the tribesmen, and ten days later, on June 20, Reno rejoined Custer, his commanding officer. All had departed Fort Abraham Lincoln on May 17, to the strains of "The Girl I Left Behind Me," with the Seventh Cavalry regimental standard streaming in the wind.

Terry, meantime, transferred from horseback to the *Far West,* a steamboat serving the military command that had churned its way up the Missouri and then the Yellowstone to the confluence of the Powder and Yellowstone Rivers. There he conferred with Custer before ordering him to trail the Indians from Rosebud Creek to the Little Bighorn.

Terry and Colonel John Gibbon, meanwhile, traveled the Yellowstone to the mouth of the Bighorn River and then proceeded to the Little Bighorn.[34] They knew that the Lakota and Northern Cheyenne bands were gathering somewhere within this triangulation and fully expected to encounter them.

---

[33]Hedren, *Traveler's Guide,* 54.
[34]Ibid., 55.

7
Beyond the Greasy Grass

VALENTINE McGILLYCUDDY WAS not yet in the Powder River Basin when George Armstrong Custer engaged in his final, fatal battle along the Little Bighorn. After their Sun Dance and the fight with Crook on the Rosebud, Lakota and Northern Cheyenne tribesmen moved west to the Little Bighorn, a stream they called the Greasy Grass. The Indians organized their large village of some seven thousand people into six major circles. Five consisted of various tribes of the Teton Sioux, and one was Northern Cheyenne. All the camp circles lay west of the Little Bighorn, with the Lakota Crazy Horse at the far western edge and the Hunkpapa Gall at the eastern end. From one end of the camp to the other, tipis were strung out over three miles. At this location the Little Bighorn meanders at the base of eastern hillsides.

As the Little Bighorn battle unfolded, Reno engaged first but was forced to retreat to a dense stand of timber beside the river. Unaided and nearly overwhelmed, he ordered his troops to fall back again. They did so in a scattered fashion, finally making a new stand on the high bluffs east of the river. There, Indians soon encircled them, throwing withering fire at the troops. As the fighting of June 26 escalated, Captain Frederick W. Benteen and Captain Thomas M. McDougall's pack train joined Reno at his position on the bluffs. Their arrival led the Indians to ease their attack on Reno's position, but already forty soldiers had been killed and thirteen wounded. Another sixteen were missing somewhere in the timber along the river below Reno.[1]

---

[1] Utley, "Little Big Horn," 252. Voluminous literature exists about the battle of the Little Bighorn. The most recent comprehensive history is Donovan, *A Terrible Glory.* See also Gray, *Centennial Campaign;* Liddic, *Vanishing Victory;* Stewart, *Custer's Luck;* and Utley, *Cavalier in Buckskin.*

Custer, with five companies, engaged in his own desperate and unsuccessful attempt to attack the village. In launching his offensive, Custer divided his command. Two companies fought in Deep Coulee, and three companies under the command of Captain Myles W. Keogh dismounted to establish a skirmish line at Medicine Tail. Although Custer likely expected Benteen to come to his aid, the latter failed to proceed beyond Reno's location.

Keogh encountered other tribesmen and died with many of his men. Custer and his command, too, engaged in a last, fatal battle. The Indians withdrew as dusk fell but resumed the attack on Reno's position the following day. Both Reno and Benteen eventually led counterattacks. They took further casualties before the Indians withdrew a final time, no doubt because they became aware that Colonel John Gibbon was moving up the Little Bighorn, a day late to save Custer but on schedule with Terry's original plan.

As Crazy Horse later told McGillycuddy, addressing him by his Lakota nickname, "Little Beard, after we closed the lines that day, no one but a bird could have escaped!"[2]

At the same time McGillycuddy recalled that statement, he erroneously added, "I was 30 miles south of the battle field [during] the fight [of] June 25, 1876, with General Crook's command, as surgeon of the 2d cavalry. We were setting up, repairing damages and caring for our wounded, Crazy Horse and Sitting Bull having attacked us on the seventeenth." In fact McGillycuddy had not yet joined Crook and was instead at Fort Fetterman, where he indeed was treating the wounded from the fight at the Rosebud on June 17. According to his own journal, McGillycuddy did not leave Fort Fetterman to travel north and join Crook until early July, reaching Crook's camp on Goose Creek on July 11. In subsequent letters, McGillycuddy often wrote that he was present during the fight at the Rosebud, but his journal effectively refutes those statements.[3]

---

[2]"Indian Wars Veteran Never Ill in 70 Years," *Oakland Tribune*, February 15, 1934. The same statement is included in V. T. McGillycuddy to Ed A. Fry, July 19, no year given, written from Berkeley, California, to Fry in Niobrara, Nebraska, acknowledging an article in the *Omaha World-Herald Magazine* of July 11, no year given, copy at Fort Robinson Museum Archives.

[3]McGillycuddy to Fry, no date.

The third prong of Sheridan's Indian offensive of 1876, Crook's command, provided no support during the Little Bighorn battle. Those troops remained in camp, first on Goose Creek and later on the Tongue River. After McGillycuddy joined Crook on July 13, he spent two weeks primarily "in camp waiting."[4] He received letters from Fanny, sent replies, took a bath on July 22, attended a trial for a soldier accused of drunkenness, endured heavy rain and hot temperatures, and occasionally saw Indians in the distance.

Finally, on July 27, a month after Custer's defeat, Crook, with reinforcement troops now in place, began moving his command. The following day, in camp on the middle fork of the Tongue River, McGillycuddy joined in a game of baseball with the troops—his team won, 30 to 17—and he read the five letters from Fanny that had arrived with a supply train. On July 30, like other men in Crook's expedition, the doctor received a thirty-one day issue of rations: thirty-five pounds of flour, twenty-three pounds of bacon, four and a half pounds each of sugar and beans, three pounds of coffee, five candles, and a bar of soap. The troopers would go on patrol once again.[5]

As he had done earlier, Tom Moore supervised the pack train that supported the soldiers. Each man had a suit of clothes, an overcoat, a blanket, and an India-rubber poncho, plus 250 rounds of ammunition.[6]

On August 4, while in camp beside Goose Creek, McGillycuddy was assigned as surgeon to the Second Cavalry by medical director Bennett A. Clements. As one of eight medical officers, he would share his mess with Captain Henry Erastus Noyes of the Second Cavalry, a Maine native who had graduated from West Point in 1857 and become a member of the Second Cavalry in 1861.[7] Noyes had earned the enmity of General Crook during the March attack by Reynolds on the Cheyenne camp and faced an indictment for failure to properly support the initial attack. Brought up on the charges at Fort D. A. Russell as soon as the expedition returned, Noyes was reprimanded but soon returned to the field.[8]

Now, in July, the Big Horn and Yellowstone Expedition crossed from the Tongue River to the Rosebud, their route scouted by men

---

[4]McGillycuddy Diary, 1876–77.
[5]Ibid.
[6]McGillycuddy, *McGillycuddy, Agent,* 47–48.
[7]McGillycuddy Diary, 1876–77; Heitman, *Historical Register,* 753.
[8]Robinson, *General Crook,* 170, 172.

including William F. Cody and Frank Grouard. They passed the site of a large but abandoned Indian village and choked in the acrid smoke from grass fires burning in the area. Like Cody, twenty-five-year-old Grouard had established himself as a frontier scout, eventually gaining the confidence of Crook, although that would be tested during the current march. Born on September 20, 1850, the middle of three sons of an American missionary in the South Pacific and his Polynesian wife, Grouard returned to California with his father, but the two were separated when the boy was five years old. Grouard lived for a time with Addison and Louisa Pratt in California and eventually in Utah. As a teenager he left the Pratt home and later became a mail rider who, at age nineteen, was captured by some Hunkpapas. He subsequently lived with the Sioux in Montana, spending time first in Sitting Bull's village and later in Crazy Horse's camp, learning Lakota ways and language—particularly sign language—before he left the tribe and found work as an army scout.[9]

It was so hot on August 8 that Crook's men lay up during the day and marched fifteen miles that night. Finally, on August 10, about twenty-five miles from the Yellowstone River, they met General Terry's command.[10] There McGillycuddy first encountered the "tired, dirty, and disgusted" remnants of Custer's Seventh Cavalry. He and other surgeons with Crook treated soldiers who had been with Reno and Benteen and learned more details of the desperate fight under a broiling sun. McGillycuddy got a firsthand account of the June 25 battle from Reno.[11]

The combined Crook and Terry expedition roamed south of the Yellowstone for two weeks, searching for Indians against whom they could retaliate for the Rosebud and Custer battles.[12] But the joint command, large and unwieldy, had no major encounters with roaming tribesmen. Needing supplies, the troops proceeded down the Powder River, reaching its confluence with the Yellowstone by August 22, where, to Crook's consternation, no supplies awaited. Scout Bill Cody quit, having served just over a month; he later claimed the command "did not want or intend to fight."[13]

[9]Greene, *Slim Buttes*, 18; Thrapp, *Encyclopedia*, vol. 2, 592–93; DeBarthe, *Frank Grouard*, 22, 30–32, 53–54; Utley, *Lance and Shield*, 352.

[10]McGillycuddy Diary, 1876–77; Robinson, *General Crook*, 190.

[11]McGillycuddy, *McGillycuddy, Agent*, 50.

[12]*Chicago Times*, September 22, 1876, reporting by John F. Finerty.

[13]Ibid.

On August 22 McGillycuddy wrote in his diary that the troops were "waiting for the *Far West* to come down the river. The wagon train came in on the other side of the river."[14] When the steamer arrived, McGillycuddy and other members of the medical corps loaded ill and wounded soldiers onto the boat. These men would now travel downriver to Fort Abraham Lincoln.[15]

Once he had settled the injured soldiers on the vessel, McGillycuddy requested a new horse to replace his lamed roan. Told that none was available, he declined the opportunity to take the *Far West* downriver, and instead mounted his weary horse to accompany Crook up the Powder. On August 26 McGillycuddy reported a "large amount of dysentery" among the troops. He remained with Crook, who headed east toward Dakota, following a faint Indian trail. The men had rations for fifteen days plus meager goods including overcoats, rubber blankets, wool blankets, and their personal mess kits, although even this last item was restricted. One reporter said the men shared forks and had no plates.[16] As if their situation wasn't already uncomfortable, it began to rain. Wool blankets, pants, and coats were soaked, and the soft ground turned into muddy mire.

During the first days of travel east into Dakota, the doctor treated the dysentery and other maladies reported by the soldiers. On August 31 a trooper was bitten by a rattlesnake and McGillycuddy administered "Lig. Ammon. Exter. Inter. & Hypoderm."[17] The translation likely would be "ligature, application of ammonia externally and possibly something internally, plus a hypodermic," probably of a pain sedative such as morphine.

While campaigning during the previous weeks, Crook's command had reduced its supplies, worn out its horses, engaged no Indians, marched and slept in the rain, and begun arguing about the best course of action. When the men reached the Heart River in present North Dakota, Crook evaluated the options. With little more than two days rations on hand, he could return west to the Yellowstone and rejoin Terry, or he could go east and make it to Fort Lincoln.[18] But he eyed a

---

[14]McGillycuddy Diary, 1876–77.

[15]Hedren, *Traveler's Guide*, 63.

[16]*Milwaukee Sentinel,* September 18, 1876.

[17]McGillycuddy Diary, 1876–77.

[18]Newspaper correspondent John Finerty reported that two and a half days' worth of rations were on hand when the column turned toward the Black Hills. Finerty, *War-Path and Bivouac.*

Tom Bell, left, and another packer tighten a mule pack during the
Big Horn and Yellowstone Expedition with General George Crook, 1876.
Stanley J. Morrow, photographer. *National Archives, image 533171.*

third route: south toward the Black Hills and the town of Crook City, just northeast of Deadwood in present South Dakota. That would be a risky move, his fellow officers reasoned, because the country was rugged and the distance to a resupply point was greater. It could take more than a week to travel to Crook City, where they could replenish their stores. "We have great confidence in Crook," Lieutenant Bourke wrote in his diary, "but cannot shake off a presentment of dread as to the possible consequences of our bold plunge, without rations, across an utterly unknown zone of such great width as that lying between us and the Black Hills, Frank Gruard [*sic*] says he knows nothing of the country this side of the Little Missouri River."[19]

Rain poured down on the Heart River camp on September 5, a day when, McGillycuddy wrote in his diary, "command put on *half rations*."[20] That evening the doctor joined General Crook as he sat alone, pondering his alternatives. Having firsthand knowledge of McGillycuddy's work in the Black Hills the previous year, Crook inquired about the distance to the hills and the conditions that faced the expedition.

McGillycuddy, well aware of the rugged country in that direction, did his best to dissuade Crook from the detour, saying it would be too difficult to make the trip to the hills on their exhausted horses and without provisions. It would take at least ten or twelve days to march from their camp to Crook City, McGillycuddy estimated. Crook then inquired whether the maps of the region could be relied upon. At this the doctor-cartographer bristled, for both men knew who had drawn the maps.[21]

"Well, watch the guidons in the morning, McGillycuddy," Crook replied, "You'll see which way we are going."[22]

Indeed, on September 6 Crook took the Big Horn and Yellowstone Expedition south toward the Black Hills. He knew that Lakota bands had scattered throughout the region and believed it fell to him and the troops he commanded to "safeguard the mining communities from incursions by warriors."[23] It was a decision, like many others of Crook's, that would have long-lasting repercussions for the troops, and more particularly for Valentine McGillycuddy.

---

[19]Diary of John Bourke, vol. 5, 878–79, quoted in Greene, *Slim Buttes*, 37.
[20]McGillycuddy, *McGillycuddy, Agent*, 53 (emphasis in original).
[21]Ibid., 54.
[22]Ibid.
[23]Greene, *Slim Buttes*, 36.

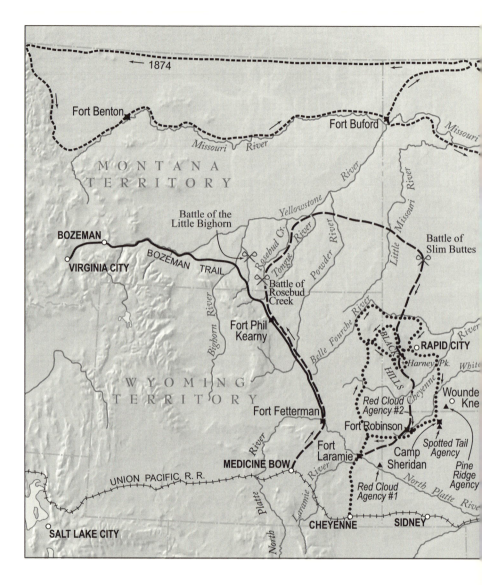

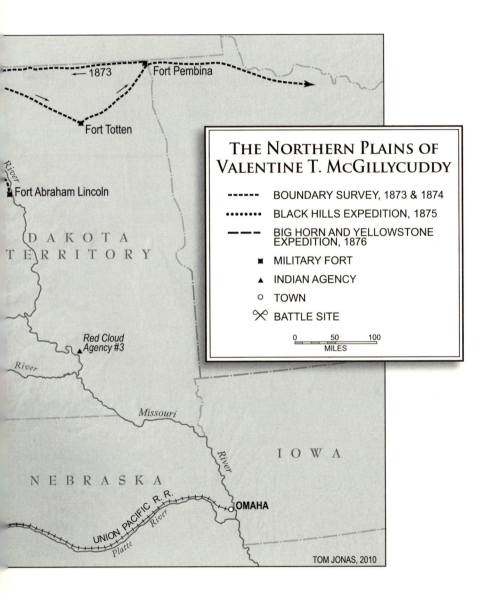

THE NORTHERN PLAINS OF
VALENTINE T. MCGILLYCUDDY

- - - - - - BOUNDARY SURVEY, 1873 & 1874
· · · · · · · · BLACK HILLS EXPEDITION, 1875
— — — BIG HORN AND YELLOWSTONE
EXPEDITION, 1876
⬟ MILITARY FORT
▲ INDIAN AGENCY
○ TOWN
⚔ BATTLE SITE

0   50   100
MILES

TOM JONAS, 2010

8

Eat Horse or Starve

E VEN BEFORE THEY struck south toward the Black Hills, the Second and Third Cavalries with Crook had been worn beyond fighting trim. The men were weary and undernourished, and well over a third of their horses "looked well fitted for the bone yard." McClellan saddles rubbed the animals raw, so the troopers cut holes in their saddle pads and smeared bacon fat on the horses' backs to reduce the friction and provide comfort. But the steeds, road weary and exhausted, got little relief. They were literally dropping from overuse, starvation, and the toil associated with travel over ground made soft by incessant rain.[1]

When Crook turned south at the Heart River, having put the expedition on half rations to stretch the two-day supply of food into four, he told newspaper correspondent John Finerty, "If necessary, we can eat horses."[2] A day later he abandoned fourteen horses and called for quarter rations. As more horses became too weak to continue, Crook ordered them shot to keep them from falling into Indian hands. Captain Anson B. Mills recalled, "Crook ordered me to shoot all played out horses. Shot 70 that day. . . . There was nothing to eat & the men were almost ready to mutiny."[3] Later, when the steady volley of shots to dispatch the equines depressed the men, the commander rescinded his directive, hoping it would improve the troops' morale.

There was no bacon, but some of the men began killing prairie dogs and rabbits for food.[4] The sight of a rabbit caused frenzy, Bourke

---

[1]*Chicago Tribune,* September 22, 1876.
[2]Finerty, *War-Path,* 245.
[3]Anson Mills, "Battle of Slim Buttes," January 24, 1914, Walter Camp documents in Robert Spurrier Ellison Papers, Denver Public Library (DPL).
[4]McGillycuddy, *McGillycuddy, Agent,* 55.

wrote, as "soldiers armed with lariats, nose bags and halters advance from all sides and keep up pursuit until the poor little jackrabbit is fairly run to death." He added, "There is enough shouting, yelling and screeching to account for the slaughter of a thousand buffaloes."[5]

Finding little wood and contending with drenching rain, many men soon fell ill from eating the poorly cooked prairie dog meat. Desperate for nourishment, they gathered prickly pear cactus pads, skinning the spines and cooking the pads into a mush. The civilian packers and scouts fared slightly better. They had been conserving their rations since leaving the Yellowstone and had a little food left, but their tobacco supply had been exhausted.[6]

Only when the troopers were facing almost certain starvation did Crook order them to take advantage of the one food supply they still had: their horses. The soldiers relied on the animals for transportation and did not want to eat them. Some, such as Third Cavalry Lieutenant Joseph Lawson, an Irishman who had served during the Civil War with the Kentucky cavalry, considered the action akin to cannibalism. "I'd as soon think of eating my brother!" he told newspaper correspondent Finerty.[7]

When faced with no better option, the men eventually butchered the dead horses. They gathered grass for weak fires so that they could roast the haunches or boil the meat with wild onions they dug from the ground as they traveled. On September 6 McGillycuddy noted in his diary, "No wood to cook the bacon we did not have." Two days later he wrote, "Shooting horses for rations."[8]

One night the men, "wet through & cold hungry," halted and decided to build a fire, "knowing, of course, that it was a dangerous thing to do," wrote Second Lieutenant George Francis Chase, of Third Cavalry Company L. They chose a secluded spot where they could make a defense if Indians found them. "We soon had a fire going and a suckling colt that had followed us all day and was about played out staggered up to the fire, among the men, to warm himself. One of the officers proposed that we kill him and eat him. I replied that I had been thinking of that myself, but had thought better of reserving him

---

[5]Diary of John Bourke, vol. 5, 881–82, quoted in Greene, *Slim Buttes*, 40.

[6]McGillycuddy, *McGillycuddy, Agent*, 55; Greene, *Slim Buttes*, 40; Finerty, *War-Path*, 248.

[7]Finerty, *War-Path*, 246.

[8]McGillycuddy Diary, 1876–77.

for an emergency, but the more we talked of the matter the more the idea struck us having a meal right there & so it was decided to kill the colt. As soon as this intention was announced an eager soldier threw one arm around the colt's neck & with his other hand drew a knife and cut the colt's throat. In 15 minutes the men were eating the raw flesh of the colt, not even waiting to roast it."[9]

As reporter Finerty noted, "hunger is a great sauce." Lieutenant Lawson, who earlier had equated eating his horse to eating his brother, "dined on horse steak, like the rest of us." Later Finerty added that "it was a tough experiment, but there was no help for it, and anything outside of actual cannibalism was preferable to starving slowly to death." One night a trooper brought the lieutenant "the hind quarters of a fine, fat Indian pony colt, on which we dined sumptuously, although the old officer made wry faces, and said again that he felt like a cannibal while eating horse flesh."[10]

With food supplies desperately low, the horses in poor condition, and the men themselves malnourished and exhausted, Crook ordered Mills, First Lieutenant John W. Bubb, commissary officer for the expedition, and 150 men to ride ahead to Deadwood City, about one hundred miles southwest of their position, to obtain rations and return to the command as quickly as possible. The relief party, made up of fifteen men from each of the companies riding the strongest horses remaining in the expedition's herd, departed the main force on September 7.[11]

In the relief force's wake, the troops with Crook settled into a camp where they boiled more wild onions and horse meat. McGillycuddy harvested wild rose hips that would benefit the ill soldiers, who were suffering from dysentery and the effects of scurvy.[12]

Bourke wrote that the men were "wet, cross, hungry, and disgusted" as they attempted to make coffee with alkaline water that "threw up to the surface a scum of saline and sedimentary matter which made the coffee look decidedly repulsive."[13] To top it off, rain continued to pour down, making soup for the men to walk and sleep in.

---

[9]G. J. [*sic*; should be F.] Chase, "The Battle of Slim Buttes," January 26, 1914, DPL.

[10]Finerty, *War-Path*, 246, 248, 271.

[11]McGillycuddy, *McGillycuddy, Agent*, 56; Hedren, *Traveler's Guide*, 76–77; Mills, "Battle of Slim Buttes."

[12]Bourke, *On the Border with Crook*, 367.

[13]Diary of John Bourke, vol. 5, 884–85, quoted in Greene, *Slim Buttes*, 45.

As Crook had ordered, Captain Mills, with Lieutenant Emmett Craw-ford and Lieutenant Adolphus H. Von Leuttwitz, left on the evening of September 7 to try to get help. They set a steady pace southward, halting on September 8 about twenty miles from Crook's camp. They were at rest when advance scout Frank Grouard backtracked to report the presence of an Indian camp ahead of their position, along Rabbit Creek near an outcrop called Slim Buttes. Mills wrote, "Grouard was ahead & made a sign to halt & came back & said he saw Inds ahead." He added, "During the night we came up to a kind [of] lake or pond, where there was considerable water. Grouard struck a match & we saw the ground all cut up with fresh horse tracks & Grouard said there must be a large body of Inds near Grouard kept a little way ahead— not far—and found the way as best he could."[14]

This discovery presented a unique problem for Mills. Should he avoid the Indian camp and proceed to Deadwood for the needed sup-plies or take advantage of the opportunity to strike a blow at the Indi-ans? They might have been among the warriors who attacked Crook's command at the Rosebud in June, and they almost certainly had played a role in the Custer fight. Joining Grouard, Mills approached the Indian camp. "We went up ahead & saw part of their herd & a few tepees up among the trees. He heard dogs bark etc. [It] had been raining all day & was cloudy."[15]

The desire for revenge and a morale boost trumped the need for sus-tenance, although certainly the men anticipated that they might find food and other supplies in the Indian camp. Mills, after consulting with his officers, formulated a battle plan, which he would carry out at dawn on September 9. With the village less than two miles from the soldiers' position, Mills withdrew to a "deep depression" and there ordered "the officers not to permit any of the men to leave the ravine but we were wet and cold and I consented to permit them to build fires, which they did. After the fires had been built I saw a peculiar thing. The clouds were low and as they passed over us the light of the fires would illuminate them much as a search light does the sky on a dark night."[16]

---

[14]Mills, "Battle of Slim Buttes."
[15]Ibid.
[16]Ibid.

The Indians, hunkered in their lodges as the rain soaked their camp, did not see the reflected firelight, and just before dawn the troops began moving toward the village. When they neared the Indian pony herd, Mills sent Grouard ahead again. He "went off and remained a long time and when he returned I noticed that he had a new horse. He had been riding an Indian pony that was thin and nearly used up. He had gone up in the herd, unsaddled, caught a fresh horse out of the Indian herd & saddled it. He was acting so cowardly and hesitatingly that I at once suspected he was getting himself in shape to get away should we get into a hot fight. I reproved him for staying away so long. I was afraid the herd would smell us & stampede into the village, and scolded Grouard for having gone among them."[17]

Although Mills said that Grouard "had a splendid knowledge of the country, and knew the ways of the Indians, and was undoubtedly the best guide we could have borrowed for such knowledge as that," he hesitated to rely on him. "I always regarded him as a coward and a big liar." Even so, as the soldiers approached the village in the predawn darkness, Mills admitted that the scout "was a good deal like an Indian and the ponies seemed not to take fright at him as he was riding an Indian pony."[18]

Mills, with Von Leuttwitz, led the center column while Lieutenant Crawford commanded the right flank in the dawn assault on the Indian camp. "I had told [Lieutenant Frederick] Schwatka to be ready to charge on the village the instant the pony herd would stampede for I knew the minute they smelled us they would start and run into the village, and this is just what they did," Mills said later.[19]

The soldiers advanced on foot, directing their fire at the lodges, which had been "laced up to keep out the rain." But the Indians cut open the opposite sides of the tipis, and all of them "got away except 17 who took refuge in a sort of cave or gully in a bend of the creek bed, which was dry except for rainwater that had settled in it here and there," Mills said.[20] It was learned later that the headmen in the

---

[17]Ibid. In his account of the battle at Slim Buttes, written for Walter Camp from Pittsburgh on October 9, 1919, J. A. Kirkwood said that when Grouard, whose name he spelled Girard, returned from his initial scout he was "leading two fine ponies, which he had taken from a herd he had located. The captain gave him a lecture on stealing ponies instead of locating the village." Kirkwood to Camp, October 9, 1919, Ellison Papers, DPL.

[18]Mills, "Battle of Slim Buttes."

[19]Ibid.

[20]Ibid.

camp of thirty-seven lodges were American Horse (also called Iron Shield, Iron Plume, and Black Shield) and Roman Nose, both of the Oglala tribe, and three Miniconjous, Red Horse, Iron Thunder, and Dog Necklace.[21]

Some Indians took cover behind rocks, firing at the troops sporadically, "so we did not crowd the village," Mills reported. The tribesmen who hid in the ravine shouted at the troops, telling them of other nearby Indian camps and saying "that they intended to hold out until assistance came." With this knowledge, Mills "mounted three men, in succession, one after another, on fresh Indian ponies, and told each of them to ride back on the trail as fast as they could and tell Crook that I had a village & was trying to hold it and needed assistance." Further, in the first wave of fighting, Von Leuttwitz had been "severely wounded and we had no surgeon with us, so we needed Crook at all events," Mills later recalled.[22]

As they entered the lodges in the hastily abandoned Indian camp, the soldiers found U.S. cavalry saddles, army blankets, a guidon that had been carried by the Seventh Cavalry at Little Bighorn, a gauntlet that had once belonged to Captain Myles Keogh, and three horses from the Seventh. They located percussion caps and ammunition, guns, harness, clothing, cloth, kitchen utensils, and several thousand deer, buffalo, antelope, and elk skins.[23] They also found food. Sergeant John Kirkwood, of Company M, Third Cavalry, said there was dried meat in abundance, "all packed in raw-hide packs."[24]

———— ❖ ————

Crook, upon learning of the attack at Slim Buttes, ordered McGillycuddy ahead to Mills's position with the first relief party. When he reached the site of the battle, before noon on September 9—just a few hours after the initial attack—the surgeon found "Lt. Von Leutwitz [*sic*] and 9 men wounded and whole Village captured & a few Indians trapped in a ravine."[25]

[21]Greene, *Slim Buttes*, 49. This Roman Nose is not the Cheyenne headman killed in the 1868 battle at Beecher Island in Colorado, and this American Horse is not to be confused with an Oglala of the same name who would later become prominent at Pine Ridge.

[22]Ibid.

[23]Ibid., 72; Hedren, *With Crook in the Black Hills*, 30. Finerty also listed these items as among those located in the village.

[24]Kirkwood to Camp, October 9, 1919.

[25]McGillycuddy Diary, 1876–77.

Although the initial attack had routed the Indians and allowed Mills to call up reinforcements from Crook's command, the fighting at Slim Buttes had only just begun. The Indians' resistance was relatively effective. General Wesley Merritt later said, "The World has not a light cavalry to match them."[26]

In the fighting, the soldiers had surrounded a ravine where American Horse, other warriors, and some Indian women had taken refuge. In an attempt to dislodge the holdouts, soldiers threw burning poles into the gorge.[27] Repeated onslaughts to rouse the Indians were met with fierce resistance, some of it fatal. Scouts Baptiste "Big Bat" Pourier, Baptiste "Little Bat" Garnier, and Charles (Jonathan) "Buffalo Chips" White, lay side by side on the east edge of the ravine, firing on the Indians who had taken refuge there. When White reared up for a shot at the entrenched tribesmen, one of them killed him. Pourier, as his companion took the fatal blow, raced into the ravine to claim a scalp and rapidly returned to his former position unscathed.[28] McGillycuddy wrote of this incident in 1920. "Big Bat was a sight that day, when we finally closed in and captured the Indians in the Gulch that afternoon, after Whites death." He described the scene: "Big Bat plunged into the ravine and scalped one of the Indians, and next appeared up on the bank swinging the bleeding scalp in a circle over his head and screeching like a demon, his red hair and beard added to the effect."[29]

The soldiers were relentless in trying to dislodge the holdouts. Early in the afternoon the Indians told Big Bat and Little Bat that they were bringing out a wounded man. Pourier reentered the ravine and emerged minutes later with American Horse, weak and wounded. Blood had soaked through a brightly covered blanket that was wrapped around the Indian's stomach. When McGillycuddy removed the cloth, American Horse's intestines spilled out. This was a mortal wound, the doctor knew, and he prepared to give the Indian a shot of morphine to ease his pain.[30]

---

[26]McDermott, *Guide to the Indian Wars of the West*, 184.

[27]McGillycuddy, *McGillycuddy, Agent*, 56–57.

[28]Greene, *Slim Buttes*, 75.

[29]McGillycuddy to Camp, August 3, 1920, Fort Robinson Museum Archives. In his 1876 diary, McGillycuddy gave a more subdued account: "Attempting to dislodge them one soldier & Buffalo Chips were killed & 2 soldiers wounded the Siouxs 3 bucks and 7 squaws at 3 P.M. found in ravine."

[30]McGillycuddy Diary, 1876–77. "Chief Am. Horse was initially wounded shot in abdomen I operated and tried to return intestines he died that night at 4½ PM."

"Put a knife through the son-of-a-bitch," one soldier demanded, according to an account by Julia McGillycuddy. Finerty wrote, "American Horse—a fine looking, broad-chested Sioux, with a handsome face and a neck like a bull—showed himself at the mouth of the cave, presenting the butt end of his rifle toward the General [Crook]. He had just been shot in the abdomen, and said, in his native language, that he would yield, if the lives of the warriors who fought with him were spared. Some of the soldiers, who had lost comrades in the skirmish, shouted, 'No Quarter!' but not a man was base enough to attempt shooting down the disabled chief."[31]

After American Horse's surrender, the soldiers captured additional Indians who had hidden in the ravine. From them they learned of the nearby camp of He Dog, Kicking Bear, and Crazy Horse. Already the troops had seen flashing mirrors and other signs that the Indians in American Horse's camp could expect reinforcements. The counterattack came from the southwest during the late afternoon.

Dr. Clements and Dr. McGillycuddy converted one of the buffalo-hide Indian lodges on the north side of the camp into a field hospital. They were sawing off Von Leuttwitz's shattered right leg when Crazy Horse and the other newly arrived warriors launched a fresh onslaught against the soldiers. The Indian reinforcements "attacked us on all sides but were forced off," McGillycuddy wrote.[32] Their withdrawal came at a cost to the soldiers. Private Edward Kennedy, of Company C, Fifth Cavalry, was mortally wounded when a bullet tore away the calf of his leg. Sergeant Kirkwood sustained a gunshot in the side while attempting to dislodge the Indians from the ravine. Kirkwood called it a flesh wound but admitted "a little more, and the backbone would have been broken."[33] The doctors treated Kirkwood's injured side and Private John M. Stevenson's ankle wound as the battle raged about them.

While Crazy Horse and his warriors fired on the camp, now overtaken by the soldiers, the troops abandoned the meals they had hastily prepared from the dried buffalo meat they had found. They began a systematic destruction of the village, smashing metal cups and cooking pots, slashing lodge coverings, and burning lodge poles. They

---

[31]McGillycuddy, *McGillycuddy, Agent*, 58; Finerty, *War-Path*, 255.
[32]McGillycuddy Diary, 1876–77.
[33]Kirkwood to Camp, October 9, 1919.

destroyed anything that could be considered useful to the Indians, before torching the lodges themselves.

With the Indians now entrenched on the hillside to the southwest, the units under Crook's command counterattacked, moving toward the enemy, firing sporadic volleys and occasional barrages with little effect. Lieutenant Colonel Eugene Carr later groused that the engagement was a "wasteful expenditure of ammunition."[34]

When the Indians finally retreated, the soldiers killed Indian ponies and roasted them, adding to their meal the dried buffalo meat and other provisions found in the Indian lodges. Finerty described that evening in an article published in the *Chicago Tribune* on September 18, 1876: "Night is here, and 1,000 camp-fires light a scene never to be forgotten. The soldiers last night, ragged, cold, weak, starved, and well-nigh desperate, are feasting upon meats and fruits received from a savage enemy, or warmly clothed by the robes which last night wrapped the forms of renegades."[35]

McGillycuddy later said it was fortunate for Mills that Crook arrived with the main command before Crazy Horse and the other reinforcements began attacking the camp, where the soldiers had taken up positions. "Otherwise there would have been a second Custer affair, for Crazy Horse would have cleaned them up that evening."[36]

While the soldiers settled down for the night, sated and relatively warm, McGillycuddy labored on, treating Private Kennedy and caring for the wounded American Horse.[37] The Indian refused a morphine hypodermic, so with nothing to relieve the man's suffering, McGillycuddy and Clements "operated & tried to return intestines."[38] During the night, both patients died. But captive Indians, including American Horse's own family members, saw the shaggy, bearded doctor work to

---

[34]Eugene Carr to his wife, September 10, 1876, quoted in Greene, *Slim Buttes,* 87.

[35]*Chicago Tribune,* September 18, 1867. This account of a thousand campfires seems highly exaggerated.

[36]McGillycuddy to Camp, August 3, 1920.

[37]On February 28, 1922, McGillycuddy wrote from the Hotel Claremont in Berkeley, California, to William Garnett, asking, "What relation was American Horse No. 2, killed at Slim Buttes in September 1876, to our American Horse?" Garnett, in a letter from Pine Ridge, South Dakota, dated March 6, 1922, replied, "In the fight at Slim Butte in 1876 there were two Indians killed, an old man whose name I do not know and a young man names [*sic*] Iron Shield. Bat Pourier killed him. Neither of these men were named American Horse and were no relation to our American Horse, the chief." Quoted in Clark, *Killing Crazy Horse,* 108–109.

[38]McGillycuddy Diary, 1876–77.

save the headman's life, and the story of McGillycuddy's efforts later spread to the Indian camps.[39]

Although the attack resumed at dawn, it was short-lived. The soldiers buried Private Kennedy and Buffalo Chips White, along with Von Leuttwitz's leg. Then they destroyed or burned any remnants of the Indian camp before resuming their march south, taking with them the Indian pony herd to replace their own weary steeds and to butcher and cook as needed.[40]

Crook placed McGillycuddy in charge of the twelve wounded soldiers. The competent doctor quickly organized nine travois, each pulled by a single horse, and three litters that the men devised by tying poles on either side of two horses in single file. They wrapped a blanket around the poles between the two horses and then placed an injured man on the litter, strapping him down securely to the poles with a surcingle.[41]

Sergeant John Kirkwood, having been injured in the fighting, was with McGillycuddy's sick party. Years later, in 1919, he wrote to Walter Mason Camp, a historian of the Indian wars, that after the burials, the men "made a big fire over the burying place, in order to fool the Indians, but the ruse did not work. The next day we started on, the wounded being carried on travoys, while Lieut. Von Ludwick was put on a stretcher between mules. The latter tried to grab a revolver from the holster of one of the packers who were leading the mules in order to commit suicide. He insisted that the Indians were rechopping his foot. And they were. The next day Major Mason was sent back with five companies of the 5th Cavalry to investigate. They found that they [*sic*] bodies had been dug up, and cut to pieces."[42]

Back on the move toward the Black Hills, McGillycuddy rode a horse or walked beside the hospital train, adjusting bandages and giving

---

[39]In his 1914 interview with Walter Camp, Anson Mills said that American Horse was brought to where "a couple of our surgeons were standing. One of them looked at this wounded Indian and made no offer to do anything, but said, 'Tell him he will die before next morning.' The interpreter told him this, but the Indian never flinched or betrayed any feeling." Mills made no reference to McGillycuddy's subsequent treatment of American Horse. Finerty wrote that "the surgeons examined the wound, pronounced it mortal, and during the night American Horse, one of the bravest and ablest of the Sioux chiefs, fell back suddenly, and expired without uttering a groan." Mills, "Battle of Slim Buttes."

[40]Greene, *Slim Buttes,* 92. John A. Kirkwood also wrote of burying Leuttwitz's leg.

[41]McGillycuddy, *McGillycuddy, Agent,* 59.

[42]Kirkwood to Camp, October 9, 1919.

medication to keep the men as comfortable as possible. Incredibly, he also took the time to write to Fanny and his mother, perhaps to assure them he had come through the fight at Slim Buttes without being injured.[43]

Rain poured down all day on September 11, and the surgeon struggled through muck and mire on a twenty-five-mile march with the wounded train. John Finerty, traveling in heavy rain with the uninjured soldiers, later wrote of the sick train: "Our eyes would often turn compassionately to the long string of travois (mule litters) on which our sick and wounded were being dragged toward civilization. The chill, merciless rain poured upon them constantly, and neither poncho nor blanket would keep it out."[44]

When Lieutenant Henry Huntington became so ill that he fell behind the others, the doctor remained with him despite the risk of Indian attack. He cut saplings from a grove of trees to fashion another travois and lashed it to Huntington's thoroughbred, which pitched a fit over the contraption dragging behind its feet. With persistence, McGillycuddy worked the horse until eventually he could transport the ill man on the drag. But the horse's skittishness slowed an already tedious form of travel, and the two men did not reach camp until ten o'clock that night. By then Crook believed that the Indians, who harassed the command from the rear, had captured the medical officer.[45]

The battle at Slim Buttes briefly rejuvenated the soldiers' spirits and gave them a fresh supply of food. But the provisions they had commandeered at the Indian camp quickly disappeared, and they soon resumed a horsemeat diet as they struggled toward Crook City. Rain came, at first sporadically and then in torrents on September 12, turning the ground into a quagmire that felled additional weak horses. The men killed the animals, and when they could not start and maintain a fire in the rain, they ate the meat raw. McGillycuddy had it no easier than anyone else. The travois were difficult to pull across muddy ground and often upset when crossing creeks, causing further trauma to the ill and wounded men. The men were "weak and despondent," many of them unable to stand without aid, and their very survival was in question. Medical officer Clements noted that almost everyone on the march had "reached the limit of human endurance."[46]

---

[43]McGillycuddy, *McGillycuddy, Agent,* 60; McGillycuddy Diary, 1876–77.
[44]Finerty, *War-Path,* 266.
[45]McGillycuddy, *McGillycuddy, Agent,* 56; Hedren, *Traveler's Guide,* 79.
[46]Clements's medical report, 18, quoted in Greene, *Slim Buttes,* 103.

Wounded man on horse travois, 1876.
In taking care of wounded soldiers after the battle of Slim Buttes,
McGillycuddy, too, used a travois for transportation. Stanley J. Morrow,
photographer. *Denver Public Library, Western History Collection, X-31751.*

While McGillycuddy laboriously transported the wounded and ill
from Slim Buttes, camping at night in a wickiup built of brush, Captain
Mills again set out to find help. This time he made it to Crook City,
where he obtained supplies from local merchants. He brought them
back to the command, arriving on September 13 at Crook's camp at
the crossing of the Belle Fourche River. Finerty, "breakfasting on pony
steak," heard the "lowing of the oxen" that heralded the relief party
and its herd of fifty head of cattle, some of which the soldiers readily

Two-horse litter.
Such litters were devised and used following the battle of
Slim Buttes, when McGillycuddy had wounded men transported
from the battlefield to Crook City. *National Archives, image 530894.*

butchered. The contingent also escorted ox-drawn wagons filled with
bacon, coffee, vegetables, eggs, butter, crackers, flour, and sugar. Later,
other supplies reached Crook's command, including onions, cabbages,
turnips, and potatoes.[47]

The medical officers told the men to eat sparingly. Nevertheless,
they soon found themselves distributing laxatives to ease the troopers'

[47]Finerty, *War-Path*, 270, 275–76.

Valentine T. McGillycuddy, 1876, while he was
with the Big Horn and Yellowstone Expedition. During
the march after the battle of Slim Buttes, McGillycuddy slept
in wickiups constructed of pine boughs. Visible here are his canteen,
a .45-55 caliber Springfield carbine, and what appear to be
homemade canvas leggings. *National Archives,
image 533168.*

overindulgence. The effects of similar gorging when the men found a grove of wild plums and berries required a reverse form of treatment by the doctors.[48]

Revitalized by the resupply of rations, the troops marched on to Crook City, a nearly deserted mining town of around 250 log and frame buildings. They camped just two miles beyond the settlement on September 18.

At Crook City, Calamity Jane met the Big Horn and Yellowstone Expedition and then rode with the troops to Deadwood.[49] McGillycuddy, who had not seen her for a year, called Jane "our old friend Calamity" and later noted that she had "blossomed out as a fully equipped border scout, beaded buckskin trousers, blue shirt, broad brimmed hat, winchester rifle, mounted on a bucking broncho, with a supply of fluid ammunition in the saddle bags."[50] Once in the embryo mining boomtown of Deadwood, with his belly full for the first time in weeks, McGillycuddy attended a dance, kicking up his heels in a schottische with Calamity Jane. "He liked to dance, and he did not know that he danced badly," the doctor's second wife, Julia, later wrote.[51]

Deadwood was a raucous mining camp. It had a "multitude of 'variety' theaters and a crowd of brazen and bedizened harlots, gambling hells, drinking 'dives' and other moral abominations," Finerty reported.[52]

General Crook had left the Big Horn and Yellowstone Expedition on September 16, under orders to report to Fort Laramie. From that point forward, Colonel Wesley Merritt assumed command of the expedition. McGillycuddy was reassigned to serve in both the Second and Third Cavalries as a medical officer to replace Dr. Charles R. Stephens, who was detached from the command.[53]

The sojourn in Deadwood was short, and the expedition soon moved on to new camps. The following day the men tramped twenty-four miles south to pitch their shelters—frames of brush covered with tattered canvas—on middle Box Elder Creek, a site that had been one of McGillycuddy's camps during the Newton-Jenney Black Hills Expedition the previous year. While they were there, two companies

---

[48]Hedren, *Traveler's Guide*, 81; Greene, *Slim Buttes*, 104.

[49]McGillycuddy, *McGillycuddy, Agent*, 62–63.

[50]McGillycuddy to editor, *Rapid City Journal*.

[51]McGillycuddy, *McGillycuddy, Agent*, 64.

[52]Finerty, *War-Path*, 280.

[53]McGillycuddy Diary, 1876–77. McGillycuddy spelled the medical officer's name "Stevens," but it is properly Stephens.

of the Fourth Artillery arrived from the Red Cloud Agency, bringing with them additional rations.[54] The long, difficult campaign had devastated the troops, and on September 20, McGillycuddy reported sixty cases of cholera among the men in the Second and Third Cavalries. He noted in his journal that he was "sick myself."[55] But he was definitely back in familiar territory, the very country he had surveyed and mapped in the company of "Old Tuttle" the previous year. During subsequent days the command, under Merritt's direction, halted at Camp Crook, so named by the members of the Black Hills Expedition, before moving to Custer City and then on to Camp Harney, another of the Newton-Jenney bivouacs in 1875.

Feeling better, and with an assured supply of rations, McGillycuddy wrote more letters to Fanny and his mother. He received messages from them as well, along with one from Captain Tuttle, when all the mail posted from July 20 through September 17 arrived at Camp Harney on September 29. That day McGillycuddy noted there had been both frost and snow on the ground.[56]

For the next two weeks, as word spread not only of the battle at Slim Buttes but also of the privations faced by Crook's men on a journey later dubbed the Mud, Horsemeat, or Starvation March, the doctor spent time in camp, wrote letters, compiled reports, and read his mail. On October 2 the soldiers and their accompanying civilian and medical corps moved to a site below a stockade on French Creek that had been built by gold seekers in 1874. There, although most of the men built new brush and canvas-covered shelters, a few had tents brought in by a relief train. McGillycuddy "camped in old log cabin," likely the first time he had slept under a real roof since June, when he left Fort Fetterman. He had that luxury for several days until ordered to accompany Colonel Merritt and six hundred men on a scout. Although Merritt likely wanted the doctor along for his medical skills, he also no doubt recognized that McGillycuddy was personally familiar with the ground they would cover as they explored to the east and north. During the next two weeks they rode through the country around Buffalo Gap and along French and Rapid

---

[54]McGillycuddy Diary, 1876–77; Finerty, *War-Path*, 276.

[55]McGillycuddy Diary, 1876–77. The official medical reports from the expedition identified the disease affecting the troops as typhoid. Cholera and typhoid had a common cause, impure water.

[56]McGillycuddy Diary, 1876–77.

Officers of the Third Cavalry,
near French Creek, Dakota Territory, 1876.

Valentine T. McGillycuddy is the second man from the top of the photograph, with a full mustache and beard. Above him is Second Lieutenant Bainbridge Reynolds. In the row below him are, from left, First Lieutenant Joseph Lawson, Second Lieutenant James F. Simpson, Second Lieutenant Charles Morton, Second Lieutenant James E. H. Foster, and First Lieutenant Albert D. King. Next row down, from left: Captain Frederick Van Vliet, First Lieutenant Emmet Crawford, First Lieutenant Alexander D. B. Smead, Captain Charles Meinhold, Second Lieutenant Henry R. Lemley. Bottom row, from left: Major Julius W. Mason, Lieutenant Colonel William B. Royal, Second Lieutenant George F. Chase, Major Andrew W. Evans, Captain William H. Andrews, First Lieutenant Augustus C. Paul, Captain Anson Mills, Second Lieutenant Frederick Schwatka. Stanley J. Morrow, photographer. *Denver Public Library, Western History Collection, X-21756.*

Field camp set up by soldiers under General George Crook,
Whitewood, Dakota Territory, 1876. The soldiers used
brush, wagon bows, and canvas to create shelters.
National Archives, image 533170.

Creeks and the Cheyenne River before turning south toward Camp
Robinson and the Red Cloud Agency.[57]

The familiar bluffs along the White River in northwestern Nebraska,
near Camp Robinson, must have been a welcome sight for McGillycuddy

[57]McGillycuddy noted his sleeping arrangements in his diary. Photographs taken by Stanley J.
Morrow, a frontier photographer who learned his craft while working as a volunteer for
Matthew Brady during the Civil War, clearly show the crude shelters used by the men on
the march and at French Creek, with canvas tents visible behind the rough lodging. Photographs reproduced in Hedren, *With Crook in the Black Hills*, 41, 42.

when the Big Horn and Yellowstone Expedition disbanded on October 24. That day Crook's army surrounded Indian bands led by Red Cloud and Red Leaf at the Red Cloud Agency, seizing horses and firearms belonging to the Indians. Crook then announced that Spotted Tail would thereafter be the "head chief" of all the Sioux, formally deposing Red Cloud and Red Leaf. In the wake of this action, McGillycuddy was ordered to report to the commanding officer at Camp Robinson, where he was formally assigned to serve as assistant post surgeon, although as a civilian he remained a contract doctor.[58]

On the morning of October 31, at Camp Robinson, McGillycuddy visited with California Joe, a friend from their days together on the Newton-Jenney Expedition. The two had resumed their acquaintance weeks earlier when the scout had brought a herd of horses from Fort Laramie to replace the worn-out mounts of the Fifth Cavalry. After reaching the troops, California Joe remained with them until they arrived at Camp Robinson.

Also at the post was civilian Thomas Newcomb, a man who had an uneasy relationship with California Joe. In his book *Frank Grouard*, Joe DeBarthe wrote that the enmity between Newcomb and California Joe stemmed from the death of scout Louis Richaud's father, who had been shot and killed along the Niobrara River in November 1875. Newcomb accused California Joe of the death. "When Joe's preliminary examination came off, Newcomb swore that old man Reshaw [Richaud] had been killed by Joe; but he had no evidence to substantiate the statement," Grouard recalled. "Nobody who knew Joe believed a word of it, and the actions of Newcomb made Joe awful mad; and I don't doubt but what he may have threatened to get even with his accuser. I don't believe, however, that Joe ever threatened to kill Newcomb, and never found a man who did believe it," Grouard said.[59]

Even so, Newcomb may have feared that California Joe would take revenge for the allegations made against him. Shortly after California

[58]McGillycuddy Diary, 1876–77; Hedren, *Traveler's Guide*, 82. Hedren reported on the action against Red Leaf and Red Cloud in *With Crook in the Black Hills*, 66. A photograph taken by Stanley Morrow shows Crook in front of the two-story wood Red Cloud Agency building, standing with Spotted Tail just after the action of October 24, 1876.

[59]DeBarthe, *Frank Grouard*, 334. John S. Gray recounted a similar story of the enmity between Newcomb and California Joe, using as a source a letter McGillycuddy wrote on April 8, 1927, to California Joe–Moses Milner's son while the latter was preparing a book about his father. Gray, "A Triple Play," n.p. The letter indicates that California Joe was killed on October 29, but in his diary, McGillycuddy correctly gave the date as Tuesday, October 31. So did the *New York Herald* in an article published on November 5, 1876.

Joe took leave of McGillycuddy on the morning of October 31, word spread across the post that the scout had been shot. Rushing to the scene, McGillycuddy found Joe dead. He soon learned that Newcomb had fled the camp. Grouard later said the fatal bullet had been fired from a double-barreled shotgun as Joe rounded the corner on his way to mess. Although the alleged perpetrator was never brought to trial for the killing, Grouard said, "I believed at the time, and still think, this was as cold-blooded a murder as I ever heard of."[60]

McGillycuddy buried California Joe near Camp Robinson (Grouard said the burial took place at the Red Cloud Agency). The doctor said California Joe "had no equal as a scout in natural ability, reliability, and wide experience."[61] Grouard noted that his "untimely end was universally regretted, for he was as popular as he was brave."[62]

<hr />

McGillycuddy must have sagged in exhaustion as he settled into the crowded quarters of the stagecoach when it rumbled from the Red Cloud Agency just after seven o'clock in the morning on November 8. He was traveling to Sidney, Nebraska, and the station that served the Union Pacific Railroad. Crammed into the confined space with McGillycuddy and three companions was Private John T. Holden, of the Fourth Cavalry, whom McGillycuddy was charged with transporting to Washington, D.C. The man had been declared insane and needed treatment. The transfer worked into the doctor's plans, because the trip would give him an opportunity to see Fanny. He telegraphed her from Sidney before climbing onto the eastbound Union Pacific train with Holden. After changing trains in Omaha, McGillycuddy and his companions reached Chicago mid-afternoon on November 11.

---

[60]DeBarthe, *Frank Grouard,* 334. In this account, Grouard called Newcomb "a first-class bluffer." He said Newcomb was "so anxious to acquire a reputation as a bad man that he never missed an opportunity of whipping a 'kid' or doing up some poor, drunken fellow" (335). Newcomb had been with the troops when the spring campaign of 1876 opened. At Fort Reno he was in the middle of a story about how he had once jumped on the back of a Texas buffalo and ridden it several miles when Indians fired on the camp, scaring him. This led the soldiers to begin calling Newcomb "Texas Buffalo" (336). In his diary, McGillycuddy noted on October 31, 1876, that California Joe had been murdered. He made no reference to handling the burial. In his 1927 letter to Milner's son, McGillycuddy said the killing took place near the corral, and he was "sitting on the porch of the hospital" when he heard the shot. These details are from Milner and Forrest, *California Joe,* 279.

[61]Watson, "California Joe."

[62]DeBarthe, *Frank Grouard,* 336.

The doctor immediately went to the Palmer House, "got Fanny & left for Washington via Balt & O. R. R. at 5:10 P.M. fare, $11.00."[63]

In Washington, D.C., on November 12, McGillycuddy got rooms at the St. James Hotel for the party, including "insane Pvt. Holden." The following day he took Holden to the asylum. Afterward he and Fanny, who had spent so little time together, made the rounds in the city. On November 17 they left for Detroit on the Pittsburgh, Cleveland and Toledo railway, reaching their destination at eleven o'clock that night. They purchased supplies, conducted business, and visited McGilly-cuddy's family in Detroit and then Fanny's in Ionia, Michigan, for four days. On November 30 they boarded a train that took them to Omaha and eventually to Sidney, Nebraska, where they transferred to the stage for the ride to the Red Cloud Agency and Camp Robin-son. On December 7, 1876, the newlyweds moved into their quarters at Camp Robinson. A week later McGillycuddy, who had faithfully kept his journal during his time apart from Fanny, turned the daily report-ing over to her.[64]

---

[63]McGillycuddy Diary, 1876–77.

[64]Ibid. The handwriting in the journal changes on December 14, and the entries from this point until the journal concludes on April 11 are written from Fanny's perspective.

9

Camp Robinson Surgeon

C AMP ROBINSON, OFFICIALLY named for Fourteenth Infantry First Lieutenant Levi Robinson, who had been killed by Indians near Laramie Peak on February 9, 1874, was a rough frontier outpost when Valentine Trant O'Connell McGillycuddy and Fanny Hoyt McGillycuddy arrived together in December 1876. Exactly which of the duplex housing units was theirs is unknown, but it stood in a row of similarly designed adobe structures on the north side of the parade ground. The commanding officer's house, two stories high and more resplendent than the others, was at the west end of the row. A line of cottonwood trees several yards away separated homes from the drill field. Across the parade ground to the south were the long barracks, constructed the year previous, and the adjutant's office and guardhouse, both raised in 1874.[1]

Back at Camp Robinson, McGillycuddy labored under the direction of Dr. Charles E. Munn. The lead doctor spent his days treating soldiers at the post hospital while his subordinate assisted. These clinicians were responsible for caring for troops stationed at Camp Robinson and Camp Sheridan, about forty miles to the northeast, and for residents of both the Red Cloud and Spotted Tail Indian Agencies. The duty of treating those who were ill or injured and away from the post often fell to the younger man.[2]

A routine day began with sick call at seven o'clock in the morning. McGillycuddy, young but now field tested, spent long hours working

---

[1]Buecker, *Fort Robinson*. Camp, later Fort, Robinson is today a Nebraska state historical park. Original buildings have been restored or replicas built, giving the place a look similar to what it was like during the years McGillycuddy lived and worked there.

[2]McGillycuddy, *McGillycuddy, Agent*, 67.

at the hospital and in the outlying camps. Once he cut his finger on a patient's splintered rib and developed a case of blood poisoning that gave him chills and caused his arm to swell and turn green. "His skin, the whites of his eyes, and his nails turned tobacco color," wrote his second wife, Julia, in her biography of him. In recounting his illness, she provided no details about any treatment he might have administered to himself—or received from Dr. Munn—but within a week noted he was recovering.[3]

Illness affected McGillycuddy in January and February 1877. On the sixth of January, first wife Fanny recorded in the diary he had started the previous year, "Dr. came home sick." This malady did not deter Fanny from attending a social gathering that evening in company of "Mr. Yeatman," undoubtedly McGillycuddy's mess partner from the summer and fall campaign. For the next ten days her diary entries commonly said, "Dr. no better." On the fourteenth she "baked him two apples. he ate them," but on the fifteenth she again reported, "Dr. no better. ate a little for his breakfast." The following day, however, she reported, "Dr little better ate two eggs for his breakfast." That day he "went through hospital and straightened things there," Fanny reported, adding, "Everybody drunk spent in at Dr. Mumms with Mr. Carpenter playing 'casino.'"

Eating eggs for breakfast, McGillycuddy soon recovered his strength. By January 19 he accompanied Fanny to the home of Major Daniel W. Burke, where the couple played euchre with the major and his wife. On January 20 both Valentine and Fanny went to the camp store, where they weighed themselves. He was 148 pounds, and she recorded her own weight as 160 and a half pounds.

During the next several days the two played euchre, attended "hops," or dances, and received carpeting and curtains for their home brought in by wagon train. But apparently McGillycuddy remained unwell, for Fanny wrote on January 27, "Our little home looks very cozy, if I could see my husband cheerful and happy, my happiness would be complete."[4] February found the doctor and his wife engaged in horseback rides, taking walks around the camp, and spending time with other couples. On February 5, Fanny accompanied Major and Mrs. Burke on an ambulance ride to a nearby lake. "Dr. was informed that

[3]Ibid., 68.
[4]McGillycuddy Diary, 1876–77.

he could not go as Dr. Munn was very sick. [Doctor] staid home much to my indignation and disgust," Fanny groused in the diary. Several days later her spirits lightened when Lieutenant Colonel George A. Forsyth, who surprised the troops at Camp Robinson with an inspection, took time to call on "all of the ladies at the post."[5]

By the middle of February, Fanny again wrote that the doctor was "feeling quite sick, came home and went to bed in a raging fever." He must have made a quick recovery, because the next day he learned that the Third Cavalry was "ordered to the Black Hills to start for Deadwood City immediately and Dr. McGillycuddy was to go as medical officer of the party." Fanny recorded her own reaction: "I thought at first it was a joke but found that it was true. how I dread the idea of leaving my comfortable, nice, little home for the uncertainties of camp life. if the weather continues fine, it will be pleasant but it is so doubtful. I fear the consequences."

Fanny set aside her concern for personal comfort, because "Dr. wants to go. Thinks he can do better up there. I am willing to do anything."[6] On February 22, Fanny, riding her horse, Charley, and easily recognizable because she wore a long green riding habit, a beaver jacket, and a cap, set out with her husband on the expedition to Deadwood and Crook City. McGillycuddy served as a surgeon with four companies of the Third Cavalry under Captain Peter Dumont Vroom, a New Jersey native who had been recognized for meritorious service during the Civil War. These troops had been ordered into the field upon reports of problems between settlers and Indians in that area. Over the next three weeks they traveled north, riding in all kinds of weather, sometimes staying in camp when snow swirled through the Black Hills. Their accommodations consisted of tents with Sibley stoves and beds made from buffalo robes. They dined on roast beef and vegetables cooked in Dutch ovens.[7]

Although often she rode Charley, when the weather was too uncomfortable Fanny huddled in the back of one of the army ambulances. At times she remarked on the stunning country, but most often she

---

[5]Ibid.

[6]Ibid.

[7]McGillycuddy, *McGillycuddy, Agent,* 70–71. Information about the military incursion into the Black Hills is also included in Buecker, "Can You Send Us Immediate Relief?" Preceding the Vroom command were sixty-one men in Company C, Third Cavalry, led by Second Lieutenant Joseph F. Cummings, who pursued raiding Indians and recovered lost stock in the area northwest of Deadwood and Crook City.

reserved her writing pages for comments about the weather and camp conditions. The tedium of campaigning was something Fanny had never before experienced. She wrote, "Dreary and lonesome is camp life. I wonder men *do not go mad.*"[8]

When the troops remained in one camp for several days in March, McGillycuddy put up the hospital tent and set up a rustic bed to share with Fanny. She wrote, "It is quite a luxury. our tent is floored and we feel a little more like human beings." But even those amenities did not make camp life truly pleasant for this frontier bride, who wrote of the foggy, snowy, disagreeable weather.

On April 4 Fanny wrote, "News came that Crazy Horse with his band has gone to Spotted Tail Agency with Spotted Tail."[9] On the tenth she indicated that she and her husband would "leave camp this morning for Crook City." But her report that Crazy Horse had moved to Spotted Tail Agency was premature. The main Miniconjou and Sans Arc village surrendered on April 14 at Spotted Tail Agency while Crazy Horse stayed out on the plains.[10] Some of the Indians had remained off the reservation following the previous year's battles with the frontier army and were only now surrendering and moving onto the land set aside for them under the 1868 treaty. Crazy Horse was not yet on the reservation, but he had made an important decision. His wife, Black Shawl Woman, was ill and needed treatment. On April 16, Crazy Horse broke his camp and headed south past Pumpkin Buttes, intending to go to the Red Cloud Agency and join the tribesmen already gathered there. By April 27, his band had halted three miles north of Hat Creek Station, an isolated log post constructed by John Bowman and Joe Walters in 1876 as Hat Creek Ranch, a stage stop on the Cheyenne-Deadwood stage road. This post was about fifty miles northwest of the Red Cloud Agency.

Lacking food and other supplies, and struggling through spring mud, Crazy Horse's followers ground to a halt and went into camp along Sage Creek. Three days later Oglala scouts accompanied Lieutenant J. Wesley Rosenquest, a New Yorker then serving with the Fourth Cavalry, as he took ten wagon loads of supplies and fifty head of cattle to the Indians. These Oglala scouts, following orders from

---

[8]McGillycuddy Diary, 1876–77.
[9]Ibid.
[10]Bray, *Crazy Horse*, 275.

American Horse, met their northern brothers along Sage Creek. The heretofore hostile warriors gave each of the approaching scouts a horse. They even handed one over to Lieutenant Rosenquest before Crazy Horse himself shook the officer's hand.[11]

In spite of these significant overtures, the surrender of Crazy Horse had not yet been concluded. The headman remained reluctant to travel the last miles to the Red Cloud or Spotted Tail Agency; he sought a separate place for his people and hesitated to give up his free life without assurance that he could hold the village together. Slowly, Crazy Horse and his followers moved toward the Red Cloud Agency, finally coming to within five miles of the buildings there. On Sunday, May 6, Second Cavalry Lieutenant William P. Clark, a man known to the Indians as Waposta Ska, White Hat, rode from Camp Robinson to meet Crazy Horse. This protégé of General George Crook knew Indian sign language and had earned respect from the tribesmen, making him an ideal emissary from the government in the final negotiations for Crazy Horse's surrender.

The two came face to face in mid-morning, riding toward each other, dismounting, sitting on the ground, and eventually standing and shaking hands before sharing a pipe. Clark told Crazy Horse he had "come to make a lasting peace, never to be broken." After some tense minutes, the Indian leaders voluntarily laid down their weapons. He Dog, one of Crazy Horse's most loyal and trusted companions, presented his own headdress to Clark, who donned it and wore it as he led the procession back to Camp Robinson. An Indian participant at the surrender said it was Crazy Horse who gave his headdress to Clark.[12]

A mile from the army post, White Hat Clark pulled up and instructed Crazy Horse to make a new camp, where he could surrender his ponies and weapons. This pronouncement, as could be expected, set up resistance, but eventually Crazy Horse complied. By the end of the day Clark had taken control of 114 weapons, including breechloaders,

---

[11]Ibid., 279.

[12]Ibid., 282–83. Thomas Dispatch, who gave his name to Walter M. Camp as "Shave Elk Eccoca Tashla, which means an elk with bare skin in spots," told of Crazy Horse's surrender this way: "At the time Crazy Horse surrendered an officer whom we called White Cap came out and met us and it was arranged to have some of our men meet some of the principal men of the soldiers when Crazy Horse met White Hat C. H. [Crazy Horse] said: 'All right I will surrender and fight no more.' He then put his head dress on White Hat and White Hat rode off wearing this head gear and he looked so comical that even we Indians laughed."

muzzleloaders, and revolvers, as well as the 145 lodges housing 899 people: 217 men, 312 women, 186 boys, and 184 girls. That evening Crazy Horse invited army scout Frank Grouard, who had served as interpreter during the day's proceedings, and First Lieutenant John Bourke, Crook's long-time aide-de-camp, to join him for supper.[13]

[13]Bray, *Crazy Horse*, 284–85.

10

Crazy Horse

BOTH BEFORE AND AFTER the 1877 spring campaign into the Black Hills, McGillycuddy gave medical aid to people in the Indian camps, where he saw a variety of injuries and ailments. In one case, while treating an eighteen-year-old Sioux woman with a difficult birth, he realized that the baby was dead and told the woman he needed to use instruments to help deliver the child. She and family members refused such care, and the doctor departed. Later, a young boy summoned him back to the woman's lodge, where, with the assistance of Dr. Munn, he delivered the stillborn infant.[1] Because of his care for them, he said, the Lakotas in the camp began calling him "Wasicu Wakan," interpreted by some as "miracle man."[2]

The McGillycuddys returned to Camp Robinson on April 19, arriving there around noon on a sunny day. The women in camp quickly called on Fanny, no doubt eager to hear about her adventures with the campaign into the Black Hills. Because their quarters were not ready for occupancy, the doctor and his wife spent their first two nights back at the post in the home of Major Burke. On Saturday, April 21, Fanny wrote in the diary, "Came into our quarters." By the following Monday they had placed carpet in the front room and begun to organize their possessions. The carpet was laid in the bedroom the next day, and by Friday, April 27, they were settled. "It seemed so nice to be at

[1] McGillycuddy Diary, 1876–77. On August 13, 1877, Fanny McGillycuddy wrote, "Dr. was sent for to go to see the squaw again. The instruments were used and Dr. [Munn] assisted. Got home at about eleven o'clock."

[2] McGillycuddy, *McGillycuddy, Agent,* 70. Elmo Scott Watson, in "Crazy Horse, Fighting Chief of the Sioux," noted that McGillycuddy "received the names Wasicu Wakan, the 'White Miracle Man' and 'Tasunka Witko Kola,' The Friend of Crazy Horse."

home once more," Fanny wrote in her own diary. "Our rooms look so nice and cozy. Everything is clean and nice."[3]

In part because he was the junior doctor at Camp Robinson, and also likely because he had established a rapport with the Indians in the camps, on the day of Crazy Horse's surrender McGillycuddy was summoned to the Oglala camp to see whether his medicine could benefit Black Shawl Woman. Accompanied by Fanny, who wore her green riding habit, McGillycuddy entered the Crazy Horse camp. The village women quickly gathered around Fanny as the doctor examined his new patient. This was the first of many trips the doctor made to Crazy Horse's lodge to treat Black Shawl Woman. Because Fanny usually accompanied him, their regular calls became "half social, and a friendship developed between the Doctor and the war chief." As Black Shawl Woman's health improved, Fanny also nurtured friendships with other women in the camp.[4]

McGillycuddy himself later said, "I became a close friend of Crazy Horse after his surrender at Fort Robinson in the spring of 1877, by reason of the fact that it became part of my duty, as assistant post surgeon, to look after such Indians, friendly or hostile, as required medical attention, and his wife, who was afflicted with tuberculosis, came under my care. Hence I was in the hostile camp, five miles from the post, every few days."[5]

On May 8, 1926, McGillycuddy wrote to William "Billy" Garnett, who had been a scout and an interpreter at the Red Cloud Agency, from the Hotel Claremont in Berkeley, California, referring to Crazy Horse: "You know his wife was very sick with consumption, and the Sunday the hostiles came in, I was sent for to come to the camp and give her medicine which was the first time I met Crazy Horse, and thus we became good friends."

---

[3]Fanny McGillycuddy Diary, April 11, 1877–October 31, 1878, South Dakota State Historical Resource Center, Pierre.

[4]Bray, *Crazy Horse,* 297. Julia McGillycuddy referred to the wife of Crazy Horse as Black Shawl, but her full name was Black Shawl Woman. She was born about 1843 in an Oglala camp, the daughter of Old Red Feather. She was Crazy Horse's second wife, married in 1871, and mother of his only daughter, They Are Afraid Of Her, who died as a child in 1873. Fanny's interaction with the women in the Indian camp is related in Kutac, "He Saw Troopers Die," 51. Unfortunately, Fanny McGillycuddy made no entry in her own diary about visiting the Crazy Horse camp. For the period from April 28 to May 20, she wrote, "Nothing of importance occurring. Col. Mills and wife arrived enroute to Sidney east for leave. Mrs. Kennington sick."

[5]Quoted in Brininstool, *Crazy Horse,* 43–48.

"There is a report that the sickness of his wife caused him to 'surrender,' what do you think about it," McGillycuddy inquired of Garnett. The scout's response, if he directly answered the doctor's question, is unknown.[6] But Black Shawl Woman's illness probably was indeed a contributing factor.

During those visits to the Crazy Horse camp, McGillycuddy had occasion to visit with the powerful war chief, who spoke of the battle at the Little Bighorn. He told the doctor, "No one got away, but the officer who put spurs to his horse and galloped to the east, and the Crow scout."[7]

In later years McGillycuddy wrote to historian E. A. Brininstool that Crazy Horse "did not have his equal as warrior and leading chief. He was a free lance—independent, intolerant of control. He gave submissive allegiance to no man, white or Indian, and claimed his inalienable right as an Indian chief to wander at will over the hunting grounds of his people. He never registered or enrolled at any Indian agency."[8]

"Circumstances and conditions resulted in a strong friendship between us, and I became known among the northern, or hostile Sioux, as 'Ta-sunko-witko-kola' or 'The friend of Crazy Horse,'" McGillycuddy told Brininstool.[9] This name would serve McGillycuddy well in years to come, when he found himself in a position of authority over the Indians at the Pine Ridge agency and reservation, in what is now southwestern South Dakota, about forty miles northeast of Camp Robinson. One writer later claimed that more than once, friendly Indians took McGillycuddy's side against angry tribesmen.[10]

———— • ◆ • ————

In the months after Crazy Horse's surrender, tension escalated throughout the Indian camps. Red Cloud, an elder Oglala statesman, in particular disliked the fact that many of the younger men were

---

[6]McGillycuddy to William Garnett, May 8, 1926, quoted in Clark, *Killing of Crazy Horse*, 116.

[7]McGillycuddy, *McGillycuddy, Agent*, 77.

[8]Brininstool, *Crazy Horse*, 43–48. This last statement is erroneous; Crazy Horse did enroll at the Red Cloud Agency when he surrendered in 1877.

[9]Ibid., 43–48. McGillycuddy to Camp, August 3, 1920, says, "Crazy Horse became a strong friend of mine on his surrender. . . . I cared for him when he was killed by bayonet wound. . . . I was afterwards known among the Indians as 'Tasunka Witko Kola,' the friend of Crazy Horse."

[10]Kutac, "He Saw Troopers Die," 52.

attracted to Crazy Horse and his camp. The Brulé chief, Spotted Tail, also had concerns about defections to Crazy Horse.[11]

"A great many of the chiefs had grown jealous of Crazy Horse's notoriety," wrote Susan Bordeaux Bettelyoun, one of eight children of trader James Bordeaux and a Brulé Sioux named Red Cormorant Woman. "Among these were Spotted Tail himself and Red Cloud. It was alleged that they were afraid he would be honored much higher than they were; he was a much younger man than they were." Susan Bordeaux spent her early years near Fort Laramie but later lived near the Spotted Tail Agency with her Brulé mother's people. She described Crazy Horse as a "very handsome man." On one occasion when she saw him at the Spotted Tail Agency, she observed that he had "nice long light brown hair. His scalplock was ornamented with beads and hung clear to his waist; his braids were wrapped in fur. He was partly wrapped in a broadcloth blanket. His leggings were also navy blue broadcloth; his moccasins were beaded."[12]

During that summer of 1877 Crazy Horse worked to gain approval of a northern reservation for his followers. With other tribal leaders, he requested an opportunity to conduct a buffalo hunt. Significant discussions were under way about organizing a delegation of Indian leaders to go to Washington, D.C., where they could meet with federal authorities, including President Rutherford B. Hayes. In late June the Indians gathered for a Sun Dance. Fanny McGillycuddy wrote on June 29, "Worst dust storm ever known here. [Indian] dances going on. Doctor could not go on account of storm. Much disappointed."[13]

In July the McGillycuddys moved to new quarters, the weather turned hot, and the army reorganized its Indian scouts. It placed Crazy Horse, who had been granted status as a sergeant in the Indian scouts in May, in a leadership role for one company. The move caused apprehension among some of the other tribal leaders, such as Spotted Tail, who had seen many of his younger men leave his camp to join with Crazy Horse. In one meeting conducted by Lieutenant Clark, Crazy Horse sat in a chair beside Clark and elevated above the other

---

[11]Clark, in *Killing of Crazy Horse*, 68, quotes He Dog's statement, written by his son, Rev. Eagle Hawk, saying that Crazy Horse was ultimately killed "perhaps due to the resentment and jealousy on the part of the chiefs and headmen of the other tribes." Bray, in *Crazy Horse*, 334, makes similar statements.

[12]Bettelyoun and Waggoner, *With My Own Eyes*, 108–109.

[13]Fanny McGillycuddy Diary, 1877–78.

Indian scouts, making the statement—symbolically, at least—that he was held in higher esteem by the military authorities. When approval came for the buffalo hunt, tribal leaders were informed at a council, during which it was announced that a feast to celebrate would be held in Crazy Horse's camp. At this news, Red Cloud and two of his followers abruptly departed the council session.[14] McGillycuddy likely missed this news, for he was "not well all of the week," according to Fanny's diary.

Tribesmen prepared for the buffalo hunt and anticipated a trip by a delegation to Washington, D.C., in mid-September. But now Crazy Horse reversed his earlier decision and desire to go to Washington. He had heard gossip from both his closest supporters, including his new wife, Nellie Larrabee, whom he had met and married after coming in to the Red Cloud Agency, and his apparent enemies. Because of their comments and warnings, he feared that if he went east he would be kept from returning to his homeland. John Provost, the mixed-blood son-in-law of Crazy Horse's uncle Black Elk and the man who worked as an interpreter for McGillycuddy, told Crazy Horse he might be imprisoned if he went to Washington.[15]

This kind of news was taken seriously. Crazy Horse and other Lakotas were aware that Southern Plains and Southwestern Indians had been transferred to prisons in Florida. Further, they knew that after the Northern Cheyennes under Dull Knife and Little Wolf, allies of the Sioux throughout their war, had surrendered at the Red Cloud and Spotted Tail Agencies, they had been transferred to Indian Territory, where they shared a reservation with the Southern Cheyennes and Arapahos.

Although Crook announced in late July that the buffalo hunt could begin in early August, just before it started he said it was cancelled. In addition, an order from the War Department rescinded permission for area traders to sell any more guns and ammunition to the Indians.[16]

Because he had always said that a visit to Washington, D.C., must be preceded by a buffalo hunt, Crazy Horse now focused his attention on the prospects for a diplomatic delegation. The military and agency leaders stressed the need for Crazy Horse to be part of any group

---

[14]For a discussion of these negotiations, promises, and plans effected during the summer of 1877, see Bray, *Crazy Horse*, 314–25.

[15]Ibid., 326.

[16]Ibid., 327.

visiting the nation's capital, but he had made up his mind not to participate. When Clark pointed out that earlier agreements had placed Crazy Horse among the Lakota delegates, the chief forcefully stated, "I am not going."[17] Neither side would breach this impasse over the next few weeks, but another issue lay on the horizon that would eventually force a showdown.

In May, Brigadier General Oliver O. Howard had ordered the Nez Perce Indians in the Columbia River Basin to leave their outlying land and relocate onto the Nez Perce reservation, centered on Lapwai, Idaho Territory. Howard's order came as a requirement of an 1863 treaty with the Nez Perces, which usurped much of their homeland. For several of the Nez Perce bands, including the one headed by Chief Joseph, the treaty had been negotiated improperly; they had not agreed to its terms and called it the "Thief Treaty." When Howard ordered them to move onto the reservation, the bands began to comply, but before they actually did so, hostilities broke out in western Idaho when some young tribesmen attacked and killed settlers. That led to army intervention and an attack on the Nez Perces at White Bird on June 17. By mid-July the Nez Perces had circled west from White Bird and crossed the Salmon River, drawing the troops behind before they recrossed the river and headed northeast.[18]

The Nez Perce bands had further clashes with soldiers in Idaho Territory before fleeing into Montana Territory's Bitterroot Valley. On August 9, Colonel John Gibbon attacked them in their camp along the Big Hole River, and they fled back into Idaho before turning around and traveling east, through Yellowstone National Park. There they repeatedly eluded federal troops as they moved forward into Montana again, angling through Crow country and heading almost due north. Howard and other military officials now believed the Nez Perces, led by Chief Joseph, Looking Glass, Toolhoolhoolzote, Poker Joe (Lean Elk), and White Bird, would strike for Canada and attempt to join forces with Sitting Bull and his Hunkpapa followers, who had fled into what they called Grandmother's Land following their own battles with the army the previous year. With Howard still pursuing the Nez Perces from the rear, the military put into effect a converging march, led by Colonel Nelson Miles, who would close on the fleeing

---

[17]Ibid., 330.

[18]For details of the Nez Perce war of 1877, see Greene, *Nez Perce War*; Josephy, *Nez Perces*; and Moulton, *Chief Joseph*.

tribespeople from the southeast. The officers planned to recruit Lakota scouts to aid them in finding and subduing the Nez Perces.

In late August, Lieutenant Clark met with Crazy Horse and Touch The Clouds, asking if they would join the army in tracking down the Nez Perces. The meeting ended with participants on both sides angry and upset. Although the Indian leaders had shown no conciliation, Clark had admittedly become confrontational, and interpreter Frank Grouard added to the acrimony when he misinterpreted statements made by both Touch The Clouds and Crazy Horse. Touch The Clouds told Clark that the Lakotas had "washed the blood from our faces and [come] in and surrendered and wanted peace." They did not want to return to the warpath. "You ask us to put blood on our faces again, but I do not want to do this," Touch The Clouds said. Even so, he agreed, with Crazy Horse's support, to engage in the chase for the Nez Perces as Clark asked. But Grouard failed to interpret this statement clearly.[19]

With the buffalo hunt already cancelled, Crazy Horse said he would go north to look for the Nez Perces, but he wanted to take with him women and children from his camp and engage in some hunting while they were out. This Clark interpreted as a sign that Crazy Horse intended to "decamp and join Sitting Bull."[20]

As the discussion continued, Grouard mistranslated statements made by both Indian leaders. In one case he interpreted Touch The Clouds' words as "If it was insisted that the Indian scouts take part in the Nez Perce war they would join the Nez Perces and fight the soldiers." In another misstatement he quoted Crazy Horse as saying that his people would go to their village and the government could "send troops and kill them all."[21] It seems clear that these were twists to the chiefs' actual words. As a result, the council became so heated that Grouard walked out.

Agency interpreter William Garnett, having missed the first portion of the meeting, was summoned. He met Grouard outside the building and then joined the session to interpret the remaining speeches. Crazy Horse concluded his portion of the discussion by having Garnett tell Clark that he and his followers intended to leave the region. "We are going out there to hunt," he said.[22]

---

[19]Bray, *Crazy Horse,* 339.
[20]*New York Tribune,* September 7, 1877.
[21]Bray, *Crazy Horse,* 341.
[22]Ibid., 342.

Following the council, Crazy Horse retreated to his camp north of the White River. Soon, Little Big Man came to the village and told the residents that the Red Cloud Agency chiefs, including Red Cloud, American Horse, Young Man Afraid Of His Horses, and others, had established a line twenty-two miles from Camp Robinson, beyond which the Sioux bands must not cross. To venture outside that boundary would be perceived as a statement that the tribesmen intended to again go to war with the federal army. Following Little Big Man's visit, roughly half the residents of Crazy Horse's northern village removed their lodges to a new site south of the White River, leaving Crazy Horse and his most loyal followers—the Northern Lakotas—more isolated than they had been since coming in to the agency in the spring.[23]

With tension boiling among the Indian bands, General Crook arrived at Camp Robinson under direct order from Lieutenant General Philip H. Sheridan. Crook had been on his way to Camp Brown, in present central Wyoming, to play a role in protecting that area from potential Nez Perce incursions, when he received a telegram from Sheridan: "I think your presence more necessary at Red Cloud Agency than at Camp Brown and wish you to get off at Sidney and go there."[24]

Crook detrained at Sidney and caught a stagecoach headed north. He arrived at Camp Robinson on Sunday, September 2, intending to avert any trouble then brewing among the Lakota bands. He prepared almost immediately to meet with Crazy Horse. Before the intended council, however, interpreters told Crook they had spoken with Woman's Dress, a relative of Red Cloud's, and learned that a plot existed to kill Crook once he was in Crazy Horse's camp. Although the plot story was untrue, Crook was unaware of Woman's Dress's duplicity at the time. It later emerged as evidence of the jealousy Crazy Horse had aroused among some of the other tribesmen in the region.[25]

---

[23]Ibid., 350–51.

[24]Telegram, Sheridan to Crook, September 1, 1877, quoted in Hardorff, *Death of Crazy Horse,* 175–76.

[25]Much of the evidence of Woman's Dress's duplicity comes from statements made by William Garnett, reported in Clark, *Killing of Crazy Horse,* 32, 68, 77, 78, 96, and Hardorff, *Death of Crazy Horse,* 33, 38. In Hardorff's account, He Dog told Garnett that Crazy Horse's death was "perhaps also due to the resentment and jealousy on the part of the chiefs and headmen of the other tribes." Clark reported that Woman's Dress made the statements he did about threats to Crook because of jealousy toward Crazy Horse. "This was all framed up against him [Crazy Horse]; not by white people, but by Indians who were jealous of him."

In spite of the apparent threats, Crook, with scout and interpreter Frank Grouard, rode to Crazy Horse's camp of approximately fifteen hundred people. There, a "heated" council took place. According to an account by McGillycuddy, the assembly "finally broke up with no results except to create the belief in Crook's mind that Crazy Horse was meditating desertion and an attempt to rejoin Sitting Bull who was still in Canada where he had found refuge under the British flag several months after the Custer battle in 1876."[26]

Crook's impression of Crazy Horse's mood and intention to desert the reservation camp resulted, according to McGillycuddy, from a "purposeful misinterpretation by the government interpreter [Grouard] who was an enemy and feared Crazy Horse."[27]

That Crazy Horse disliked Grouard was no secret, even though he had dined with him months earlier when first surrendering to the authorities. The war leader believed Grouard had deserted Sitting Bull and joined the enemy when he became a scout for Crook during the Powder River Expedition the previous year.[28]

Crazy Horse's reply, first to "White Hat" Clark and later to Crook's request for Lakota scouts to track the Nez Perces, is one of the most egregious incidents of misinterpretation to occur during the Northern Plains Indian wars. Crook, angered by what he believed to be the chief's response, quickly departed Crazy Horse's camp with no further thought of recruiting the Lakota fighter and his allies to help bring in the Nez Perces.

McGillycuddy was not at the council with Clark on August 31 or at Crazy Horse's camp when Crook and the war leader met, but he certainly had an opportunity for firsthand knowledge. Years later he wrote to William Garnett that he had been on his way to the Crazy Horse camp after Crook had arrived at Camp Robinson. "I saw the Generals four mule ambulance coming on the jump towards me from the camp, and the General halted me and ordered me back to the post for the reason that it would not be safe for me to go into the camp as there had been trouble in the council."[29] Because he had so frequently

---

[26]McGillycuddy, *McGillycuddy, Agent*, 79, 81. The reference to a "heated" council comes from Watson, "Crazy Horse." Other accounts of this period, specifically Clark's in *Killing of Crazy Horse*, suggest that Crook never actually met with Crazy Horse once he arrived in the area on September 2. I rely on McGillycuddy's letters and reminiscences for my statement that the council did at least begin.

[27]Watson, "Crazy Horse."

[28]McGillycuddy, *McGillycuddy, Agent*, 79.

[29]Quoted in Clark, *Killing of Crazy Horse*, 122; Brininstool, *Crazy Horse*, 43, 48.

visited the village, often accompanied by Fanny, the doctor said he had experienced no hostility from Crazy Horse and his followers, and he requested permission to be allowed to continue to the Indian camp. Crook denied the appeal.[30]

McGillycuddy returned to Camp Robinson and at about eight o'clock that evening had a visit from Louis Bordeaux, who had been present during the session in Crazy Horse's camp that day. The brother of Susan Bordeaux Bettelyoun, Louis Bordeaux had been educated in Hamburg, Iowa, before returning to Dakota Territory and becoming an interpreter. His boisterous voice and mannerisms made him known to the Lakotas as Louis Mato (Bear). He had accompanied a Sioux delegation to Washington in 1869 and now served as the official interpreter for the Spotted Tail Agency and Camp Sheridan.[31]

Discussing the situation that had developed in Crazy Horse's camp that day, the interpreter had details to share: "Doctor, that damn Gruard raised hell in the council today, for I was there and when Crook asked Crazy Horse to take his young men, and help the Great Father, by going North and helping to round up Nez Perces, Crazy Horse said, you sent for me, I came in for peace, I am tired of war, but now that the Great Father, would again put blood on our faces, and send us on the war path, we will go North and fight until there is not a Nez Perce left[.] Gruard interpreted it, we will go North and fight until there is not a white man left."[32]

Although Bordeaux was present at the council and knew of Grouard's misinterpretation, he had not had an opportunity to correct the statement at the time it was made, because Crook immediately departed.

---

[30]McGillycuddy, *McGillycuddy, Agent*, 79–80; Fanny McGillycuddy Diary, 1877–78. In some of her diary entries for the period, including the one for Monday, September 3—probably the day Crook met with Crazy Horse—Fanny wrote, "All quiet."

[31]Hardorff, *Death of Crazy Horse*, 95, 96; Bettelyoun and Waggoner, *With My Own Eyes*, 20–33. Bettelyoun provided details about her family, including brother Louis Bordeaux. The siblings spent their early years living near Fort Laramie, where her father had a trading post, but later settled near her mother's people at Whitstone Agency and also at Spotted Tail Agency.

[32]Brininstool, *Crazy Horse*, 43–48. Bordeaux reiterated his statement to Eli Ricker in 1907; see Jensen, *Indian Interviews of Eli S. Ricker*, vol. 1, 295–97. Julia McGillycuddy, in her account of the conversation, wrote that Crazy Horse said, "Myself and my people are tired of war. We have come in and surrendered to the Great Father and asked for peace. But now, if he wishes to go to war again and asks our help, we will go north and fight till there is not a Nez Perces [*sic*] left." She quoted Grouard's translation the same way Brininstool did. McGillycuddy, *McGillycuddy, Agent*, 80.

Bordeaux, like others, believed that Grouard feared the Indians would kill him because of his earlier desertion of Sitting Bull.

McGillycuddy told Bordeaux, "There's goin' to be the devil to pay if this thing ain't straightened up."[33]

Once Bordeaux left McGillycuddy's quarters, the doctor went to find General Crook to clarify the translation and perhaps avert trouble. "But Gen. Crook said there was no mistake. Crazy Horse is figuring on going North to join Sitting Bull."[34] Crook's belief in the veracity of Grouard's translation—in spite of evidence to the contrary—likely rested on the general's having traveled with Grouard for months in 1876 and come to trust him.

Susan Bordeaux Bettelyoun wrote that Grouard "knew he had done treachery" with his misinterpretation at the council. He "feared for his life," she said. "He wanted to see Crazy Horse put out of the way so he could be free from the fear of losing his life." At the council, according to Bettelyoun's account, Touch The Clouds "reprimanded Frank Grouard about this [misinterpretation] and called him a liar. Everyone knew that Spotted Tail and Red Cloud were jealous of Crazy Horse and wished him out of the way."[35]

Why would Grouard misinterpret Crazy Horse's statement? Because, according to what McGillycuddy told Brininstool, "Frank Grouard was afraid of Crazy Horse and the northern hostiles, for he had been raised by them, and then deserted them and joined our troops under Crook in the spring of 1876, *and he had reason for wanting to get rid of Crazy Horse.*"[36]

In fact, several of the army officers and Indian leaders had met privately in Lieutenant Colonel Luther Prentice Bradley's quarters—although the commanding officer was not present—to discuss a plan to kill Crazy Horse. William Garnett later said that he, Grouard, and scout Baptiste "Big Bat" Pourier, along with General Crook and Lieutenant Clark, met in Bradley's office with Red Cloud, Little Wound, Red Dog, Young Man Afraid Of His Horse, American Horse, Three Bears, No Water, Blue Horse, and a number of other Lakotas. The tribal leaders agreed that they would each select two to four of their top warriors, who would go to Crazy Horse's camp with the intention

[33]McGillycuddy, *McGillycuddy, Agent*, 80.
[34]Brininstool, *Crazy Horse*, 43–48.
[35]Bettelyoun and Waggoner, *With My Own Eyes*, 109.
[36]Brininstool, *Crazy Horse*, 43–48 (emphasis in original).

of killing him. The man who actually carried out the fatal attack would receive $300. Before the plan could be put into action, however, Bradley heard about it, and the intended strike was scuttled.[37]

The next morning Crook, who may still have feared for his life because of the message conveyed by Woman's Dress, struck out for Fort Laramie. That day, McGillycuddy later recalled, "a courier arrived from Ft. Laramie with orders to arrest Crazy Horse and put him in the guard house, and I received orders to report next morning before daylight as medical officer to accompany the expedition to make the arrest."[38]

Following those directives, "a force of three troops of cavalry and a field piece and myself as medical officer left the post an hour before daylight [on September 4] for a march of five miles to the camp to make the arrest," McGillycuddy said. Also with the troops was a contingent of Sioux leaders including agency chiefs Red Cloud, Little Wound, American Horse, Young Man Afraid Of His Horse, and Yellow Road, and three leaders from Crazy Horse's northern band: Little Big Man, Big Road, and Jumping Shield.[39]

"We arrived at daylight and found a deserted camp ground," McGillycuddy said. "Crazy Horse and his people, lodges and everything had scattered and gone." That evening a courier arrived from Major Daniel Burke, commanding at the Spotted Tail Agency forty miles east, saying that Crazy Horse had arrived alone and was in Spotted Tail's Camp.[40] Fanny McGillycuddy wrote, "The whole command starting out to capture 'Crazy Horse' when they got there he had skipped out."[41]

Second Lieutenant Henry L. Lemley, of Company E, Third Cavalry—a man who had been with Crook throughout the summer of 1876, participating in the battles at the Rosebud and Slim Buttes—took part in the march on Crazy Horse's camp that day. He later wrote, "The column of cavalry was directed to so time its arrival, after a night march, that it could surround the village of Crazy Horse at

[37]Garnett interview, related in Clark, *Killing of Crazy Horse*, 79–81.

[38]McGillycuddy to Garnett, June 27, 1927, quoted in Clark, *Killing of Crazy Horse*, 122–23.

[39]Watson, "Crazy Horse." Names of the Indian chiefs present are from Clark, *Killing of Crazy Horse*, 33.

[40]Watson, "Crazy Horse." Similar information is related in McGillycuddy to Garnett, June 27, 1927, quoted in Clark, *Killing of Crazy Horse*, 122–23: "When we arrived at the site of the village at daylight, there was not a lodge or Indian to be seen, they had scattered and gone."

[41]McGillycuddy Diary, 1876–77.

daybreak. . . . when they arrived upon the bluffs supposed to overlook the village there were no tepees in sight. The bird had flown!"[42]

While Crazy Horse may have actually reached the Spotted Tail Agency alone, when he departed his own village earlier in the day he rode with Black Shawl Woman, Kicking Bear, and Shell Boy. They paced themselves on the long trip, arriving hours later at the Lakota village, where Black Shawl Woman had relatives. Crazy Horse left her with them and rode on alone to the Spotted Tail village.[43]

After Crook departed from Camp Robinson, and before the orders came to arrest Crazy Horse, McGillycuddy approached Bradley and asked for permission to go to Crazy Horse's village, as he had been doing on a regular basis. He wanted to check out the Bordeaux story from Crazy Horse himself. But the commander refused permission, saying it was unsafe. To make his point that he trusted Crazy Horse, the doctor said he would take Fanny with him. According to Julia McGillycuddy's account of the circumstances, "Bradley said he was crazy."[44]

Even the residents of Camp Robinson and Camp Sheridan were uncertain about events during those tense early days in September. Lucy Lee, who was at Camp Sheridan with her husband, Second Lieutenant Jesse M. Lee, the acting agent at the Spotted Tail Agency, wrote on September 18, 1877, to the *Greencastle* (*Indiana*) *Star.* She described how reports had circulated that Crazy Horse had been killed, and then that he had not. She said that troops had ridden to his village to surround it and take his people captive, but everyone had fled. She said Crazy Horse had taken his sick wife to her uncle's camp.[45]

In a 1934 statement made to a newspaper reporter, McGillycuddy recalled that when the order was sent to Captain Daniel W. Burke, commander at Camp Sheridan and the Spotted Tail Agency, to arrest Crazy Horse and return him to Camp Robinson, the Brulé chief Spotted Tail had a response: "Crazy Horse is a chief. He is my guest. He cannot be arrested, but if the soldier chief will set the time we will council with him."[46]

---

[42]"The Death of Crazy Horse," *New York Sun,* September 14, 1877.

[43]Bray, *Crazy Horse,* 366–68.

[44]McGillycuddy, *McGillycuddy, Agent,* 81.

[45]Quoted in Hardorff, *Death of Crazy Horse,* 252.

[46]Watson, "Crazy Horse"; McGillycuddy, *McGillycuddy, Agent,* 81–82.

On the morning of September 5, Spotted Tail and Crazy Horse reported to Burke's office at Camp Sheridan and learned that Crazy Horse was wanted for a council with Colonel Bradley at Camp Robinson. Lieutenant Lee accompanied Crazy Horse to Camp Robinson. Some reports indicate that Lee was unaware that the chief was actually under arrest, but a telegram from Lieutenant Clark to General Crook on September 4 said, "I urged the arrest of Crazy Horse strongly to Lee."[47]

When it was time to depart from Camp Sheridan for the forty mile ride to Camp Robinson, Crazy Horse was placed in an army ambulance—one account called it a yellow buggy—which was surrounded by Indian scouts and a cavalry escort.[48] The entourage, which included Black Crow, Swift Bear, High Bear, Touch The Clouds, a few other headmen, and Bordeaux, halted for lunch under cottonwood trees beside Chadron Creek.[49]

That day McGillycuddy "had been ordered to keep within the limits of the post, as in case of trouble with the Indians I would be wanted."[50] Like others at Camp Robinson, he watched for the incoming party, which eventually trailed in during the late afternoon from the north, tracking along Soldier Creek to the military ground.[51] Even before Crazy Horse reached Camp Robinson, the doctor had apprehensions: "Well I sort of smelled it in the air that trouble was coming."[52]

Lieutenant Lee and Spotted Tail Agency interpreter Bordeaux also sensed pending problems. Upon arriving at Camp Robinson, they met Captain James Kennington, officer of the day, and told him they had brought Crazy Horse so that he could meet with Bradley. Kennington told them he had "orders to put Crazy Horse in the guardhouse."[53] As usual, two soldiers were posted outside that structure, under directive of officer of the guard Henry Lemley.[54]

Lee and Bordeaux left Crazy Horse with Captain Kennington and went to find Colonel Bradley, presumably at his quarters across the

[47]Hardorff, *Death of Crazy Horse,* 177.
[48]Watson, "Crazy Horse."
[49]McGillycuddy, *McGillycuddy, Agent,* 82; Clark, *Killing of Crazy Horse,* 35.
[50]Clark, *Killing of Crazy Horse,* 124.
[51]Watson, "Crazy Horse."
[52]Clark, *Killing of Crazy Horse,* 124.
[53]McGillycuddy, *McGillycuddy, Agent,* 82.
[54]Hardorff, *Death of Crazy Horse,* 147.

parade ground. While crossing the open area, the two met McGillycuddy and Lee told him, "I'm not going to be made a goat of in this affair."[55]

The surgeon quickened his pace toward the adjutant's office. There he met Crazy Horse striding between Captain Kennington and Little Big Man as they moved toward the guardhouse. Near the buildings were "about half a dozen line officers standing around, and crowds of Indians gathering," McGillycuddy recalled.[56]

Crazy Horse "recognized me as usual," the doctor later said, adding that the chief extended the greeting *How kola,* "hello friend."[57]

Bordeaux, seeing Crazy Horse nearing the guardhouse, whispered to Lee, "We better get out of here, if they try to put him in the guard house, there will be a fight and we will get killed for bringing him over here."[58]

From his position in front of the adjutant's office, McGillycuddy watched as Crazy Horse "walked quietly from the adjutants office and entered the guard room with Capt. Kennington an [*sic*] Little Big Man, the next thing I saw was Crazy Horse jumping out of the guard house, a knife in each hand, and Little Big Man on his back trying to hold his arms down," McGillycuddy wrote to Billy Garnett on June 7, 1917. To E. A. Brininstool he said that Crazy Horse entered the guard room "quietly, and I thought it all over, when suddenly there was a howl from Crazy Horse and he jumped out the door, striking with his long knife at Kennington."[59]

Garnett said one weapon "was a long, glittering knife," and Lieutenant John G. Bourke wrote that it looked like a stiletto.[60]

After Crazy Horse bolted from the guardhouse, "Kennington and Little Big Man who was standing near caught hold of him, but he slashed Little Big Man across one wrist and freed himself, but the double guard of twenty men closed in around him with fixed bayonets," McGillycuddy said. "Officers, orderlies, and interpreters had all disappeared and I was left standing alone about twenty five feet away." Crazy Horse "lunged from side to side trying to break through, when

---

[55]McGillycuddy, *McGillycuddy, Agent,* 83.

[56]Hardorff, *Death of Crazy Horse,* 63, n. 7.

[57]Brininstool, *Crazy Horse,* 43–48; Clark, *Killing of Crazy Horse,* 124–25.

[58]Clark, *Killing of Crazy Horse,* 124.

[59]Ibid., 124–25.

[60]Hardorff, *Death of Crazy Horse,* 63, n. 7.

suddenly one of the guard a private of the Fourteenth Infantry made a lunge and Crazy Horse fell to the ground."[61]

In one account McGillycuddy said, "One of the guard, a private of the Ninth Infantry, [thrust] his bayonet into the chief's abdomen, and he fell to the ground."[62] He added, "By that time as the cow boys would say 'Hell was popping' the Indians milling around and yelling at us." He wedged his way between the guards, found Crazy Horse with a bayonet wound above the hip, and "saw that he was done for." Working his way out of the throng again, McGillycuddy informed Kennington, who said, "Well I have orders to put him in the guard house, and if you will take one shoulder, I will take the other, the men will take his feet, and we will carry him in." They tried it, Kennington said, but "a big Northern Sioux gripped my shoulder and partly lifting me, began making motions to leave him alone, which we were forced to do."[63]

McGillycuddy later wrote in an understated way that "things got warm in the mixup between the hostiles, the friendlies, and the troops." But clearly, the northern band Indians on hand at Camp Robinson were incensed that Crazy Horse had been wounded. The troops were on high alert. As the doctor surveyed the scene, he noticed Grouard peering from around the commissary building, but "he refused to come to us."[64]

"The officers were at their quarters, orderlies had vanished and no one could carry orders," McGillycuddy said. "So I tried to arrange matters and advised Kennington to hold the grounds while I crossed the parade ground to the general's [sic] quarters to explain matters."[65] Rushing toward Colonel Bradley's quarters, McGillycuddy saw his interpreter, John Provost, "up in front of my quarters and called him

[61]Clark, *Killing of Crazy Horse*, 124–25.

[62]McGillycuddy to "Friend Garnett," June 7, 1917, copy in McGillycuddy Papers, Fort Robinson Museum Archives. A similar account by McGillycuddy is quoted in Brininstool, *Crazy Horse*, 43–48. The wound was caused by a bayonet thrust delivered by Fourteenth Infantry Private William Gentles, although that would not be known for some time. Gentles, a native of County Tyrone, Ireland, had enlisted in the United States Army on April 2, 1856, served with the Tenth Infantry, Company K, was with Colonel Albert Sidney Johnston during the 1857 Mormon War, and concluded his first enlistment period at Fort Laramie in 1861. He went on to serve with the First Missouri Volunteer Engineers in the Civil War and later joined the Fourteenth Infantry. Following the stabbing of Crazy Horse, Gentles hid from the Indians at Camp Robinson, withdrew to Camp Sidney, and died at Fort Douglas on May 20, 1879.

[63]Clark, *Killing of Crazy Horse*, 124–25.

[64]McGillycuddy to "Friend Garnett," June 7, 1917.

[65]Watson, "Crazy Horse."

across the parade ground to interpret." With Provost now available to translate, McGillycuddy explained to American Horse that "Crazy Horse was badly hurt, that orders were that he be put into the guard house and I would care for him." American Horse refused to see Crazy Horse, a chief, be placed in the guardhouse.[66]

"So I made another trip across the parade ground to see the General [*sic*]." McGillycuddy explained to Bradley that he "had men enough to put Crazy Horse in the guard house, but I said 'General it will mean the death of a good many men and Indians before you succeed, for the Indians are ugly." As the doctor described the scene, "the old chap hated to give in, but finally agreed to my proposition to put [Crazy Horse] in the Adjutants Office where I could care for him."[67]

Years later, McGillycuddy told the story to E. A. Brininstool this way: "I volunteered my services as an orderly, and crossed the parade ground to General [*sic*] Bradley's office and explained the situation. However, the general had evidently received his orders, for all I got out of him was: 'Please give my compliments to the officer of the day, and he is to carry out his original orders, and put Crazy Horse in the guardhouse.' So I returned with the 'compliments' and nervy old Kennington made another try. Then more strenuous objections and cocking of carbines began, and we were apparently on the edge of an explosion, so another trip across the parade ground was incumbent upon me. I explained the latest developments to the general, with the suggestion that the Indians were becoming somewhat irritable, and that while there were one thousand men under arms at the post [earlier he had said eight hundred], and that they could possibly imprison Crazy Horse, there were ten thousand Indians around us, and it would mean death to a good many people, and knowing the Indians, I suggested that we effect a compromise and put Crazy Horse in the Adjutant's office, where I could care for him until he died."[68]

[66]Clark, *Killing of Crazy Horse*, 125. In his letter to "Friend Garnett" of June 7, 1917, McGillycuddy wrote, "I finally got my interpreter John Provost, and after a talk with American Horse we arranged with the permission of Col. Bradley to put Crazy Horse in the adjutants office where I took charge of him."

[67]Clark, *Killing of Crazy Horse*, 126.

[68]Brininstool, *Crazy Horse*, 43–48. That McGillycuddy increased the number of soldiers and Indians at the camp in his second message to Bradley is perhaps consistent with the tension at Camp Robinson that day, or it could be an error of memory, since he made these statements years later. It might have seemed as if more people were present as he made another trip across the parade ground in an effort to diffuse the situation.

To this arrangement, McGillycuddy told Brininstool, "the general *reluctantly consented*." The doctor returned to the scene in front of the guardhouse and again spoke to the Indians assembled there, telling them of the plan to move Crazy Horse to the adjutant's office. American Horse, no real friend of Crazy Horse, now stepped down from his mount, spread a blanket beside Crazy Horse, and motioned two young warriors to move him. Billy Garnett said that Red Shirt and Two Dogs helped carry Crazy Horse to the adjutant's office.[69]

There, the doctor examined the warrior's wound. The Sioux He Dog, who had examined Crazy Horse shortly after he was stabbed, "recalled that the penetration had occurred between the lower ribs in the back, to the right of the spine column."[70] He Dog's description revealed "that the blade of the bayonet had traversed diagonally through the body, and that hemorrhaging had caused a lump to rise under the skin just below the heart." He Dog noticed a second wound in the small of Crazy Horse's back. It, too, had been "caused by a bayonet which, he thought, had penetrated both kidneys."[71]

"The bayonet did *not* penetrate the kidneys," the doctor said, but had "traversed the length of the bowel mass which lay in the front of it." Even so, both He Dog and McGillycuddy noted the bloody froth coming from Crazy Horse's mouth and nose, which indicated that he might have had other stab wounds as well, including one that possibly punctured a lung.

Once in the adjutant's office, He Dog took his blanket, threw it over Crazy Horse, and made a pillow of it.[72] As he had told both Colonel Bradley and American Horse he would do, McGillycuddy remained with Crazy Horse to care for him in his final hours, administering morphine to "ease his pain." Also in the adjutant's office that evening were Big Bat Pourier; Crazy Horse's father, Old Crazy Horse or Worm; his uncle Touch The Clouds; Captain Kennington; Lieutenant Lemley; and, for a time, the post surgeon, Captain Charles E. Mumm.[73]

While still lucid, Crazy Horse said to McGillycuddy: "It was one of the knives on the soldiers' guns that wounded me. It passed across my body. I shall die before sunup."[74]

[69] Ibid. (emphasis in original); Clark, *Killing of Crazy Horse*, 95. Julia McGillycuddy, in *McGillycuddy, Agent*, 84, reported on American Horse's actions.

[70] Hardorff, *Death of Crazy Horse*, 148, n. 10.

[71] McGillycuddy, *McGillycuddy, Agent*, 83; Hardorff, *Death of Crazy Horse*, 148, n. 10.

[72] Hardorff, *Death of Crazy Horse*, 150.

[73] Ibid., 111.

[74] McGillycuddy, *McGillycuddy, Agent*, 85.

Although more than once McGillycuddy, too, said the fatal wound had been made by a bayonet, that evening as the Oglala headman lay dying, he attempted to explain to Worm and Touch The Clouds that the wounds had come from a knife. He went so far as to demonstrate the attack by pushing a knife through a piece of paper.[75]

It was "dismal and lonesome" in the adjutant's office, the doctor later noted.[76] A kerosene lamp threw little light within the log building. Two guards paced outside. McGillycuddy himself recalled, "The old father made many remarks as time passed, and I remember them; they were as follows: 'We were not agency Indians, we preferred the buffalo to the white man's beef, but the Gray Fox [Crook] kept sending his messengers to us in the north, saying, 'Come in, come in.' Well. We came in, and now they have killed my boy; hard times have come upon us, but we were tired of fighting. Red Cloud was jealous of my boy. He was afraid the Gray Fox would make him head chief. Our enemies here at the Agency, were trying to force us away, so probably we would have been driven soon back to our hunting grounds in the north."[77]

At about ten o'clock that night, Crazy Horse's vital signs weakened. McGillycuddy started to give him some brandy, but "Worm protested making signs that his sons 'brain whirled.'"[78] Instead McGillycuddy "administered several hypodermics of morphine to Crazy Horse, which seemed to ease the pain, but which did not prevent his death."[79]

Big Bat was the first to discover that Crazy Horse was dead. He urged McGillycuddy to give Worm a drink of grog—the *New York Sun* called it whiskey—before Big Bat told Worm, "Don't take it hard; your son is dead."[80]

McGillycuddy said, "About 11:30 P.M. Crazy Horse made a last struggle and passed away. Touch The Clouds crossed over to the body lying on the floor, drew the blanket over the face and pointed to it, with the remark: 'That is the lodge of Crazy Horse.' Then, standing to his full height of seven feet, pointed upward with the remark, '*The Chief has gone above!*' It was a tragic scene in that dimly-lighted room,

---

[75]*New York Sun*, "Death of Crazy Horse."

[76]Clark, *Killing of Crazy Horse*, 126. Similar information is included in Brininstool, *Crazy Horse*, 43–48.

[77]Brininstool, *Crazy Horse*, 43–48.

[78]McGillycuddy to Garnett, May 10, 1926, quoted in Clark, *Killing of Crazy Horse*, 117–18.

[79]Hardorff, *Death of Crazy Horse*, 112; McGillycuddy to Garnett, May 10, 1926, and June 24, 1927, quoted in Clark, *Killing of Crazy Horse*, 117–18; Hinman, "Oglala Sources on the Life of Crazy Horse."

[80]Hardorff, *Death of Crazy Horse*, 91, 92; *New York Sun*, "Death of Crazy Horse."

an epic of our Indian history, and listening to the death wail from the neighboring camps brought back to me Crazy Horse's rallying cry to his warriors as we heard it the previous year at the battle of the Rosebud and at Slim Buttes: 'It is a good day to fight! A good day to die! Strong hearts, brave hearts, to the front! Weak hearts and cowards to the rear!'"[81]

In 1917 McGillycuddy wrote to William Garnett, "I was sorry to see him die that way, he was a good man, a brave man, and he was my friend."[82]

"If Crazy Horse had not been killed he would have been taken that night, to the rail road, and Fort Marion Florida," McGillycuddy said.[83] Big Bat agreed. He believed Crazy Horse had been intentionally stabbed. Before that happened, he said, the army had planned to take Crazy Horse by ambulance to Fort Laramie and then on to Omaha, with Big Bat, No Neck, and Yankton Charlie to accompany him.[84]

Indeed, on September 5, 1877, the day Crazy Horse was arrested at Camp Sheridan, Lieutenant Clark had sent a telegram to General Crook at Cheyenne suggesting that once taken into custody, Crazy Horse "should be started for Fort Laramie to-night and kept going as far as Omaha." Two or three other Sioux should go with him, "so that they can assure people on return that he has not been killed." Clark concluded, "I hope you will telegraph Gen. Bradley. Everything quiet and working first-rate."[85]

Crook responded with a supportive telegram to Colonel Bradley at Camp Robinson: "Send Crazy Horse with a couple of his own people with him, under a strong escort, via Laramie to Omaha. Make sure that he does not escape."[86] As a follow-up to that message, Crook sent another telegram on September 5, this one to General Sheridan: "Crazy Horse is now a prisoner & I have ordered Bradley to send him

---

[81]Brininstool, *Crazy Horse*, 43–48.

[82]McGillycuddy to "Friend Garnett," June 7, 1917.

[83]McGillycuddy to Garnett, June 27, 1927, quoted in Clark, *Killing of Crazy Horse*, 126. In Brininstool, "Chief Crazy Horse," McGillycuddy is quoted as saying, "Had the arrest been carried out successfully in imprisoning him in the guardhouse, he would have been sent through to the railroad that night, and thence to the Dry Tortugas as a prisoner for life."

[84]Hardorff, *Death of Crazy Horse*, 93.

[85]Telegram, Clark to Crook, Camp Robinson, September 5, 1877, quoted in Hardorff, *Death of Crazy Horse*, 179.

[86]Telegram, Crook to Bradley, Camp Robinson, September 5, 1877, quoted in Hardorff, *Death of Crazy Horse*, 180.

here [to Omaha]. I wish you would send him off where he will be out of harm's way."[87] Sheridan, from his headquarters in Chicago, immediately responded with a telegram back to Crook: "I wish you to send Crazy Horse under proper guard to these Hd. Qs."[88] All this planning was for naught. Crazy Horse's death precluded any need to transfer him to Omaha, Chicago, or any other distant location.

———— ·◄► · ————

When McGillycuddy left the adjutant's office after the death of Crazy Horse, he felt tension pulsing across the parade ground and a "great deal of excitement" at the camp. The surgeon went to his own quarters, where Fanny was still awake; the two retired about midnight.[89] "Touch The Cloud went with me and slept on the floor until morning, things looked scary," McGillycuddy said. The Indian "rolled himself in his blanket, and lay down outside [the] door, on guard lest any harm come to the man who, in after years, was known as Tasunka Witko Kola, Crazy Horse's friend, while he slept."[90] Even then the doctor asked the question, "Who was responsible for his death?"[91]

Fanny McGillycuddy sat up until her husband returned home on the night Crazy Horse died. About that day she wrote in her diary, "'Crazy Horse' went to Spotted Tail gave himself up and they brought him here to be confined here. Arrived here at about six o'clock. He would not go to the guard house and he got injured so that he died at eleven o'clock. There was a great deal of excitement. Went to bed at twelve o'clock." She made no reference to the doctor's role in treating Crazy Horse or to the fact that Touch The Clouds spent the night at their home.

"I was standing about thirty feet from Crazy Horse when he fell, and never quite understood the thing," McGillycuddy later wrote to Garnett. "I always liked Crazy Horse, he was a brave man, and a good man, but Lieut Clark distrusted him, and I think Gruard prejudiced Gen. Crook and Clark against Crazy Horse." He told Garnett, "I

[87]Telegram, Crook to Sheridan, Cheyenne, Wyoming Territory, September 5, 1877, quoted in Hardorff, *Death of Crazy Horse,* 180.

[88]Telegram, Sheridan to Crook, Cheyenne, Wyoming, September 5, 1877, quoted in Hardorff, *Death of Crazy Horse,* 180–81.

[89]Fanny McGillycuddy Diary, September 5, 1877.

[90]McGillycuddy to Garnett, June 27, 1927, quoted in Clark, *Killing of Crazy Horse,* 126; McGillycuddy, *McGillycuddy, Agent,* 87. This information is also reported in Watson, "Crazy Horse."

[91]McGillycuddy to Garnett, June 27, 1927, quoted in Clark, *Killing of Crazy Horse,* 126.

never had any use for Gruard." After Crazy Horse fell that day, he said, "I saw Gruards head projected out from around the corner of the old commissary, and I tried to get him over to me to interpret, but he was too scared to come, in fact I did not feel very well myself."[92]

The stress of the day must have been almost unbearable. McGillycuddy had seen Crazy Horse, a man he considered a friend, fatally stabbed. He had found himself at the center of the conflict when no interpreter could at first be located and no soldiers were available to relay messages from Captain Kennington to Colonel Bradley. To top it off, when Kennington first ordered the guard to move Crazy Horse back into the guardhouse, the Indian soldiers "cocked their guns." Crazy Horse's father tried twice to shoot but was prevented from doing so.[93]

McGillycuddy later noted, "We had a close call that day while Crazy Horse was lying on the ground writhing in agony, for had a single shot been fired on either side, there would have been a killing unequalled in this history of our Indian troubles. We all felt it, and each side held back."[94]

Lieutenant Lemley, also close by when the stabbing occurred, called the situation "every bit as harrowing as the Rosebud battle, when, as if with a single click, thirty carbines were cocked and aimed at us by as many mounted Indians, who had formed a semi-circle around the entrance to the guard-house. Fortunately for all concerned, the soldiers were able to diffuse the situation, partially by assuring the Sioux that Crazy Horse was 'ill' since most had not actually seen what proved to be the fatal bayonet thrust."[95]

"Capt. Kennington and Dr. McGillycuddy deserve great credit for the cool and collected manner in which they acted under such trying circumstances and not knowing who were soldiers or who were not, and whom to trust," the *Chicago Tribune* reported on September 11, 1877.[96]

Word of Crazy Horse's death flashed across Camp Robinson and on to the nearby Indian camps. The *Tribune* reported on the scene: "Indians were rushing to and from the post, women and children were crying, and matters indeed looked dubious for a while. The post

[92]McGillycuddy to Garnett, May 10, 1926, quoted in Clark, *Killing of Crazy Horse*, 118–19.
[93]"Crazy-Horse, the Death of the Indian Chieftain," *Chicago Tribune*, September 11, 1877.
[94]Brininstool, "Chief Crazy Horse."
[95]Lemley, "The Passing of Crazy Horse."
[96]*Chicago Tribune*, "Crazy-Horse, the Death of the Indian Chieftain."

was well guarded, and a party of Brulé Indian soldiers slept inside the Agency-stockade. Many northern Indians stampeded during the night,—it is supposed for Spotted-Tail Agency."[97]

"Crazy Horse had the reputation among the whites and Indians generally of being a man of his word, and never breaking a promise," McGillycuddy told Brininstool. "Hence, it is my opinion that he had no intention of again going on the warpath and joining Sitting Bull, as charged at the time of his arrest." He concluded that "a combination of treachery, jealousy and unreliable reports simply resulted in a frame-up, *and he was railroaded to his death*."[98]

Crazy Horse's parents claimed his body, took it to a site near Chadron Creek and the Spotted Tail Agency, and later removed it to a different location on Pine Ridge. Fanny wrote, "They took Crazy Horse's remains to Spotted Tail to be buried. It is feared there will be an outbreak among Crazy Horses friends to avenge his death."[99] Almost simultaneously, Black Shawl Woman also died. Lucy Lee wrote, "The sick wife, whom Crazy Horse brought up here has since died, and today was laid by his side; and I can now hear the dismal howling of the mourners. My husband went over to the grave of the dead chief to superintend the erection of a fence around his body. He found there the old father and mother, who had been keeping watch over their son's remains for three days and nights, that nothing should molest them."[100]

The Nez Perces, whose own hegira had precipitated some of the events that transpired along the White River in early September 1877, continued their northern journey, finally engaging Colonel Nelson Miles at a place called the Bear's Paw in northern Montana Territory. The battle began on September 30, turned into a siege, and ended with the surrender of Chief Joseph on October 4. Although some of the Nez Perces reached Canada with White Bird and there found refuge with Sitting Bull, those with Chief Joseph were taken to Tongue River Cantonment, transported downriver to Fort Abraham Lincoln, and eventually shipped to Fort Leavenworth, Baxter Springs, and then Indian Territory. There they remained until 1886, when they were finally allowed to return to the Columbia Basin.

---

[97]Ibid.

[98]Brininstool, *Crazy Horse*, 43–48 (emphasis in original).

[99]Fanny McGillycuddy Diary, September 6, 1877.

[100]Lee to *Greencastle* (*Indiana*) *Star*, September 18, 1877.

II

On the Move

WEEKS AFTER THE DEATH of Crazy Horse, a delegation from the Lakota bands met with President Rutherford B. Hayes in Washington, D.C., intent on solidifying their position in the Black Hills. But as Crazy Horse had feared, final orders soon came to relocate the Brulés with Spotted Tail and the Oglalas with Red Cloud to new agencies nearer to the Missouri River. This removal had been in the works for years. As early as 1875, officials in Nebraska had sought to have the Indians ejected from the northwestern corner of the state. A Nebraska legislative resolution approved on February 4, 1875, indicated that the state had never "agreed or consented" to having the Indians living in that area. The Red Cloud and Spotted Tail Agencies served thousands of Indians who were "occupying a large and valuable portion of the state." State leaders perceived this situation as preventing "the growth, development, and prosperity of that portion of the state."[1]

The resolution demanded that the "general government" immediately exclude "from within the boundaries of the State of Nebraska, the Indian agencies of Red Cloud and Spotted Tail." The state action could not supersede federal treaties with the tribes, and although Nebraska

---

[1]Nebraska Legislative Resolution, February 5, 1875, copy at Fort Robinson Museum Archives. The council proceedings for the Lakota delegation to Washington, D.C., that met with President Rutherford B. Hayes on September 26 and 27, 1877, record that the participants were Red Cloud, Big Road, Little Wound, Little Big Man, Iron Crow, Three Bears, American Horse, Young Man Afraid Of His Horses, Yellow Bear, He Dog, Spotted Tail, Swift Bear, Through The Clouds, Red Bear, and White Tail, together with the Arapahos Black Coal and Sharp Nose. Among those representing the government were General George Crook, Lieutenant William P. Clark, Commissioner of Indian Affairs E. A. Hayt, four Indian commissioners, and other persons.

citizens and leaders were howling for removal, it did not take place rapidly.[2]

The latter portion of September 1877 passed pleasantly for McGilly-cuddy and Fanny. They took horseback rides around Camp Robinson and attended a performance of the Third Cavalry Band. The wives of several other men arrived at the camp, including Mrs. Lemley, Mrs. Henry, Mrs. Monahan, Mrs. Lawson, and Mrs. Palmer, in addition to a Miss Von Sturteford. The presence of those additional women led to a number of social affairs. The doctor joined his wife in decorating for a hop held on September 25, and as Fanny recalled in her diary, "dance passed off elegantly, supper was elegant everybody pleased."

McGillycuddy left Camp Robinson for the Spotted Tail Agency on October 2 to care for a sick man. Three days later he was back home, where his patients were none other than General George Crook and Colonel William Royal, who had been injured when the stagecoach they were riding from Sidney overturned. Although Colonel Royal was "badly hurt" and the stage driver had a dislocated shoulder, Fanny reported that the general was "not much hurt."[3]

Five days later McGillycuddy returned to the Spotted Tail Agency, where its physician, Dr. Kemper, was "very ill." Word at that camp began circulating about the removal of the Indians to new agency sites. This transfer involved the Spotted Tail tribesmen and their families, who would be sent to the Ponca Agency on the Missouri River in eastern Nebraska, and the Red Cloud followers, who would relocate to the Missouri, to a new agency on Yellow Medicine Creek not far from the Crow Creek Agency and Pierre, in Dakota Territory. On October 21, Fanny noted that Crook told "Doctor," as she always referred to her husband in her writings, that he "had his choice of going with the Indians or staying." Who could have been surprised that this intrepid medical man, who was experienced as a topographer and cartographer and already familiar with some of the country along the Missouri, decided to "go with the outfit"?[4]

On October 22, Captain Joseph Lawson was ordered to command Companies E and L of the Third Cavalry and assist with the Indian transfer. Packing twenty-five days' worth of rations, the troops left Camp Robinson on October 25, making three short marches to the

[2]Nebraska Legislative Resolution, February 5, 1875.
[3]Fanny McGillycuddy Diary, 1877–78.
[4]Ibid.

Spotted Tail Agency. There they were "joined by the Indian Agent and the beef cattle."[5] McGillycuddy and Fanny remained at Camp Robinson when the troops left and had their photograph taken on the twenty-sixth before departing in the late afternoon for the Spotted Tail Agency. Although she gave no reason why, Fanny wrote that day, "Dr. in a stew."[6]

The McGillycuddys were back on the trail by mid-morning the following day, marching seven and a half miles as storm clouds gathered. "What a sight to see the Indians all over the country 6 or 7000 of them," Fanny wrote. On October 28, a plains storm hit this mass of humanity with full force, making it impossible for the command to move forward for the next three days. The roads were "very muddy." The soldiers also needed to wait for the beef issue that would feed the Indians as they undertook the relocation journey.

The party struck out again on Wednesday, October 31, going ten miles to Bordeaux Creek. Supported by more than "one hundred big freight wagons," the people slowly moved north, traveling from eight to twelve miles a day.[7] McGillycuddy and Fanny spent one night at Camp Sheridan and others in the field. Fanny, as she had done earlier in the year, rode a horse some of the time and took shelter in the ambulance when the weather was particularly disagreeable. Two stray cats had taken up "residence" in the ambulance, sitting on the back seat in a "dignified manner" as the conveyance rocked across the prairie. Fanny preferred the out-of-doors to the companionship of the cats.[8]

The migration was necessarily slow, because of the weather, difficult terrain—one day they crossed the White River ten times—and the large number of Indian families, including children and old people, in the party. The soldiers also needed to halt periodically to kill some of the beef cattle and distribute meat to the Indians, who dried it for later use. On November 9, Fanny wrote, "Broke camp this still morning. Lovely day. roads excallant [*sic*] made camp at mouth of Wounded Knee creek. 14⅓ miles."

The travelers saw prairie fires, had accidents, and endured cold, snowy weather before reaching the site of the new Red Cloud Agency on November 24. Two days later Fanny reported that she and her husband

[5]Captain Joseph Lawson to Adjutant General, Department of the Platte, December 4, 1877, RG 393, Box 54, NARS, Kansas City, Missouri.
[6]Fanny McGillycuddy Diary, 1877–78.
[7]Hyde, *Spotted Tail's Folk*, 287.
[8]McGillycuddy, *McGillycuddy, Agent*, 88.

were staying at the agent's house at Crow Creek "until our quarters are finished at the Post."

Captain Lawson, in a letter about the transfer he wrote to the adjutant general of the Department of the Platte on December 4, 1877, noted that the new agency site had some shortcomings. The land was arid, and it lacked wood and water resources. The Indians "moved slowly and reluctantly towards the Missouri," he said, partly because they feared the possibility of disease. "They say that it is very unhealthy and when here before they lost large numbers from Small Pox and Phneumonia [*sic*]."[9] In fact the Indians did not proceed all the way to the agency that fall but halted and formed winter camps some sixty miles short of the new location.[10]

The new headquarters was known as Red Cloud Agency No. 3, to distinguish it from the first agency, near Fort Laramie, and the second, near Camp Robinson.[11] The trip there gave McGillycuddy an opportunity to engage in one of his previous pursuits, cartography. On December 13 he wrote to President Ulysses Grant from "New Red Cloud Agency," Dakota Territory, "I enclose plats of trail from South fork and also one of the Agency and Post."

While the McGillycuddys settled into their new post, American Horse's band, the Loafers, camped about a mile from the mouth of the South Fork of the White River, McGillycuddy wrote. A Sioux band known as the Cut Offs, under Little Wound, camped "on the small wooded bottom of creek coming in from the North opposite the South Fork," he said. Red Cloud and Young Man Afraid Of His Horses had halted on the White River about sixty miles from agency headquarters near the Missouri River. "It is hard to say how long they will remain where they are," the doctor told Grant. He added, "The heads of the families will be in here to day to draw their annuities and rations, leaving their lodges behind at the camp."[12] The Indians had begun coming to the agency to draw their rations even as the weather turned disagreeable, with rain most days through December.

McGillycuddy had shown his adventurousness on many occasions; now Fanny, too, made it clear that she was ready for a challenge. At

---

[9]Lawson to Adjutant General, December 4, 1877.

[10]McGillycuddy to Ulysses S. Grant, December 13, 1877, copy at Fort Robinson Museum Archives.

[11]Information about the agency's name is from Bettelyoun and Waggoner, *With My Own Eyes*, 112.

[12]Ibid.

this new posting for her husband, she was the only white woman present. She spent time riding horses with her husband or another escort from the camp. On Christmas Day, 1877, the doctor and Fanny rode horses over from their temporary lodgings to their new quarters at the agency and the following day occupied them. On December 29, Fanny wrote that she was still organizing her new home: "2 men papering and it seems a hopeless job." She spent the following day writing reports for McGillycuddy and on New Year's Eve busied herself making wine jelly and a cake to serve on New Year's Day to all the officers and gentlemen at the post.

The new year got off to a rough start for Red Cloud Agency No. 3. On January 2, a Company E soldier was killed when he fell from the wagon he was driving. Fanny wrote that the "wheel passed over his head killing him instantly."[13] The weather then turned bitterly cold and windy, so the funeral was delayed for two days. Throughout the winter, Fanny most often wrote about the weather and noted that many days she had headaches and was otherwise "sick." But when the weather moderated, she and the doctor took walks or went on horseback rides.

For the Indians, that winter was particularly difficult. They had gone into camp some sixty miles from the new agency, which required them to make biweekly trips from their village to the agency to draw rations. This situation caused a "terrible mortality," because the Indians did not always have the supplies they needed, and transporting the goods subjected them to severe weather conditions. The result, Susan Bordeaux Bettelyoun later reported, was "hundreds of tree graves" along the White River—a reference to the Lakotas' traditional way of placing their dead on scaffolds set in trees.[14]

In early March McGillycuddy applied for a leave that would enable him and Fanny to visit family and friends in Michigan. Two months later the couple packed belongings for the journey east. They waited for a boat that would take them down the Missouri, finally stepping aboard on May 27, with a cold wind blowing. Although she had earlier recorded the arrival of the *Far West* and another Missouri River steamboat, the *Red Cloud,* when the boat that they would board reached the post, Fanny did not name the vessel. They steamed down the river to Fort Randall and then to Yankton. From there they took a train to Chicago. Fanny wrote of eating strawberries for supper and of

[13]Fanny McGillycuddy Diary, 1877–78.
[14]Bettelyoun and Waggoner, *With My Own Eyes,* 113.

arriving in Chicago on May 30, "just in time for the parade, it being Decoration Day."

The McGillycuddys stopped at the Palmer House for the night and set out the following day for a reunion with Fanny's mother, which took place on June 1. Although the couple surprised Fanny's mother upon their arrival, the doctor did not stay long. Instead, he hopped a train at noon en route to Detroit for a quick visit to his own mother, before he boarded the ten o'clock Canada Southern Railroad train that night, bound for New York.[15]

Fanny and Valentine reunited in Detroit on June 4, spent the next few days shopping, and on June 9 visited the Marine Hospital, where McGillycuddy had begun his medical practice. There he met with one of his former colleagues. Fanny had time to shop for silk, velvet, and silverware. They took tea with friends, attended church, and "had a lovely time," she reported. On June 17, McGillycuddy prepared to "start for the West, but when it came time to start I could not let him go," Fanny wrote. Torn between remaining with her family and separating from her husband, even temporarily, Fanny "got all ready to come back home with Doctor." The following day they set off, spending another night at the Palmer House in Chicago before catching the train for Sioux City. On June 26 their steamboat chugged into Red Cloud Agency No. 3. "All came down to meet us," Fanny noted, adding that the weather quickly turned very hot and the mosquitoes were dreadful.[16]

When the tribes had been relocated from the Spotted Tail and Red Cloud Agencies in the fall of 1877, they had received assurance that they would be situated along the Missouri River only for one winter and then could return to agencies closer to the Black Hills. Throughout the spring, Spotted Tail, at the Ponca Agency in eastern Nebraska, pushed for relocation. Red Cloud, who had remained farther west, had fewer difficulties with the military and agency representatives, but he nevertheless joined Spotted Tail in seeking new sites for their people and demanding a council with Indian commissioners.

In response to these appeals, Colonel David S. Stanley, of the Twenty-second Infantry, arrived at the Ponca Agency on July 5, along with Protestant missionary A. L. Riggs, former Kiowa Indian agent

---

[15]Fanny McGillycuddy Diary, 1877–78.
[16]Ibid.

J. M. Haworth, and Ezra Hayt, the newly appointed commissioner of Indian affairs. These federal representatives met with Spotted Tail in a formal council and also privately. In both settings Spotted Tail stressed one fact: His people wanted to move west. Once the meetings at the Ponca Agency had concluded, the commissioners proceeded up the Missouri, where they were taken to the site Red Cloud eyed for his new agency, a place on Pine Ridge in southwestern Dakota Territory. The commissioners preferred a site on Wounded Knee Creek, farther east and therefore more accessible to the Missouri River for shipment of annuities and other goods needed to sustain the Indians.[17]

The temperature soared while the commissioners met with Red Cloud and topped one hundred degrees when the commissioners went "with the Indians to select a place."[18]

As of July 1, 1878, McGillycuddy had a new appointment as physician at Red Cloud Agency No. 3, where he earned $600 a year.[19] This kept him busy and often away from Fanny, who was at their home at the nearby military camp while he tended people at the agency and in the Indian camps. As a diversion from the routine at the agency, Fanny joined a Mrs. Daugherty in mid-August on the *Far West,* taking the steamer up the Missouri past Fort Pierre to Standing Rock, Fort Rice, and eventually Bismarck. She returned to Red Cloud Agency No. 3 on August 28 to find that "Doctor had gone to the 'Forks' to see the Indians. How disappointed I was." The "Forks" she referred to was Red Cloud's camp, near the forks of the White River. Fanny wrote that she was "lonesome and disagreeable" as she waited for her husband to return, which he did on September 1.

While at the agency, Fanny, who was trained as a teacher, began learning Spanish from one of the officers, but the lessons ended abruptly. In her biography of McGillycuddy, Julia McGillycuddy said the soldier had exhibited rude behavior toward the doctor because on one occasion he was "too much engrossed with the lesson" and failed to salute him. Fanny, when informed of the "rudeness," appears to have been unaware of it, but she "immediately discontinued the Spanish

---

[17]Hyde, *Spotted Tail's Folk,* 292–93. Additional details about these councils are included in Olson, *Red Cloud and the Sioux Problem,* and Larson, *Red Cloud.*

[18]Fanny McGillycuddy Diary, July 13, 1878.

[19]Fort Robinson records, September 3, 1878, Fort Robinson Museum Archives.

lessons and the visits ceased." Although she hinted of no impropriety, it could be that McGillycuddy believed the man was "too much engrossed" with his wife.[20] As one of very few women present with the agency command, Fanny had no real alternative but to visit with the men if she wanted conversation beyond that with her husband. Yet this is the only clear reference to Valentine's placing any restriction on her, perhaps a sign that jealousy had reared its head.

That fall, anxiety grew when word circulated about a breakout of Northern Cheyennes from their reservation in Indian Territory. Hundreds of Cheyennes had been moved in 1877 to the Darlington Agency near Fort Reno—a place that became a hell hole. Hot, sultry air combined with disease and starvation to decimate the Indians. By September 1878, fewer than 350 survived.

By September the Northern Cheyennes could stand the suffering no longer. Late in the evening on September 7, nearly the entire group of surviving warriors, women, and children, led by Little Wolf, Dull Knife, and Wild Hog, fled the Darlington Agency. They were going home to the northern plains. Their 750-mile, forty-four-day trek would take them across western Oklahoma, Kansas, and Nebraska. Along the way they engaged in attacks and raids on settlers as federal troops quickly massed and set off in pursuit.[21]

Some troops had organized at Sidney Barracks in Nebraska shortly after the Indian breakout. Located on the Union Pacific Railroad line, Sidney Barracks had access to trains that could carry soldiers east or west to intercept the Cheyennes should they make it that far north. Major Thomas Tipton Thornburgh, of the Fourth Infantry (who would die in the 1879 White River battle with Utes in Colorado), failed to stop the Cheyennes. They crossed the railroad just east of Ogalalla, Nebraska, and then disappeared into the Sand Hills.

Now back in Nebraska, but with troops closing in from various directions, the Indians split their ranks. Little Wolf and his band

---

[20]McGillycuddy, *McGillycuddy Agent,* 89. In her diary, Fanny McGillycuddy noted on September 12, 1878, that she "wrote for Spanish Reader." Just eight days later, on the twentieth, she wrote, "Took my last lesson in Spanish." Nothing in her diary indicates any conflict between Dr. McGillycuddy and any of the men, although months earlier, on December 4, 1877, she had written, 'Mr. Cummings and Dr. had a few words." Subsequent references to Cummings appear in the diary, making it clear that the couple continued to have him visit their home. This was no doubt Third Cavalry Second Lieutenant Joseph Cummings. Julia McGillycuddy's reference to an officer failing to salute McGillycuddy is incongruous. Because he was a civilian medical officer, it would have been unnecessary for anyone to salute him.

[21]Monnett, *Tell Them We Are Going Home.*

headed toward the Powder River and eventually reached Montana Territory. Dull Knife, Wild Hog, Old Crow, and their followers turned toward the old Red Cloud Agency, near Camp Robinson, expecting to find sanctuary with Red Cloud and other Lakotas. They did not know that the agency had been moved and was now situated along the Missouri River.

McGillycuddy, like others at Red Cloud Agency No. 3, heard about the Cheyenne breakout by early October. Captain Peter Vroom came to the McGillycuddy house "to say that he had orders to be ready at a moments notice to go out in the field after the 'Cheyennes' who had escaped from their reservation and who were murdering settlers all along their route. Through Kansas coming North it is supposed to join Red Cloud and scatter among his band," Fanny wrote on October 5. The following day, orders came for the troops to respond, and McGillycuddy accompanied them, leaving the agency by about two o'clock. "So lonesome," Fanny wrote. "How I dread the time they are to be gone 20 days, possibly longer."[22]

As the campaign to round up the Northern Cheyennes began, Fanny fretted, "Everybody is frightened. A rumor came that 'Spotted Tails' band had broken out and they had burned their store house and were coming this way." Such was not the case, and by October 9 she said she was "getting over the fright a little." The next day she wrote that the Indians "were going to be allowed to move," an indication that the delay in relocating the Spotted Tail and Red Cloud Agencies had finally ended. A letter she received from McGillycuddy on the eleventh must have eased Fanny's mind over the outbreak, for the next day she wrote in her diary, "Went to the Agency *alone* on horseback." The wind was howling on October 21 when Fanny had another note from the doctor, informing her that the troops would return to the agency that afternoon. She was on hand to meet him when they came in, writing that she was "very glad to see them, all came in in good spirits."[23]

The soldiers with McGillycuddy had not seen the Northern Cheyennes, but in a foggy accident on October 25, troops from Major Caleb H. Carlton's Third Cavalry, based at Camp Robinson, stumbled onto the camp of Dull Knife and Wild Hog. Following tense negotiations, the Indians were taken into custody and moved to Camp Robinson, where they were held in an abandoned barracks.

[22]Fanny McGillycuddy Diary, 1877–78.
[23]Ibid. (emphasis in original).

Sergeant Carter P. Johnson was with the troops and later told
Indian wars historian Walter Camp that "Dull Knife said his people
were hungry & if we would give them something to eat they would
follow. We set out some rations & the Indians took them & followed
us. This was about 10 A.M. We went down into the valley & camped
that night on Chadron creek. Dull Knife's band camped in the creek
bottom and we had only 2 companies at that time camped on both
banks right over them."[24]

Buffalo Hump was with Dull Knife and also later told Camp about
the Cheyennes' surrender: "When Dull Knife surrendered there was
no firing on the part of either soldiers or [Indians]. . . . When they
surrendered most of them gave up their arms, but a few concealed
them under their clothing and in this way retained possession."[25]

In early December McGillycuddy received a letter ordering him to
report to Omaha and appear before the Medical Board. This sum-
mons, once answered, could make him a military medical officer. Up
to this point he had been a contract doctor. The relocation of Indians to
the Missouri River agencies had lasted less than a year. By the time the
doctor was ordered to go to Omaha, the Red Cloud Agency had been
moved again, to White Clay Creek northeast of Chadron, Nebraska,
where new, substantial buildings were under construction. The Brulé
Sioux left the Ponca Agency and were relocated to Rosebud Agency.[26]

With the Red Cloud bands at their new agency at Pine Ridge, troops
were unnecessary at Red Cloud Agency No. 3. When the soldiers set out
to return to Camp Robinson, the doctor made plans to ride with them.
Winter had begun to ensconce the northern plains, and he prudently
decided that his wife should not accompany him but instead travel east
for a visit with her family. Fanny dressed warmly, encasing her legs in
wool stockings and pulling on a fur coat before bundling up with her
husband under a pile of buffalo robes in a stagecoach that took her a
dozen miles to the Brulé agency. There she began the trip to Detroit.[27]

The doctor's journey back to Camp Robinson, in northwestern
Nebraska. took place in the face of early winter storms and extreme
cold. Prairie fires had raged earlier in the season, so the soldiers found

[24]Interview with Major Carter P. Johnson, September 19, 1913, Camp documents, Ellison
    Papers, DPL.
[25]Account by Buffalo Hump, Camp documents, Ellison Papers, DPL.
[26]Bettelyoun and Waggoner, *With My Own Eyes*, 114–15.
[27]McGillycuddy, *McGillycuddy, Agent*, 92.

little firewood. The medical officer controlled the whiskey available to the troops by keeping in the pocket of his heavy buffalo coat the key to the locker holding the stash. McGillycuddy warned the men that although they believed a drink of whiskey would warm them, in fact, from a medical viewpoint, it had the opposite effect and lessened their ability to withstand the frigid temperatures. He carefully dispensed the alcohol only in the evening, when they were in camp, unlike on some of his earlier trips—such as the 1875 explorations of the Black Hills with Newton and Jenney, when the men often imbibed at every rest break on a day-long trail.

The soldiers arrived at Fort Robinson—it had been renamed in December—on January 3, 1879, to find that the Cheyennes were crammed into a log barracks. One guard was posted outside the building and there were more inside, "with a sentry pacing up and down, armed with a six-shooter, among the Indians," Sergeant Carter P. Johnson recalled. In the early days of the Indians' incarceration, soldiers prepared food for them. The women and children were allowed to go outside the barracks freely, and the men were permitted to be outside with supervision. "The Indians were pleasant and agreeable to their guards inside and often talked and smoked with us in the little room. They had their dogs with them in the barracks and a heating stove, and were comfortable enough," Johnson said.[28]

The atmosphere changed when orders came to once again remove the Cheyennes to Indian Territory. The tribespeople made it clear that they would die first. When negotiations with the headmen failed, Captain Henry W. Wessells removed leaders Wild Hog and Old Crow from the barracks and cut off food, water, and fuel supplies to the people remaining inside. Lacking basic supplies, the Indians "now became very ugly to the inside guards, having changed their demeanor completely, and were getting to be very unruly," Johnson said.[29]

Though just returned to the post, McGillycuddy heard the talk that the Cheyennes intended to break out once again. The troops were on heightened alert while the Indians reportedly sang and danced, tore up the floorboards, and barricaded the windows. Tribeswomen who had earlier been allowed outside had picked up corn that had fallen through the flooring of the post storehouse, and this may have been

[28]Interview of Major Carter P. Johnson by Walter M. Camp, Denver Public Library.
[29]Ibid.

the captives' only food—although Johnson believed the Indians might also have killed and eaten some of their dogs.

After dark on January 9, the Cheyennes were suspiciously quiet, according to Sergeant Johnson, who said, "I declared then and there that they were getting ready to come out." Upon hearing the first gun-shot later that evening, the sergeant ordered his men toward the fort. "We doubled-quicked to the fort, over a mile away, not waiting even to fully dress."[30]

Buffalo Hump recalled, "When it became evident that the soldiers intended to starve us to death we thought we might as well die fighting as to starve so it was decided to break out." As he described the action: "The soldiers had boarded up their windows of the guard house & built a fence around the house a little way from it and guards were patrolling outside the fence. When the time came to [break] out I busted the boards from the window and was first out and knocked a hole through the fence with an ax. A fight started right there."[31]

Once outside the barracks, Buffalo Hump joined his mother and sister, Dull Knife, and other members of the band. "We were out 10 days without anything to eat and we nearly perished," he recalled. Eventually some of the 149 Northern Cheyennes who had escaped found refuge with the Lakotas at Pine Ridge. More than thirty Indians were killed and another thirty wounded during the outbreak from Fort Robinson. Eleven members of the Third Cavalry died, and ten were wounded.[32]

McGillycuddy, while serving as a physician at the Red Cloud Agency, had been involved in councils with the Cheyennes before their outbreak. Armed with his firsthand knowledge, and having decided not to go to Omaha to appear before the medical board, he left for Washington on the very night of the incident. There he met with Commissioner of Indian Affairs Ezra A. Hayt and Secretary of the Interior Carl Schurz, giving them a personal account of the tension at Fort Robinson and across the region. They had a proposition for him as well. The role of this frontier doctor was about to change.

---

[30]Ibid.
[31]Account by Buffalo Hump.
[32]Monnett gives the Indian casualty numbers in *Tell Them We Are Going Home*, 137.

III

INDIAN AGENT

12

Pine Ridge Agent

A SNOWSTORM HERALDED THE arrival of Valentine T. McGillycuddy when he returned to the Black Hills with Fanny in March 1879. Having already labored as cartographer and topographer, doctor and frontier contract military surgeon, he was about to engage in a new, equally challenging career—that of Indian agent. In January, Commissioner of Indian Affairs Ezra Hayt and Secretary of the Interior Carl Schurz had reached a decision about the management of one of the largest, potentially most volatile Indian agencies in the country. They would accept the resignation of Agent James Irwin, of the Pine Ridge Agency, and replace him with a man they had seen involved in Indian affairs in that region for the past two years: Dr. McGillycuddy.

Ambitious and engaged, McGillycuddy, to his credit, when offered the position during his visit to the nation's capital, deferred until he could hear from Fanny. But his acceptance just hours after the offer was tendered made it clear that he had no doubts about taking the job. He sailed through Senate confirmation, which was granted on January 29, 1879.[1]

The newly appointed agent spent two months preparing for the post—arranging necessary bonds, organizing household goods, even hiring a woman to assist Fanny at the agency. "I wish to leave for Pine Ridge as soon as possible, my appointment has met with universal favor both in civil and military circles, especially so with the Indians who have heard of it," McGillycuddy wrote Hayt on February 11 from Omaha, where he was arranging the $50,000 bond required for his

---

[1]McGillycuddy, *McGillycuddy, Agent,* 97.

service. "All I ask is a chance to [manage] Pine Ridge Agency and I think that neither the government nor the Indians will ever have cause to regret my appointment."[2]

The McGillycuddys and Louisa Duggett, the woman hired to assist Fanny, took the train to Sidney, then the stagecoach to Fort Robinson, where they transferred to an army ambulance for the forty-mile ride to Pine Ridge Agency. Buffalo robes warded off the cold, but Fanny and Valentine were both glad to arrive at the Indian post and the house that would be their home. It was not yet fully constructed, but it did have a stove, in which a fire burned, thanks to the effort of James R. O'Beirne, the man who had charge of constructing the Pine Ridge Agency buildings. Once they had washed down some venison sandwiches with hot coffee, the young couple headed to their bed, which had been placed in the dining room.[3]

James Irwin, the man McGillycuddy was to replace, reluctantly relinquished his position. Upon his arrival on March 10, McGillycuddy "called upon Agt. Irwin and demanded posesion [*sic*] of the agency." Instead, Irwin instructed J. W. Alder, who had served as agency clerk, "to take possession of all official papers, records, documents and government property belonging to the office of U.S. Indian Agent here."

McGillycuddy might have been a bit "in a stew" as efforts to assume his new position were temporarily thwarted. He acknowledged Irwin's opposition to his taking over as agent when he wrote to Hayt from Pine Ridge on March 12, 1879, "There appears to be a tendency here to retard my assuming charge as much as possible and on consulting with Col. O'Beirne I decided to send the before mentioned telegram [of March 10] and leave it to your office to issue a more preemptory order."[4]

In a reply telegram that same day, the commissioner instructed McGillycuddy to take charge, prompting the doctor to call on Irwin at his home. There, in the presence of Alder, he served Irwin with the papers ordering the change, but to no avail. "He again refused to deliver posesion [*sic*] of this agency, etc.," McGillycuddy told Hayt.

On March 15, McGillycuddy posted notices around the agency, saying "I have taken charge and entered upon my duties under full instruction of the Office of Indian Affairs. I shall expect to be obeyed

[2]McGillycuddy to Hayt, February 11, 1879, NARS 724, p. 444, Kansas City, Missouri.
[3]McGillycuddy, *McGillycuddy, Agent*, 4.
[4]McGillycuddy to Hayt, March 12, 1879, NARS 724, p. 487, Kansas City, Missouri.

and respected accordingly."[5] He enumerated the following orders: "1st Unauthorized persons are not allowed on the reservation. 2nd All traffic with the Indians is strictly forbidden. 3rd The bringing of liquors on the reservation is forbidden."[6]

That same day Irwin wrote to McGillycuddy regarding the transfer of the agency: "I am worn out by oppressive authority my very best efforts for the good of the service and for your success appears to be still misunderstood. For the sake of [peace] and safety, under protest I surrender all government property belonging to this agency to you, to take effect tomorrow morning."[7] That did not mean Irwin would leave the agency quickly. He added, "Your clerk can have free access to the office and all public records therein, providing I am allowed a desk for the use of my clerk and free access to all books, papers, blank forms and stationery in order that I may complete my final accounts, agreeable to my instructions, and that I may take copies of such official papers as I may require agreeable to my instructions."[8]

The delay in transferring agency control, according to Irwin, could be attributed to factors such as the size of the agency and his belief that he should not be removed from the position even though he had tendered his resignation months before. "It was not possible that I could run this large agency and have property in such a shape as to transfer at a days notices [*sic*] especially as the time of my relief has been indefinite," Irwin wrote in his March 15 letter. "I believe sir, that you cannot find a case under the administration of . . . Indian Affairs when an Agent resigning with no charges against him is required to surrender government property for which he is responsible under his bonds to a successor before he is indemnified by official receipts," he added.

These claims were unsubstantiated, for Irwin had known of McGillycuddy's appointment for nearly two months.

Having just marked his thirtieth birthday, Valentine T. McGillycuddy, still sporting a flamboyant mustache and a neatly trimmed Van Dyke beard—a look that earned him the Indian name "Little

---

[5]McGillycuddy U.S. Indian Agent notice, March 15, 1879, NARS 724, p. 493, Kansas City, Missouri.
[6]McGillycuddy, Diary, 1879.
[7]James Irwin to McGillycuddy, March 15, 1879, NARS 724, p. 497, Kansas City, Missouri.
[8]Ibid.

Beard"—wasted no time in establishing himself as Pine Ridge agent. This was a job of almost authoritarian rule. Governors of the states and territories in which Indian reservations were located held no authority over Indian agents. Instead, the agents answered to the president of the United States through the Bureau of Indian Affairs, which had been organized in 1849 under the office of the Secretary of Interior.[9]

As he began taking stock of the resources available on the reservation and at the agency, McGillycuddy asserted his own firm style of governing and managing. He had charge of some eight thousand Indians, who lived in a region encompassing about four thousand square miles.[10] To effectively manage such a place, he quickly obtained a spring wagon and team of horses, which he could use to inspect the reservation. He also bought a single-door, fire-proof safe for the agency's records and other important documents.[11]

In one of his first appointments, McGillycuddy selected Dr. E. J. DeBell, of Dakota City, Nebraska, to serve as physician at Pine Ridge, a position no doubt of particular importance to the agent, who had until recently worked in that capacity himself. The candidate was married and a graduate of Albany Medical College in New York. More important, he had spent nine years "in the practice of medicine on the frontier which of course is very much the same as practice among the Indians. For this reason I consider him much superior to a physician whose life has been spent in the more settled regions East," McGillycuddy wrote to Hayt in recommending the appointment.[12]

Once he had wrestled management away from Irwin, McGillycuddy set about working with the Indians. He quickly organized councils with Red Cloud, the first held on March 24 and another two days later in the agency office.[13] The two shared a pipe, and then McGillycuddy fastened a map of the reservation to the wall. He showed the chief and his companions the agency's location, near which most of the people had their camps, and told them to disperse to "plow the land, and earn a living."[14]

---

[9]McGillycuddy, *McGillycuddy, Agent*, 18.

[10]Ibid., 5.

[11]McGillycuddy to Hayt, March 1, 1879, NARS 724, p. 473, Kansas City, Missouri. The safe arrived at the agency on June 4, according to the 1879 diary.

[12]McGillycuddy to Hayt, March 12, 1879, NARS 724, p. 491, Kansas City, Missouri.

[13]McGillycuddy, Diary, 1879.

[14]McGillycuddy, *McGillycuddy, Agent*, 103. The 1879 diary noted on March 26 that McGillycuddy "held Council with Chiefs in regard to Boundary lines—Referred as on the 24th inst. Also in regard to division of farming lands and other less important things."

Sioux chiefs, 1869.
During his years on the northern plains,
McGillycuddy worked with many tribal members.
Here, Red Cloud stands at the right, next to interpreter Julius Meyer.
Seated, from left, are Sitting Bull, Swift Bear, and Spotted Tail.
Nebraska State Historical Society, RG2246 PH 0 8 a.

Early on, Julia McGillycuddy wrote in her biography, McGilly-cuddy "conceived the idea of having the tribal system abolished and the bands scattered. He imagined farms and homes covering the valleys and schoolhouses filled with red-skinned children. He envisioned a home government with a native police force, and Indian teamsters transporting their own freight from the railroad."[15]

The reaction to the agent's suggestion that the Lakotas plow and plant came from Red Cloud quickly—and negatively. He said, "Father, the Great Spirit did not make us to work. He made us to hunt and fish. He gave us the great prairies and hills and covered them with buffalo, deer, and antelope. He filled the rivers and streams with fish. The white man can work if he wants to, but the Great Spirit did not make us to work. The white man owes us a living for the lands he has taken from us."[16]

Little Wound added that if the Indians moved away from the agency, they would be unable to obtain rations. McGillycuddy responded that he would increase the quantity of rations depending on the distance the people lived away from the agency. In an even bolder move, he said he would organize an Indian police force to replace the soldiers then responsible for maintaining order on the reservation.[17]

Those who doubted McGillycuddy's ability to bring about these sweeping reforms had not yet seen the tenacity of the Irishman. It would take him years and engulf him in long-lasting controversy, but this young agent intended to follow the policy being dictated by the Office of Indian Affairs. He would push his charges toward assimilation into white civilization and away from tribal traditions.

"The rule in regard to the employment of relatives is general in its application to all Agencies," Commissioner Hayt wrote to McGillycuddy in a telegram sent March 24.[18] It can be surmised from this answer that McGillycuddy had inquired about regulations pertaining to his hiring relatives at Pine Ridge. In general practice, the Office of Indian Affairs did not allow such nepotism, but McGillycuddy would find ways to circumvent the rules.

---

[15]McGillycuddy, *McGillycuddy, Agent*, 12.
[16]Ibid., 103.
[17]Ibid., 104.
[18]Telegram, Hayt to McGillycuddy, March 24, 1879, RG 75, Series 11, Box 722, NARS, Kansas City, Missouri.

On March 31, 1879, he requested approval of agency workers and received confirmation of appointments in an April 26 letter from E. J. Brooks, acting commissioner of Indian affairs.[19] Among those appointed were John B. Provost, interpreter, to be paid $600 a year; William Allman, assistant blacksmith, earning $60 a month, Frank Stewart, storekeeper, starting the job on April 1 at a recommended wage of $720 a year; three Indians, identified as Iherruka, Takuya wanica, and Hauska, as laborers earning $15 a month; John W. Marshall, chief herder, $800 a year; and Louis Hawkins, Roy DeLion, Jack Lebou, and Canumpa, herders, at $15 a month. Equality of pay was not a feature of the Indian Service. Herder Charles Cuny, who was white, received $40 a month, and laborer James Fielding, also white, earned $600 a year. In his April 26 letter Brooks noted, "Your action in increasing the salary of the following employees during the present fiscal year is not approved. Frank Stewart, storekeeper, April 1, 1879 from $720 to $840 per annum[;] George A. White, Laborer, April 1, 1879, from $40 to $50 per month."[20]

The most interesting appointment included in this routine list is that of Stewart, the new storekeeper at Pine Ridge, for he was McGillycuddy's older brother, Francis Stewart McGillycuddy. He became "Frank Stewart" in order to take the job at Pine Ridge and retained that name until his death many years later in Rapid City.[21]

In making his appointments, McGillycuddy started with two men he knew he could trust: his brother and John B. Provost, who had long served as the doctor's interpreter. Provost had been with him at least since 1877, when he provided critical service at the time Crazy Horse was stabbed and killed.

* ◆ *

Having treated Indians for a variety of medical ailments while attached to the army at Fort Robinson and later at Red Cloud Agency No. 3, McGillycuddy no doubt had experience with some of their family relationships and had encountered their cultural beliefs. It might not have been a surprise, therefore, when he dealt with Keeps The Battle when the Lakota's wife was "stolen" by an Indian identified

[19]Brooks to McGillycuddy, April 26, 1879, RG 75, Series 2, Box 2, NARS, Kansas City, Missouri.
[20]Ibid.
[21]V. T. McGillycuddy, Affidavit, sworn in Alameda County, California, March 2, 1929; copy in private collection of Daniel Stanton.

as Eleven.[22] McGillycuddy knew the woman had been taken to the Rosebud Agency and notified H. G. Bullis, the agent there, of pending trouble as a result.

On April 6, Bullis replied with a letter: "'Keeps the Battle' whose wife was stolen and brought to this agency by one of my people and of whom you wrote some days back, reached here today and instead of reporting to this office as directed by you on his pass, proceeded to the village where his wife was staying and in sight of her [relatives] attempted to kill her." Bystanders prevented Keeps The Battle from "carrying out his design," and although several shots were fired, no one was injured.

Following the shooting, Keeps The Battle was taken to the Rosebud Agency office, and Bullis sent for Spotted Tail, who helped resolve the conflict. Bullis reported, "According to the Indian custom the Indian receives back his wife and condones her offense, promising not to ill-treat or abuse her, and agreeing if he breaks his promise to let her go forever." The woman preferred to remain at Rosebud but returned to Pine Ridge with her husband. Bullis told McGillycuddy, "At the request of Spotted Tail I write you this letter asking if the woman ever complains to you of ill treatment to advise him through me."[23]

As part of the agreement, Eleven received permission to visit Pine Ridge to check on the woman. In spite of his action in this case, Bullis confided to McGillycuddy, "I consider it the wiser plan for an Agent to keep clear of these family troubles and let them settle their affairs according to the Indian law and usages; and therefore as the agreement was mutual between all parties concerned in this difficulty, I grant a pass to 'Eleven' to carry out his part of the program as agreed upon, feeling assured that if called upon you will decide impartially between them."[24]

In a postscript Bullis noted, "'Eleven' desires me to add that he wishes you to understand that he does not return to your Agency for the purpose of creating any trouble in 'Keeps the Battle's' household, and that if you should hear he came for that purpose you must not believe it for it is not true."[25]

---

[22]H. G. Bullis, special agent at Rosebud Agency, to McGillycuddy, April 8, 1879, RG 75, Series 2, Box 25, NARS, Kansas City, Missouri.

[23]Bullis to McGillycuddy, April 6, 1879, RG 75, Series 2, Box 25, NARS, Kansas City, Missouri.

[24]Bullis to McGillycuddy, April 8, 1879.

[25]Ibid.

On April 14, McGillycuddy recorded in the agency diary that Keeps The Battle and his wife "have family difficulty settled."[26]

Next the agent turned his attention to a council with chiefs on the rain-washed morning of April 22. Little Wound complained that the tribe had not received $25,000 it had been promised in exchange for land it had relinquished between the North and South Platte Rivers. Young Man Afraid Of His Horses objected to the establishment of an Indian police force on the reservation. American Horse and No Flesh, however, agreed to serve as McGillycuddy's "body guard" during a trip he planned to the Missouri River, where he would oversee the arrival and disposition of annuity goods and other supplies intended for use at Pine Ridge.[27]

Within the week McGillycuddy, with American Horse and No Flesh, departed Pine Ridge for the Missouri. Before leaving, he placed James R. O'Beirne, U.S. special Indian agent, in charge at Pine Ridge. Not long after the doctor set out, Little Big Man arrived at the agency, blood streaming from his legs. He had stabbed them following an accident involving his little girl, in a traditional way of showing concern and grief. O'Beirne and Dr. DeBell immediately went to Little Big Man's camp, where they found the child badly burned, but with care she survived.[28] On May 15, McGillycuddy returned to Pine Ridge, reaching the agency the same day a supply of seed corn arrived.[29]

In McGillycuddy's absence, chiefs and headmen at the Pine Ridge Agency petitioned President Rutherford B. Hayes, addressing concerns about the departure of former agent James Irwin. Their May 1 document referred to the council between some of the chiefs and the president in 1877. "We talked with you in your city," they wrote. "We told you that so long as we had an Agency or so long as he lived we wanted the old man—Dr. Irwin—for our Agent. . . . And now Great Father we wish that you would not send us any other Agent to take his place until after his death." Although they had "no desire to say anything against the agents you have sent us nor to find fault with them," the chiefs said, "We are here and we have brains and hearts, and we have eyes also, so that when White-men come among us we are soon able to judge whether their work is for good or for evil."

---

[26]McGillycuddy, Diary, 1879.
[27]Ibid.
[28]Ibid.
[29]Ibid.

Young Man Afraid Of His Horses in front of his lodge,
Pine Ridge Agency, January 17, 1891. This is the type of camp
McGillycuddy visited regularly as a doctor and agent for the Red Cloud
and Pine Ridge Indian Agencies. *National Archives, image 533072.*

In their petition, Red Cloud, Old Man Afraid Of His Horses, Young
Man Afraid Of His Horses, and Little Wound asked for payments not
yet received for the Black Hills, along with wagons, harness, mowing
machines, cows and bulls, oxen, hogs, chickens, and sheep.

Further, they said, "There were [*sic*] $25,000.— promised to the
Oglalas. To be paid them for relinquishing their right to hunt on the
Republican Fork. Cannot that be given to us this year?"

Raising several other grievances, they sought a stop to the theft of
Indian horses from "bad white-men," reinstatement of agency butcher
Benjamin Tibbitts and clerk C. P. Jordan, and the opportunity to
"hunt deer and buffalo in our old country."[30]

A similarly worded petition, also prepared on May 1, 1879, was
signed by twenty-two chiefs and headmen, including the four already
named and American Horse, Red Dog, Blue Horse, High Wolf, Slow
Bull, White Bird, Three Bears, Little Big Man, No Water, Woman's

---

[30]Petitions, Pine Ridge Agency, Dakota Territory, May 1, 1879, RG 75, Series 71, NARS, Kansas
City, Missouri.

Dress, No Flesh, and Keeps The Battle.[31] The signatures, or marks, of American Horse and No Flesh are particularly interesting, because those two had departed on April 26 with McGillycuddy to serve as his bodyguards. It is unknown whether they escorted him to the Missouri and immediately returned to the agency to take part in the petition writing and signing or whether their names were added in absentia.

———— ·•◆•· ————

It took little time for McGillycuddy to raise the ire of Bullis at the Rosebud Agency. On April 16 the new agent wrote the commissioner of Indian affairs to request "24000# Bacon, 10000# Coffee and 20000# Sugar be purchased and shipped to [the Pine Ridge] Agency," on the grounds that a large number of Indians had departed Rosebud and relocated at Pine Ridge.[32]

In a May 2 letter to McGillycuddy, Bullis thundered, "Nothing could exceed my surprise at your audacity in making a Statement of this character. For every person transferred from this Agency to Pine Ridge, four have been transferred from that Agency to this." He added, "The books in this office show that while but forty nine (49) persons have been transferred *from* this Agency to Pine Ridge since Jan'y 1st 1879, one hundred and eighty six (186) persons have been transferred from Pine Ridge to this Agency during the same period."[33]

Bullis charged that McGillycuddy was "grossly misrepresenting the condition of affairs" and added, "If you have taken up any larger number of Indians than above stated, you have done it without authority and in direct violation of the rules governing the transfer of Indians from one agency to another, and you alone are responsible for the consequences."[34]

That letter was not enough to diffuse Bullis's ire, and he fired off another to the commissioner of Indian affairs on May 3. "I have to inform you that the excession [*sic*] to the number of Indians at Pine Ridge Agency, so far as Spotted Tail Indians are concerned, is purely imaginary." He reiterated the figures he had provided to McGillycuddy in the previous day's correspondence and added, "In obedience to instructions from the Department, I have uniformly refused

[31]Ibid.
[32]Bullis to McGillycuddy, May 2, 1879, RG 75, Series 2, Box 25, NARS, Kansas City, Missouri.
[33]Ibid.
[34]Ibid.

rations to Indians of other agencies desirous of making this their home, unless regularly transferred, and it is a law now well understood among them.—I have no hesitation in saying if Agent McGillycuddy would enforce that law, his rations would hold out, during the period for which sent."

More important, Bullis said that if he transferred supplies to Pine Ridge, then the Rosebud Agency would lack goods to issue to residents there. "In conclusion, allow me to suggest, that if the Pine Ridge Indians have not enough energy, with a competent director, to have their rations from their base of supplies, they had better be moved back to the Missouri River, where their food can be laid at their feet and no such exigencies as the present arise."[35]

This confrontation spilled over into May as McGillycuddy struggled to get adequate provisions for the Indians under his charge. While he was at Fort Robinson on May 23, he sent the commissioner a telegram expressing his concern: "This is nearest the office to Rosebud. One hundred & ninety miles distant. Information I sent you this day I got from Rosebud by mail as I left Pine Ridge seventy miles from here. I want to get back to Pine Ridge. please hurry up matters."[36]

Acting Commissioner Brooks immediately responded, "Rosebud was ordered yesterday to loan you ten (10) thousand lbs coffee and twenty (20) thousand sugar. Has he [Bullis] refused since receipt of telegram?"[37]

McGillycuddy sent another telegram to the commissioner that day, asking that he "instruct receiving clerk Rosebud Landing to certify to me by mail receipt of freight at landing to enable me to sign bills of lading.[38]

The immediate response from Brooks: "Do as you have been instructed. Borrow Coffee, Sugar and if unavoidable Bacon from Rosebud, ten, twenty and eight thousand pounds respectively of each—We have no funds to warrant double issues the year round."[39]

---

[35]Bullis to Commissioner of Indian Affairs, Washington, D.C., May 3, 1879, RG 75, Box 3, folder dated April 8, 1879–June 30, 1879, NARS, Kansas City, Missouri.

[36]Telegram, McGillycuddy to Commissioner of Indian Affairs, May 23, 1879, RG 75, Series 6, Box 53 A and B, folder 1877–79, NARS, Kansas City, Missouri.

[37]Telegram, Brooks to McGillycuddy, May 23, 1879, RG 75, Series 11, Box 722, NARS, Kansas City, Missouri.

[38]Telegram, McGillycuddy to Commissioner of Indian Affairs, May 24, 1879, RG 75, Series 6, Box 53 A and B, folder 1877–79, NARS, Kansas City, Missouri.

[39]Telegram, Brooks to McGillycuddy, May 24, 1879, received at Fort Robinson, Nebraska, May 25, 10 A.M., RG 75, Series 11, Box 722, NARS, Kansas City, Missouri.

"Tel. rec'd. I leave for Pine Ridge at daylight," McGillycuddy responded. "Indians have rec'd both bacon and beef for years [past] notwithstanding the beef has no fat on it. it is a dangerous experiment to cut off bacon. do you intend to cut off coffee. do you mean if I have beef I must draw no bacon from Rosebud. can I issue double rations of beef if I can procure it."[40]

At 1:20 P.M., another telegram arrived from Brooks. "The Commissioner says 'Inform McGillycuddy that if he has Beef for regular ration no more is required. Treaty rations calls for Beef or Bacon—not—Beef and Bacon—If you have neither Beef or Bacon, present this telegram to Agent Newell [who] will lend you eight thousand pounds bacon.'"[41]

At that McGillycuddy fired back to Hammond and O'Beirne at Rosebud Landing: "Examine my telegraphic correspondence with Indian Office for past two days and do something."[42]

Apparently they did so, for on May 27 McGillycuddy's agency diary noted, "Sent 10 wagons to Rosebud for coffee & bacon."[43]

An ongoing problem on the reservation involved illegal traders and men who provided contraband to the Indians. From his first orders as agent at Pine Ridge, McGillycuddy set a standard regarding alcohol and inappropriate people on the reservation. Traders had long-standing relationships with the Indians. Many of them had married Indian women, and these couples had children who carried on their own trading operations. McGillycuddy received his first official correspondence related to trade on the reservation less than two weeks after becoming agent.

On March 27, Commissioner Hayt wrote, "The office is in receipt of information that a certain Half Breed is carrying on trade with the Indians of your reservation, he being only the representative of a worried party at Sidney, Neb. Who supplies him with goods, and who is in fact *the trader*, only using the name of the 'Half Breed', who has no capital of his own, in order to evade the law regulating trade

---

[40]Telegram, McGillycuddy to Commissioner of Indian Affairs, May 24, 1879.

[41]Telegram, Brooks to McGillycuddy, May 24, 1879, RG 75, Series 11, Box 722, NARS, Kansas City, Missouri.

[42]Telegram, McGillycuddy to Hammond and O'Beirne, May 24, 1879, RG 75, Series 6, Box 53 A and B, folder 1877–79, NARS, Kansas City, Missouri.

[43]McGillycuddy, Diary, 1879.

with Indian tribes. A half-breed has the right to trade, with members of his own tribe, without a license from this office, provided he is the *bonafide* owner of the stock in which he deals, but he will not be allowed to be the stool-pigeon of others for an illegal purpose. You will make a thorough investigation of this matter, and report the result without unnecessary delay."[44]

In late May, having finally established the flow of supplies for the Indians, McGillycuddy turned his attention to reports that a man named McDonald, who had a ranch along the agency road a mile and a half from Camp Sheridan, was "selling liquor to half breeds contrary to laws of the United States." McGillycuddy had already ordered McDonald to cease the practice when, on May 28, the agent encountered "half breeds returning from there, this afternoon where they have been drinking intoxicating liquor and one half breed who works in the Commissary was very drunk and acted very unbecomingly and was notified by Mr. Alder [the agency clerk] of his discharge from his job at the agency commissary."[45]

Two days later, Woman's Dress and Big Fork came to the agency "from 'Camp Sheridan' and McDonalds ranch where they have been for one day—and both were very drunk, and claimed that McDonald and Buese gave them or sold them liquor."[46]

On Sunday, June 1, Agent McGillycuddy, accompanied by his brother and a laborer, took action against the McDonald and Buese operations, even though they were not on reservation land. The agency diary noted, "Dr. McGillycuddy with Mr. Steward (Commissary clerk) [and] Fielding (laborer) started for McDonald Ranche and Camp Sheridan for the purpose of taking all intoxicating liquor from them arrived at Camp Sheridan, and with the Comandg Office proceeded to Buese store and took what liquor they had and placed it in the Commissary at that place and after making a thorough examination of the premises, proceeded thence to McDonalds where they found Whiskey bottles in profusion but the birds had flown."[47]

On Monday McGillycuddy obtained sworn statements from his

---

[44]Office of Indian Affairs to McGillicuddy (*sic*), March 27, 1879, RG 75, Box 3, folder September 3, 1877–April 8, 1879, NARS, Kansas City, Missouri.

[45]McGillycuddy, Diary, 1879.

[46]Ibid.

[47]Ibid. This reference to Mr. Steward mostly likely meant Frank Stewart, McGillycuddy's older brother, since he held the position of agency storekeeper.

interpreter, John Provost, and Woman's Dress that "they have received liquor from McDonalds and Bueses store at Camp Sheridan, and that it was gave or sold to them by the above named parties." The agent immediately took "proper steps for the arrest" of the proprietors. Buese did appear at the agency to say he did not sell liquor, but there was no sign of McDonald.[48]

On June 4, 1879, the ten wagons that had been sent to the Rosebud Agency returned with bacon, coffee, and other supplies.[49] The following day, Acting Commissioner Brooks wrote authorizing McGillycuddy "to expend a sum not to exceed $2,500, in the purchase of materials and the employment of skilled labor necessary in the construction of a dwelling, in according with the plans this day mailed to your address for occupancy by Chief Red Cloud; and also a further expenditure of not to exceed $3,000, in the erection of *six* small dwellings for the Chiefs at your agency."[50]

By this time McGillycuddy had already begun purchasing many of the goods the Indians would need if they were to change their lifestyles as dictated by current Indian policy. These included tools and materials for use in the shops, twenty cases of axle grease, and shovels.

The chiefs, however, were not preoccupied with accommodations or tools. Red Cloud and others asked permission "for three half breeds and six Indians" to travel east where they could hold exhibitions, but Commissioner Hayt wrote to McGillycuddy on June 20 that "many applications of this character have been made to the office from various sources, on behalf of Indians of different tribes during the past two years which have invariably been refused. Such expeditions are not conducive to the permanent good or welfare of the Indians and I must decline Red Clouds request."[51]

Tribal chiefs and headmen Red Cloud, Young Man Afraid Of His Horses, Red Dog, American Horse, Black Bear, No Water, Red Shirt, Big Foot, Slow Bull, and Little Wound met with McGillycuddy and First Lieutenant George Francis Chase of the Third Cavalry on June

[48]Ibid.
[49]Ibid.
[50]Brooks to McGillycuddy, June 5, 1879, RG 75, Series 2, Box 2, NARS, Kansas City, Missouri.
[51]Hayt to McGillycuddy, June 20, 1879, RG 75, Series 2, Box 2, NARS, Kansas City, Missouri.

1.[52] Red Cloud told McGillycuddy he wanted white people to stop stealing Indian horses. He added, addressing the distant U.S. president, "This Agent we have had but a few days and don't know much about him, our present rations of beef and annuity goods were left by old agent. Great Father, I intend here after to let you know when our agent is good and when bad." The old chief had thrown down the gauntlet. He had already dealt with five previous Indian agents and knew what he wanted for his people. He would be determined, stubborn, and often inflexible in holding onto tribal beliefs. His determination would be met by McGillycuddy's own obstinacy and resolve.[53]

Chase responded to Red Cloud that he would take soldiers to stop the horse theft that had been occurring on the reservation. "If you lose any horse [*sic*] send some of your young men upon the trail and also send some of them to find and tell me, so I can follow them," he said.[54]

When No Flesh offered to help the soldiers in pursuing horse thieves, Chase replied, "We will do what we can but can't follow the trail I want your young men to help me in this." No Flesh said that if he trailed the thieves, he would find them, and "I'l' [*sic*] kill them." Chase told him, "All right, but be sure and kill right men." At that, No Flesh backed away, telling Chase, "You attend to it yourselves."[55]

Given an opportunity to speak, Red Dog told McGillycuddy and Chase that he opposed "the Kearney [*sic*] Road" through the region, and he warned travelers to guard their belongings. In response the agent told Red Dog he had appealed to both the president of the United States and governor of Nebraska to halt traffic over the road from Fort Kearny and other points along the Union Pacific Railroad in Nebraska. "I asked them to tell all people starting over the road to stop and not come this way but go around by the way of [Camp] Sheridan," McGillycuddy said.[56]

At the council, McGillycuddy learned of plans for a Sun Dance to be held later in the month. Red Cloud told him, "This Sun Dance is a rule of the Great Spirit. On this day we give horses and cloth to

---

[52]"Proceedings of Council held at Sun Dance, June 1, 1879," RG 75, Series 4, Box 53 A and B, NARS, Kansas City, Missouri. McGillycuddy and Chase knew each other from their days together in 1876 on the Starvation March and at the battle of Slim Buttes, when they were in company with Crook.

[53]Ibid.

[54]Ibid.

[55]Ibid.

[56]Ibid.

the poor to make them rich and happy. We are doing all this for our children and praying to god for them. You dress up and wash and go to church. My young men for the same reason put on paint. We want the Great Father to give us paint."[57]

This ritual would take place in the area between Black Pope and Gap Creeks and would involve Indians from several agencies, including Pine Ridge. Brooks, in a June 6 letter to McGillycuddy, said, "As the 'sun dance' is a relic of barbarism and tends to retard and destroy all efforts made to promote the welfare and civilizing influences of the Indians, you will immediately take measures to prevent your Indians from attending it, and also induce the leading members of the tribe to cooperate with you in discouraging such heathenish practices."[58]

There is little to indicate that McGillycuddy actually instructed the Pine Ridge residents not to participate in the ceremony, and indeed, he outwardly supported it. When Chase and a *Chicago Tribune* reporter arrived to witness the event, McGillycuddy accompanied them to the Indian village, where preparations for the Sun Dance were under way from June 8 through June 10. "On the 12th the Sun dance took place, they were quite a number of them danced and all passed of [*sic*] smoothly, Dr. and company went out to see it returned about 4 oclock," the agency diary noted.[59]

A couple of hours after their return to the agency, a severe storm swept through, "breaking window glasses in the office, Drs house and employes buildings." Lightning struck very near the agency but caused no harm, and by about ten o'clock that night, "everything was quiet."[60]

At the time, Lieutenant Chase, with troops from Company A, Third Cavalry, was at the agency again, looking for horse thieves known to have been stealing Indian stock. While he was there, the agency diarist noted, "Lieut. Chase goes out to see the sun dance and is welcomed."[61]

Few Indians reported to the agency on June 29, beef issue day, because they were still out participating in the Sun Dance at the Spotted Tail Agency.[62]

[57]Ibid.
[58]Brooks to McGillycuddy, June 6, 1879, RG 75, Series 2, Box 2, NARS, Kansas City, Missouri.
[59]McGillycuddy, Diary, 1879.
[60]Ibid.
[61]Ibid.
[62]Ibid.

A freight wagon train driven by Indians arrived at Pine Ridge on Sunday, July 6, carrying fencing material. After unloading three wagons, the Indian teamsters went to their lodges, saying they would return the following day to unpack the remaining wagons. McGillycuddy paid little heed to this development; he was preoccupied by a visit from Little Wound and No Flesh questioning whether there had been any response from President Hayes to their inquiry of the previous month.[63]

Indeed, the agent could give them information not only regarding their concerns about flour still stockpiled at Rosebud Landing but also about other issues. Three days earlier he had received a letter from Acting Commissioner of Indian Affairs E. J. Brooks, concerning the road from Fort Kearny to the Black Hills.[64] This road, running north-south from the town along the Union Pacific Railroad line to the Black Hills, had been embraced by white residents of Nebraska but violated provisions of the treaties with the Lakotas. McGillycuddy supported the Indians' objections to the road, "on the ground that crossing the reservation by emigrants results in the introduction among the Indians of liquor and ammunition, and the running off of the Indian Ponies, thus creating a bad feeling generally." On his own he had stopped emigrant wagon trains from using the road, and on July 3 he received support from the Indian Office. Brooks, citing treaty provisions, wrote, "You will continue to prevent the passage of these trains across the reservation, by any North and South road."[65]

If needed, McGillycuddy could instruct his police force to remove emigrants and all other unauthorized people found trespassing on the road. "And if they return, and are afterwards found within the Indian Country," Brooks wrote, "you will report them to the U.S. District Attorney, together with the names and residences of the witnesses by whom the trespass can be proven, for prosecution."[66]

---

[63]Ibid.

[64]Brooks to McGillycuddy, July 3, 1879, RG 75, Series 2, Box 3, NARS, Kansas City, Missouri.

[65]Ibid. The second article of the agreement entered into between the United States and the "bands of the Sioux Nation of Indians and the Northern Arapahoes [*sic*] and Cheyennes," on September 26, 1876, contained this stipulation: "The said Indians also agree and consent that wagon and other roads, not exceeding three in number, may be constructed and maintained, from convenient and accessible points on the Missouri river, through said reservation to the country lying immediately west thereof, upon such routes as shall be designated by the President of the United States; and they also consent and agree to the free navigation of the Missouri River."

[66]Brooks to McGillycuddy, July 3, 1879.

Red Cloud, date unknown.
The Lakota chief wears a combination of traditional
and European clothing, holds a pipe, and has a peace medal
around his neck. *Nebraska State Historical Society, RG2845 PH 3 4.*

On July 15, McGillycuddy met with Red Cloud, Little Wound, Young Man Afraid Of His Horses, and "all the principal chiefs and men of Influence of the 'Ogallallas,'" telling them he had cows and bulls to distribute. "You are expected to take care of them and not to kill them. They are of a fine breed, and a good start for stock."[67]

---

[67]McGillycuddy, Diary, 1879, July 15.

Accepting the cattle, Red Cloud told McGillycuddy he wanted the mixed-blood people living on the reservation to share in annuities and provisions. "What Indians receive[,] Half Breeds should share," he said. Not only should mixed-blood people and non-Indian men married to Indian women help the Indians and teach them to farm, Red Cloud said, but also they should "cut hay with us on shares."

"This is my agency! This is my land!" he stated firmly, adding that he wanted Indian teamsters to haul the freight from the Missouri River, "to prevent outsiders from hauling for us and taking the money." As further proof that he recognized the provisions of the treaties with the Sioux, Red Cloud stated, "This is Ind[ian] land I want these people who are cutting down my timber to pay for it." He also wanted the wagons that had been promised to the tribe.

"The Great Father has kept pushing us back West, and taking land from us. Are not those wagons in part pay for our land? . . . When we went to see the Great Father we asked him for three styles of [wagons] Namely Heavy Wagons, medium [wagons,] and Buggies." Although the annuity goods generally arrived in the spring, Red Cloud said he wanted them distributed in the fall.[68]

McGillycuddy agreed that the annuities would be disbursed before winter and that the Indians should not need to pay for wagons. Surprisingly, he also supported cooperation with the mixed-bloods on the reservation, saying, "I think the Idea of having half breeds help the Indians is a good one. They can show them how to care for their cows. According to a law of the Great Father's a half-breed is considered to be the same as an Indian." But McGillycuddy told Red Cloud he had "closed up McDonald's ranch" for selling whiskey, and some of the non-native men married to Indian women caused a "great deal of trouble" in transporting freight from the Missouri River.

"There are some of them especially who cause trouble, and if you take their advice they will surely lead you into trouble," he warned Red Cloud.[69]

The chief groused that the Spotted Tail Indians would take Red Cloud Agency annuities if they had a chance. "They have done it and we know them," he told the agent.[70]

---

[68]McGillycuddy, Diary, 1879.
[69]Ibid.
[70]Ibid.

But McGillycuddy insisted that the freight needed to be transported by steamboat on the Missouri and delivered to Rosebud Landing during the summer, and then hauled to Pine Ridge. He also told the chiefs, "[You] have the power in Your own hands and if you don't want Squaw men to cut hay and trees—Just stop them." He said mowing machines would be available to cut hay for winter, and he would soon distribute other tools, including band saws and spades.

In the days immediately after the council, the Indians received an issue of cows and bulls along with spades, saws, and other tools. Then, on July 19, another contingent of chiefs—Little Wound, Blue Horse, Bear Brain, and Young Man Afraid Of His Horses—arrived at the agent's office. They had been involved in the earlier meeting with McGillycuddy and also in discussions among the tribal leaders. They wanted to make it clear that Red Cloud did not speak for all Lakotas on the reservation.[71]

Bear Brain, a member of Red Cloud's band and cousin to that chief, urged a transition from traditional beliefs. "I went to the council To-Day and heard the chiefs talk," he said. "They spoke of 'Red Cloud.' I told them to throw off their Indian clothes and be white men. I am not a chief, but I talked to them. We will stay here as if we were stuck in the land and take time to think of these things." Later he added, "American Horse is the only one at the council who said mind the agent!"[72]

———— • ◄► • ————

Secretary of the Interior Carl Schurz, with half a dozen associates, arrived at Rosebud Landing to begin an agency inspection in late August. After a two-day tour of the Rosebud Agency, he rode horseback to Pine Ridge, escorted by Indian police. The party reached Wounded Knee on September 1 at nearly ten o'clock in the evening but pushed on to make the agency at eleven thirty. The following morning Agent McGillycuddy accompanied the secretary to the camp of Young Man Afraid Of His Horses, where "A number of Indians pay their respects to Great Chief."[73]

This visit to the camp of Young Man Afraid no doubt irritated Red Cloud, but it likely took place as a result of Young Man's past support

---

[71]Ibid.
[72]Ibid.
[73]Ibid.; Hayt to McGillycuddy, August 6, 1879, RG 75, Series 2, Box 2, NARS, Kansas City, Missouri.

for McGillycuddy. On September 3, Schurz and his party engaged in a morning of target practice before meeting with "All Chiefs." Those addressing the secretary were Young Man Afraid Of His Horses, Red Cloud, Red Dog, and Three Bears, although the agency diary noted that the last "got excited and made a   of himself. He didn't want Indian soldiers." According to the diary, "Sectr'y Schurtz replied firmly and the Indians seemed to understand that he was not to be 'twisted out of shape' at their will."

Schurz rode his horse to Young Man Afraid's camp again on September 4. There, the women gave a dance, which was "followed by a regular scalp dance" performed by the Indian men. After the dancing, the Indians and the secretary had a "feast," followed by more dancing and then a meeting. The Indian spokesmen again raised concerns about obtaining wagons and about the establishment of an Indian police force, and they "*of course* brought up the Black Hills' question," according to the agency diary. A dozen mounted Indian policemen accompanied Secretary Schurz when he set off the following morning for Fort Robinson.[74]

Moving the Red Cloud Agency from its location on the Missouri River and reestablishing it as the Pine Ridge Agency farther west required the construction of new buildings. Much of the work was under the direction of James R. O'Beirne. In mid-September Commissioner Hayt instructed him to "complete his work without delay and to transfer to [McGillycuddy] all property in his hands."[75]

Accordingly, on September 30, the buildings were transferred. Among them were a sawmill and a gristmill, a two-story carpenter shop, a schoolhouse, a barn, a two-story warehouse, a wagon and blacksmith shop, five sets of quarters for employees, the agent's residence, a two-room warehouse issue house, an agency office, a council room, and a building to serve as a hospital, dispensary, and orphanage. There were also a privy, a store shed, a coal shed, a scale house, a well house, and a corral for the cattle, where the regular issuing of livestock occurred.[76]

[74]McGillycuddy, Diary, 1879 (emphasis in original).
[75]Hayt to McGillycuddy, September 18, 1879, RG 75, Series 2, Box 2, NARS, Kansas City, Missouri.
[76]"List of Public Buildings transferred by Jas R. O'Beirne Special U.S. Indian Agent to V. T. McGillycuddy U.S. Indian Agent at Pine Ridge Agency D.T. on the 30th day of September 1879," RG 75, Series 2, Box 3, NARS, Kansas City, Missouri.

Most the buildings were in need of further work. Almost all required outside battens, most needed chimneys, and some needed doors and partitions, besides work on walls and ceilings. The house meant for Red Cloud seems to have been virtually uninhabitable; O'Beirne reported that it required "floors, partitions, chimneys, battoning, doors & windows." The agent's house, where Valentine and Fanny had lived since March 11, was apparently in the best shape, for O'Beirne wrote, "All buildings except Agts house require painting."[77]

An inspection of the agency by C. V. Curry, an official with the Department of Interior, took place late in the summer, and already McGillycuddy had begun to effect change. "The condition of the Indians appears to be good, and they are fully as much advanced as the Rosebud Indians, if not more so," Curry wrote to Commissioner Hayt on September 4, 1879, from the Pine Ridge Agency. "I have seen more corn fields here, and more successful efforts at agriculture than at the former place."[78]

But there were deficiencies, "The buildings here are almost all—I might say all—of an inferior character, and scarcely fit for anything more than temporary use. They do not seem to have been well planned and have been executed in very poor style. It will require a great deal of work to make them serviceable for the winter." Among the problems with the buildings: the storehouse was too small and had been built on "piles without mud-sills," so the floor was collapsing, and a portion of the agency building was designed as a hospital, for which "at the present moment I can see no use whatever," Curry reported to Hayt.

Both the Rosebud and Pine Ridge Agencies lacked suitable housing for employees. Although McGillycuddy had employed a doctor, Curry wrote that he found "no building here which can accommodate the physician and his family." Even the home where the agent and Fanny lived was "too small, and too badly located that in rainy weather it literally stands in the water."[79]

Ultimately, the McGillycuddy house had a thick gray Brussels carpet with a flowered border and a square piano made of mahogany, which was notoriously out of tune. There was a large music box the size and shape of a coffin, which the doctor purchased for $250. Each

---

[77]McGillycuddy, Diary, 1879, April 11, refers to Dr. and Mrs. McGillycuddy's moving into the house that had "previously been occupied by his predecessor, Dr. Irwin."
[78]C. V. Curry to Hayt, September 4, 1879, NARS 724, p. 364, Kansas City, Missouri.
[79]Ibid.

of its four large cylinders played six tunes. Double doors opened to the bedroom, with a pink-bordered blue carpet. A swinging bed hung from the ceiling by four iron rods fastened to a huge iron hood. A pair of hand-darned net curtains featuring a patterned border and lined with blue silk and an edging of lace, along with a matching spread and pillow sham, completed the décor.[80]

While living at the agency, Fanny had assistance from Louisa Duggett and an Indian boy she called Tommy. Eventually she had chickens, ducks, and turkeys, as well as two buffalo calves given to her by some of the Indian boys. These buffalo were placed in a paddock near the agency, and a cow was obtained to nurse them.[81] Later, some Indian boys brought McGillycuddy two eaglets. He fed them but they were never tamed.[82]

In spite of the facility deficiencies, Pine Ridge had good news to report. During the summer, McGillycuddy had employed a number of Indian freighters to haul goods from the staging point at the Missouri River to the agency, paying them $5 to $8 per day for their work. "The freighting experiment has been as complete a success here as at Rosebud, and I think it will be well to turn the wagons definitively over to the Indians. They have done so well as to deserve it." But Curry suggested the Indians be made aware that if they failed to perform their freighting duties efficiently, the wagons could be taken away from them.[83]

Although payment for freighting duties could be made "one-half in silver," in no case were checks to be distributed. This regulation was to avoid a situation in which the Indians would take the check to a trader "and be induced instead of receiving change to make more purchase than would be condusive [*sic*] to their interest," Curry wrote. He added, "We may have to pay some express charges on the silver, but the result will be very beneficial to the Indians."[84]

Anticipating the completion of land surveys and subsequent allotments to the tribal members, Curry called for "some large breaking plows."[85]

---

[80]McGillycuddy, *McGillycuddy, Agent*, 106.

[81]Ibid., 112.

[82]Ibid., 113.

[83]Curry to Hayt, September 4, 1879. For information about the use of the Indian teamsters, see Curry to Department of the Interior, April 29, 1879, NARS 724, p. 257, Kansas City, Missouri.

[84]Curry to Hayt, September 4, 1879, pp. 369–70.

[85]Ibid.

"Begin immediately and break up as much land as your facilities will permit during September," McGillycuddy was instructed in late August. "Plow four inches deeper than the common plowing in Dakota. Sow half the land so plowed with winter wheat as an experiment, and remainder next spring & have the furrows turned over flat so as to cover the grass as much as possible. Deep plowing will require doubling your [teams]."[86]

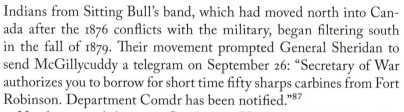

Indians from Sitting Bull's band, which had moved north into Canada after the 1876 conflicts with the military, began filtering south in the fall of 1879. Their movement prompted General Sheridan to send McGillycuddy a telegram on September 26: "Secretary of War authorizes you to borrow for short time fifty sharps carbines from Fort Robinson. Department Comdr has been notified."[87]

Nearly a month later, on October 22, Hayt wired McGillycuddy: "Require Sitting Bull Indians surrender their arms and ponies. Place them by themselves under the surveillance of police, and feed them. Further orders will be sent shortly.[88] In a follow-up message, Hayt admonished McGillycuddy for allowing someone at Pine Ridge to telegraph the *Chicago Herald* about Sitting Bull's Indians. "Secretary desires the practice discontinued. Discharge anyone guilty of making such publications. No government employee can at the same time be [a] newspaper employee," Hayt ordered.[89]

The commissioner told McGillycuddy: "The Secretary desires me to say 'Sitting Bull' Indians returning must be looked upon virtually as prisoners of war. They must surrender arms and ponies. The idea must not be permitted to spread that they can simply come back and be fed—Everyone of them if fed must be made to earn his rations by work."[90]

---

[86]Telegram, Office of Indian Affairs to McGillycuddy, August 26, 1879, received at Fort Robinson, Nebraska, August 26, 3:04 P.M., RG 75, Series 11, Box 722, NARS, Kansas City, Missouri.

[87]Telegram, Sheridan to McGillycuddy, September 26, 1879, received at Fort Robinson, Nebraska, 6:00 P.M., RG 75, Series 11, Box 722, NARS, Kansas City, Missouri.

[88]Telegram, Hayt to McGillycuddy, October 22, 1879, received at Fort Robinson, Nebraska, October 23, RG 75, Series 11, Box 722, NARS, Kansas City, Missouri.

[89]Telegram, Hayt to McGillycuddy, October 23, 1879, received at Fort Robinson, Nebraska, October 24, RG 75, Series 11, Box 722, NARS, Kansas City, Missouri.

[90]Ibid.

Earlier in the year, Cheyenne headmen Horse Roads, Hump, Tall Bull, and Spoken Wolf had sent a letter to Young Man Afraid Of His Horses and Little Big Man, saying they had relatives then living with the Lakotas whom they wanted to have join them on Tongue River.[91] They inquired whether Big Rascal and Dull Knife were then with the Lakotas and said they had heard "that our relatives, Man Afrd of his Horses and others had some Cheyenne prisoners down there, mostly women and children, that where they are hungry there's no one to give them food. We wish you to help them to come and be with their friends they [*sic*] Cheyennes at this place."[92]

"We earn our living here and would like to have some of our relations with us—no rations or annuities are given to us but we raise our food and we have our cattle, there is Buffalo plenty fat, and we expect some day to raise an abundance of food and have many cattle and we want you to do the same as we have done," the Cheyenne message said.[93]

The Cheyennes the letter referred to were some of those who had fled Indian Territory in the fall of 1878, been taken into custody by troops at Fort Robinson, broken out of the barracks there in January 1879, and been rounded up and kept with the Lakotas. Recognizing the "discontent" of these tribal members, McGillycuddy, in a letter to the commissioner of Indian affairs on November 22, asked for authority "to transfer renegade Cheyennes left here last winter to Tongue River to their relatives with Gen. [*sic*] Miles." He added, "Request Miles to allow no more of his Cheyenne messengers to come here they make nuicane [nuisance.] Police will be instructed to treat them as hostiles."[94]

With authority for the transfer approved, 119 men, women, and children were sent to Fort Keogh, in Montana Territory. They included Dull Knife, Big Rascal, Long Frenchman, Black Moccasin, Two Bulls, Red Bear, Elk Looks Standing, Pretty Face Elk, and William Rowland, along with their women and children, among others. In

---

[91]Message from Horse Roads, Hump, Tall Bull, and Spoken Wolf to Young Man Afraid Of His Horses and Little Big Man, 1879 (from period January 11, 1879–April 30, 1879), RG 75, Series 2, Box 26, NARS, Kansas City, Missouri.

[92]Ibid.

[93]Ibid.

[94]McGillycuddy to Commissioner of Indian Affairs, November 22, 1879, RG 75, Series 4, Box 3, Letterbook vol. 1, p. 85, NARS, Kansas City, Missouri.

the Rowland family group were listed four men, one woman, and ten children. Dull Knife had two women and three children in his family group.[95]

In one report, McGillycuddy wrote of the intermingling of tribal bands on the reservation. He noted that the Cheyennes had been sent to Indian Territory, but in their first breakout, they had crossed a "broad stretch of packed scabbed country" to return to their northern hunting grounds, which put them among the Lakotas.[96]

"Is it to be wondered that these people have been at times rebellious and that they are not as yet *self supporting*. The old maxium [sic] that a rolling stone gathers no moss was never more applicable," he wrote.[97] "Another cause of the [illegible] condition of these Indians in former years has been the turning of the agency into an asylum or rendezvous for dissatisfied and rebellious members of other agencies and tribes, such as Cheyennes, arrapahoes [sic] and Northern Sioux from Sitting Bulls hostiles. The influence of turbulent outsiders, coming to an agency is also bad and the taking in of any more people of that class is to be protested against."[98]

McGillycuddy added, "If the large bands of Northern hostiles are to be taken back by the treaty, which circumstances will certainly force us to do inside of one or three years, I would suggest that they be given an Agency by themselves. The Ogallalas do not wish for them. The experience of locating the Crazy Horse band of fifteen hundred persons, after the Custar [sic] Massacre of 1876, at this agency, and the subsequent jealousies and troubles, finally resulting in the death of that Chief and the departure of his people back north again, should be a sufficient test of the sorridness [sic] of this policy."[99]

In laying out his concern over the influence of chiefs and the tribal system, McGillycuddy wrote in a report that the only possible way for the agents to control and feed the Indians was "through and by the assistance of the Chiefs," for the chiefs "hold undisputed and absolute sway" over their followers. He abhorred allowing chiefs such as Red

[95]McGillycuddy to Colonel Nelson A. Miles, November 19, 1879, RG 75, Series 4, Box 35, Letterbook vol. 1, p. 112, NARS, Kansas City, Missouri.

[96]McGillycuddy report, 1879, RG 75, Series 4, Box 35, Letterbook vol. 1, NARS, Kansas City, Missouri.

[97]Ibid.

[98]Ibid.

[99]Ibid.

Cloud to have such power, believing it kept the Indians from improving their lot in life.[100] Sarcastically he added, "If we wish to continue them as savages and feed them until they finally die out, I would recommend the tribal system as the most feasible one."[101]

McGillycuddy, by the end of his first nine months as agent at Pine Ridge, had fully embraced the principles being touted by the Office of Indian Affairs and the Interior Department: Quash tribal beliefs. Require the Indians to abandon their hunting and gathering traditions and instead begin plowing the land and planting and harvesting crops. Send their children to boarding schools or require them to attend schools on the reservation. Most of all, break the power of the old chiefs who embraced those traditions.

---

[100]Ibid.
[101]Ibid.

13
Indian Police

THE PRESENCE OF THOUSANDS of Indians on a large reservation presented unique challenges for keeping order. Knowing that the tribesmen disliked and distrusted soldiers, McGillycuddy "called their leaders together and told them [he] was in favor of moving the American troops from the agency." He said to the chiefs and headmen, "'I trust you. Give me 50 of your best men and we will have 'home government.'"[1]

In the view of the Indian Department, this realignment of power—taking from the old chiefs the authority to deal with issues of order and law among the tribespeople—was necessary in order to force the people to follow more progressive rules.

Although McGillycuddy would say in later years that it was his idea to form the Indian police at Pine Ridge, he certainly had orders from Washington and was carrying forward a plan begun by his predecessor, James Irwin. But Irwin had never created an effective Indian police organization, and McGillycuddy assuredly did so.

Just after arriving at Pine Ridge, and before he had even wrested control of the agency from Irwin, McGillycuddy was instructed by Indian Commissioner Ezra A. Hayt to "forward as soon as practicable a statement showing the number of men, and also, as far as possible, the sizes of the uniforms and hats required. It is deemed advisable that the present police force at your Agency should be doubled if a sufficient number of men possessing the proper qualifications can be obtained."[2]

---

[1]*Oakland Tribune,* "Indian Wars Veteran Never Ill in 70 Years."
[2]Circular 28, Hayt to U.S. Indian Agent, Pine Ridge Agency, Dakota, March 2, 1879, RG 75, Series 2, Box 2, Accounts 1879, NARS, Kansas City, Missouri.

Indian police unit, Pine Ridge Agency, 1890.
Captain George Sword stands at left foreground.
Clarence Grant Morledge, photographer.
Denver Public Library, Western History Collection, X-31356.

Although McGillycuddy had information that Irwin had appointed four policemen in November 1878, the organization of the police force the following spring was obviously haphazard. McGillycuddy sent more than one letter to Hayt's office regarding pay for the officers, but the commissioner responded that he had no record that the men had been hired.[3]

Finally, in June, Acting Commissioner of Indian Affairs Brooks wrote to McGillycuddy, "The total number of Indian Police at your agency for the fiscal year 1880 will be 50. The force will be organized under section V of the Rules and Regulations for the government of the U.S. Indian Police service of July 1st 1878. These nominations will be submitted at once on the proper form."[4]

That McGillycuddy's Indian police force worked well was due in large part to the man he placed in the necessary role of captain, Man Who Carried The Sword. Young, strong, and fiercely loyal, this Lakota

---

[3]Hayt to McGillycuddy, April 16, 1879; Brooks to McGillycuddy, June 9, 1879; Brooks to McGillycuddy, June 13, 1879: all in RG 75, Series 2, Box 3, NARS, Kansas City, Missouri.

[4]Brooks to McGillycuddy, June 30, 1879, RG 75, Series 2, Box 2, NARS, Kansas City, Missouri.

officer would eventually take an American name, George Sword. That he was opposed by Red Cloud is not surprising, for that leader stood against virtually all progressive action on the reservation, particularly when it had the potential to upset traditional tribal roles.

Other Indian men soon hired for the police force included those who would be privates, earning $5 a month: Kills A Hundred, Standing Soldier, Fast Horse, White Horse, Weasel Bean, Long Bean, Last Horse, Little Bear, Lone Wolf, Red Kettle, No Flesh, White Wash Face, Hollow Wood, Thunder Ball, Standing Bear, Long Cat, Eagle Thorn, Black Bear, Lone Bear, Pumpkin Seed, Man Above, Iron Crow, and others.[5]

Initially McGillycuddy tapped Sword as a lieutenant in the force, along with Cloud Shield. But when the Indian Office denied the appointments for the reason that there could be only one lieutenant and one captain, Sword was placed in the higher rank. This move would prove a good choice for McGillycuddy. Sword stood steadfast in his resolve to enforce the laws of the government. Cloud Shield would eventually leave the force and align himself with Red Cloud.[6]

By early September 1879, the force had thirty-seven members. It is "very fine, and it will not be difficult to fill the whole allowance of fifty," C. V. Curry wrote to Hayt, adding, "I think more police is needed here than at Rosebud, for the simple reason that the Nebraska line is near, and that line will now and then have to be patrolled to prevent horse stealing. We must find some way to increase the pay of the policemen, by their employment as laborers or otherwise, until we can ask Congress for an increase of pay by law."[7]

Curry recommended a change in the color of the men's uniforms, saying, "The grey is not acceptable at all." He suggested the men should have arms, "if possible the U.S. carbine."[8]

In November the police received Sharps rifles after McGillycuddy contacted General Philip H. Sheridan with a request for the weapons.[9] This allocation came about partly because of concern that potentially hostile members of the Sitting Bull band of Lakotas might

[5]Hayt to McGillycuddy, September 4, 1879, RG 75, Series 2, Box 2, NARS, Kansas City, Missouri.

[6]Ibid.

[7]Curry to Hayt, September 4, 1879, NARS 724, p. 372, Kansas City, Missouri.

[8]Ibid.

[9]McGillycuddy, Diary, 1879.

move toward Pine Ridge. The army was equally concerned over the intentions of the Northern Cheyennes who had been living with the Lakotas since their breakouts from Indian Territory and Fort Robinson the preceding year.[10]

Policemen Lone Bear and Tobacco reported to the agency office on September 8 that four Cheyenne men, six women, and a child had fled, taking several ponies stolen from the village of Young Man Afraid Of His Horses, and were moving north. McGillycuddy quickly ordered twenty policemen to ride in pursuit. The following day, their ponies worn out, four of the policemen returned to the agency and reported, "Cheyennes heading for Tongue river remainder still in pursuit say they will be overtaken tonight or tomorrow."[11]

McGillycuddy, receiving a telegram that his mother was gravely ill, immediately departed for Detroit. The Indian police tracked the fleeing Cheyennes and ran them to ground on September 10 along Sage Creek, west of the Black Hills. A fight ensued in which Spotted Wolf was shot and killed. The remaining Cheyennes were brought back to Pine Ridge by Sword and his associates, who turned the Indians over to the supervision of Young Man Afraid.[12]

J. W. Alder, by then serving as McGillycuddy's clerk, upon learning that the Cheyennes had been captured, fired off a telegram to associates in Omaha, asking them to meet McGillycuddy, who was on the train headed east toward Detroit. In the choppy style of a telegram, he added, "Cheyenne Captured at Sage Creek west of Black hills By Sword and Police one Cheyenne Killed Stolen horses recovered."[13]

In reporting on the incident later, McGillycuddy wrote, "'Spotted Wolf' was a very troublesome Indian constantly breeding discontentment among the Cheyennes here and the principal object in his leaving here was for the purpose of stealing horses and eloping with the daughter of 'Dull Knife.'"[14]

This had been a good test of the police force's ability to pursue and bring fugitives to justice both on and off the reservation. McGillycuddy

---

[10]Telegram, Sheridan to McGillycuddy, September 26, 1879, received at Fort Robinson, Nebraska, September 26, 6 P.M., RG 75, Series 11, Box 722, NARS, Kansas City, Missouri.

[11]McGillycuddy, Diary, 1879; McGillycuddy to Commissioner of Indian Affairs, October 2 [or 7], 1879, RG 75, Series 4, Box 35, pp. 5–9, NARS, Kansas City, Missouri.

[12]McGillycuddy, Diary, 1879.

[13]Telegram, J. W. Alder to H. and J. S. Collins, Omaha, Nebraska, received at Omaha, September 12 [1879], 9:10 P.M., RG 75, Series 11, Box 722, NARS, Kansas City, Missouri.

[14]McGillycuddy to Commissioner of Indian Affairs, October 2 [or 7], 1879.

said, "Sword and Party deserve great credit for their persistence in the chase and feel [justifiably], proud of their achievements." He added, "The Agency Police force are a very reliable lot of young men and feel the importance of their position and are ready at any and all times to obey orders given them."[15]

That fall the policemen also protected surveyors marking reservation boundaries.[16] A headquarters for the police that had been turned over to McGillycuddy in September was finally completed on November 22, and five days later—on Thanksgiving Day—thirty-four members of the Pine Ridge Indian police gathered in front of the guardhouse and stood for a photograph.[17]

Over the next six years this Indian force would maintain order on the reservation, consistently backing McGillycuddy.

Life at the Pine Ridge Agency began routinely in 1880 as workers cut and stored ice for the following summer. The place lit up on January 4 when a lamp in the room occupied by Frank Stewart exploded. Apparently there were no injuries. Early that month, detectives arrived at the agency and arrested a man identified as Mexican Joe for horse theft. Supplies were issued to residents of the area, including coffee mills, which were handed out on January 19.[18]

Over the course of the winter McGillycuddy made more than one trip to Deadwood to attend a court trial that involved his interpreter, John Provost. The big news in early February was a report of small-pox at the Rosebud Agency and "the probability of [a] railroad running through reservation."[19] On February 11 the agent, again showing his authority on the reservation, performed a wedding ceremony for William Allman, the assistant blacksmith, and Louise Richard. The following day McGillycuddy had one man arrested for improperly trading with Indians and another "for stealing another man's wife."[20]

Everyone at the agency had a break on February 14, McGillycuddy's

[15]Ibid.

[16]Telegram, unknown sender in Washington, D.C., to McGillycuddy, October 25, 1879, received at Fort Robinson, Nebraska, October 25, 10:45 A.M., RG 75, Series 11, Box 722, NARS, Kansas City, Missouri.

[17]McGillycuddy, Diary, 1879.

[18]Stewart was identified in McGillycuddy, Diary, 1879, as Steward.

[19]McGillycuddy, Diary, 1879.

[20]Ibid.

birthday. That day "Mrs. McG gives him a surprise party which was quite a break to every one present," the diarist penned in the agency journal.[21] Three days later Fanny and Valentine departed for Washington, D.C.

On March 7, Captain Sword and the police guard returned from Rapid City, where they had been assisting the local sheriff with a prisoner. That same day the agency physician investigated a report of smallpox at Wounded Knee, and on March 8 he went to Porcupine Creek to see about a similar rumor from that district. The agency record that day noted, "Thinks it all a mistake; some slight breaking out caused probably by poison."[22]

Spring was definitely on the way in the region, for on March 22 workers "spent the day looking for trees suitable to transplant in Agency yard." Over the next few days, agency employees hauled and set out oak trees. Presumably they wanted some shade for the houses and other buildings. As spring came to the area, agency employees distributed farming implements. On April 6 the McGillycuddys returned to Pine Ridge, having already experienced warm weather and budding trees in Washington.[23]

Planting, gardening, and other spring chores were the order of business over the next two weeks, until McGillycuddy called the chiefs and headmen together for a council on April 20 to discuss plans for the railroad that was to push across reservation land. "Gave the Indians beef for a feast before coming to the Council. Gathered about 3 o'clock to hear the words of the Inspector," the agency diary noted. The railroad officials asked the tribal leaders to "sign papers conveying the rights to the Rail Road company to build the Road to the Black Hills through their Res. North of White River. The R. R. to pay the 6 tribes 20,000 head of 2 year old heifers." The council ended abruptly after Red Cloud spoke, saying that he would not sign the papers but wanted instead to visit Washington.[24]

The following day, having reflected on the preceding day's council, most of the Indians "wished to sign" the agreement, although a "few held back in the hope of going to Washington." Further discussion ended when the chiefs and headmen pledged to grant the railroad

[21]Ibid.
[22]Ibid.
[23]Ibid.
[24]Ibid.

right-of-way if they could sign the agreement "in Washington before the 'Great Father.'"[25] It would take months for this visit to occur.

In December 1880, the postmaster general ordered the dismissal of John W. Dear as postmaster at Pine Ridge. He subsequently insisted that the entire Dear family, including trader H. C. Dear, leave Pine Ridge and ordered McGillycuddy to carry out their removal. The agent could use the police force for the eviction if necessary. John Dear had been involved with the Lakotas since the establishment of the Red Cloud Agency in 1874, serving as a trader under the administration of agent John J. Saville. Now McGillycuddy came into his own disagreement with the family. He precipitated its removal by citing "disorderly conduct" by H. C. Dear while living on the reservation. Dear and his family had not yet departed the reservation by late January 1881, which prompted McGillycuddy to write to the commissioner of Indian affairs for instructions on how to proceed.[26] Eventually the Dears were removed, but because they had been staunch friends of Red Cloud, the action would cause further difficulties for McGillycuddy in his administration of Pine Ridge.[27]

McGillycuddy again cited the work of the Indian police in his monthly report for May 1881, in which he wrote, "The police have sustained good order and discipline on the reservation. No signs of intoxicating liquor have been at the agency. Two prisoners have been confined in the guard house and a half breed name Peter Jangrau, two days, for stealing a pair of boots[,] and the other Pvt Locke of the 5th U.S. Cavalry for four days on march from Fort Niobrara Neb to Deadwood Dak for trial for the murder of Lt. C Norty USA[;] while confined here he was entirely under the charge of the Indian Police who took most excellent care of him."[28]

---

[25]Ibid.

[26]McGillycuddy to Commissioner of Indian Affairs, January 24, 1881, RG 75, Series 4, Box 35, Letterbook vol. 2, 1880–1882, p. 62, NARS, Kansas City, Missouri.

[27]Larson, *Red Cloud,* 230; Olson, *Red Cloud,* 160, 271, 273; Buecker, *Fort Robinson,* 8, 25, 152. John W. Dear allowed his trading license to expire at the Red Cloud Agency near Fort Robinson in 1879 but moved to Pine Ridge, where he again began trading operations. He filed a claim for compensation from the government for his former store and stage station at Fort Robinson in 1880 but was denied.

[28]McGillycuddy, monthly report to Commissioner of Indians Affairs, May 1881, RG 75, Series 4, Box 35, Letterbook vol. 2, "Copies of letters sent to the commissioner of Indian Affairs, 1879–1914 this vol. 1880–1882," NARS, Kansas City, Missouri. The spelling of the perpetrator's name, Jangrau, is as McGillycuddy wrote it, but this likely was Peter Shangrau. The soldier killed was Lieutenant Samuel Cherry, who was murdered by a trooper on May 11, 1881. Cherry had been involved in the fighting with Utes in northwestern Colorado in 1879. Cherry County, Nebraska, is named for him.

Valentine McGillycuddy and Lakota representatives from
the Pine Ridge Agency while visiting Washington, D.C., 1883.
(*from left*) Standing Soldier, a member of the Pine Ridge Indian police;
George Sword, captain of the Indian police; McGillycuddy;
William Garnett, a top Indian interpreter; and Young Man Afraid Of
His Horses, an important ally of McGillycuddy's at Pine Ridge.
Nebraska State Historical Society, RG2845 PH 3 4.

"Everyone at the agency is happy and contented[,] fraudulent petitions and newspaper reports to the contrary notwithstanding," he
added.[29]

But there was discontent at Pine Ridge. It had bubbled for two years
between Red Cloud and McGillycuddy, having begun over the twin
issues of schools and Indian police who were loyal to the government

[29]Ibid.

and not the chiefs. Dear's removal as postmaster had exacerbated the situation, because he was a known supporter of Red Cloud's.

In the fall of 1881, tribal leaders including Red Cloud and Young Man Afraid Of His Horses traveled to Washington for a meeting with Indian Commission authorities. They asked that McGillycuddy accompany them, but the appeal was denied. McGillycuddy did obtain permission, however, for Indian police captain George Sword to accompany the group. In a letter to the commissioner of Indian affairs written in late July, McGillycuddy said of Sword, "He is the representative young man of the tribe and to him belongs the credit of enlisting the company of Indian police, numbering fifty, and comparing well in discipline and efficiency with that of any other agency in the service. He is destined to take a leading part in the affairs of the tribe in the future and has rendered valuable service to the government. He expresses a strong desire to visit Washington and has had my repeated promise that I will aid him toward the accomplishment of his desire."[30]

Although Sword more than lived up to the expectations McGillycuddy had when he appointed him captain of the Indian police, Cloud Shield fell short. By early 1882 relations between McGillycuddy and Red Cloud had become so strained that the agent condemned by association anyone who supported the chief. This led to removal of Cloud Shield from the police force. McGillycuddy told Indian Commissioner Price that the suspension came "for counciling with Ex Ch. [ex-Chief] Red Cloud and other disrespectful Indians against the management of agency affairs and causing dissention in the police force."[31]

---

[30]McGillycuddy to Commissioner of Indian Affairs, July 20, 1881, RG 75, Series 4, Box 35, Letterbook vol. 2, 1880–82, NARS, Kansas City, Missouri.

[31]McGillycuddy to Price, March 32 [*sic*] [1882], RG 75, Series 4, Box 35, General records, Letterbook vol. 3, 1882, p. 164, NARS, Kansas City, Missouri.

14

Educating the Children

IN THE FALL OF 1878, Pine Ridge Agent Irwin had been informed that fifteen orphan Indian girls from both his agency and the Spotted Tail Agency were to be chosen for education at the boarding school on the Santee reservation in Nebraska. But apparently none was transferred, perhaps because during that period all the tribespeople were being moved from their agencies in western Nebraska to new sites closer to the Missouri River.

In early June 1879, Agent McGillycuddy was asked to report on whether the girls had been sent to Nebraska, and if not, to "make the proper transfer."[1] By July, additional efforts to provide education for the Indian children were implemented, with schoolhouses being built across the reservation. On July 24, Episcopal bishop William H. Hare wrote to McGillycuddy from the Yankton Agency in Dakota Territory to say that he would visit soon with "two clergymen whom I propose putting in charge of the Mission work, and also of the school until I can find by experience how large the school work will be."[2] Hare sought the use of a schoolhouse and a teacher's house and wanted to know when a boarding school would be ready for use at Pine Ridge.[3]

Upon their arrival in late August, Bishop Hare, the two clergymen, and a missionary, Reverend John Robinson, who was to remain in residence, made do with tents because there was no building suitable for a teacher's residence. The school, too, remained unfinished.

[1]Brooks to McGillycuddy, June 5, 1879, RG 75, Series 2, Box 2, NARS, Kansas City, Missouri.
[2]William H. Hare to McGillycuddy, July 24, 1879, RG 75, Series 2, Box 25, NARS, Kansas City, Missouri.
[3]Ibid.

Undaunted, Hare wrote to clerk J. W. Alder at the agency, "I beg to request that you will have the kindness to erect two temporary partitions at the South end of the School-house, one running East and West and the other North and South, so that the clergy may have one room for a School-room and another for a bed-room. If temporary benches are also made, a school can be begun at once and the clergy can be housed until other provision can be made for them."[4]

By September 1879, the schoolhouse at Pine Ridge was still "in an unfinished condition, and a large part of it unfit for use," according to a report by C. V. Curry. He wrote to Commissioner Hayt, "I suggest that you instruct Dr. McGillycuddy to finish the building as best he can, so that it may be used until we can establish boarding schools and day schools after the allotment of land has taken place, and the different tribes can be divided into school districts."[5]

While some native children would attend the schools on the reservation, others would be sent to boarding schools elsewhere. On September 7, McGillycuddy and the Rosebud agent were instructed to "get ready immediately twenty-four boys & twelve girls from twelve to eighteen years old from each agency seventy-two in all have them examined by competent surgeon & none but absolutely sound & healthy children. children of chiefs preferred."[6] These youngsters would be educated at Carlisle Indian School in Pennsylvania.

An army officer arrived on September 21 to escort the selected children to the boarding school, but there was opposition from some of the chiefs. On September 22 agency officials met with the chiefs to discuss sending children to the school. "'Little Wound' objects. High Wolf and Am Horse send some," the agency diary recorded.[7] Over the next two days, at least two dozen Indian children headed east with First Lieutenant Richard H. Pratt, who had opened the Carlisle Indian School on November 1, 1878.[8] Pratt, a New Yorker, had considerable experience with Indians, having commanded native scouts on the southern plains a few years earlier. He had served with the

---

[4]Hare to J. W. Alder, August 23, 1879, RG 75, Series 2, Box 25, NARS, Kansas City, Missouri.
[5]Curry to Hayt, September 4, 1879, NARS 724, p. 376, Kansas City, Missouri.
[6]Telegram, unknown sender, Office of Indian Affairs, Washington, D.C., to Agents McGillycuddy and Newall [*sic*], September 7, 1879, RG 75, Series 11, Box 722, NARS, Kansas City, Missouri.
[7]McGillycuddy, Diary, 1879.
[8]Ibid.

Indiana infantry during the Civil War and earned commendations for gallantry and meritorious service. He joined the Tenth Cavalry as a second lieutenant in 1867 and would be promoted to captain in 1883. He had served under Lieutenant Colonel John W. "Black Jack" Davidson at Fort Sill in 1873, fought Kiowas and Comanches at Adobe Walls in 1874, and taken charge of Indian scouts during the ensuing Red River War of 1874–75.

McGillycuddy, who had been called east in mid-September by the serious illness of his mother, returned to Pine Ridge on September 21. On October 9 he received a telegram from Indian Commissioner Hayt, saying, "Replying to your communication of the 30th, ult. Relation to sending another company of children from your agency to the school at Carlisle, I have to say that I do not consider it best, at present, to take any steps in that direction, the quota from other agencies having been increased so as to make the whole number of pupils equal to the original estimate."[9]

By the summer of 1880, efforts were begun to establish a boarding school on the Pine Ridge reservation itself. In May McGillycuddy had inquired about the possibility, but the federal Indian Office did not reply until July, when Acting Commissioner Brooks wrote, "I regret to say that your communication of May fourteenth was overlooked; but I hope the delay in giving it due attention will not prevent the opening of some sort of a boarding school this fall, and to this end I trust you will use your very best endeavors. Will it not be possible for you to put up some temporary partitions in the large building which was erected for a day school, and make it habitable for twenty five pupils, or even less, until a new building substantial and comfortable can be erected in the spring, for which, in the meantime you can be getting out the necessary lumber." To propel the construction, Brooks told McGillycuddy that if he had no employees who could do the work, it could be contracted to outsiders.[10]

The agent had already outlined a recommendation to establish four day schools, to be located at "White Bird's Camp, Red Dog's Camp, Orphan's Camp, and at Hiyaska Loafer [Little Worm] Camp." Acting

[9]Telegram, C. D. Child to McGillycuddy, September 8, 1879: "McGrow & Clelland says that your mother cannot live[.] C. D. Child"; Hayt to McGillycuddy, October 9, 1879, RG 75, Series 11, Box 722, NARS, Kansas City, Missouri.

[10]Brooks to McGillycuddy, August 5, 1880, RG 75, Series 2, Box 2, NARS, Kansas City, Missouri.

Commissioner Brooks inquired about "plans and estimates for said houses," to enable the Indian Department to know "the amount of the contemplated expenditure."[11]

In September, Joseph Kocer and his wife, Julia, were appointed teachers at Red Dog's Camp—an indication that at least one building had been constructed during the late summer. The two teachers would be paid $720 and $480 a year, respectively. Joseph Marshall, appointed teacher of the day school at the Little Worm camp, also earned $720 a year. In all cases these teachers were placed in their positions by Bishop Hare.[12]

An additional four schoolhouses, costing $500 each, would be constructed as soon as labor and materials could be obtained. These presumably would serve the students in the other camps noted in the early August correspondence.[13] As the weather turned colder, McGillycuddy was authorized to purchase five heavy iron box stoves for use in heating the schools.[14]

By early November the school system was under control of the Indian agent, and McGillycuddy immediately appointed a new superintendent of schools—his wife, Fanny. In spite of this family relationship, Acting Superintendent of Indian Affairs E. M. Marble supported the recommendation, saying that "the appointment of Mrs. McGillycuddy as recommended by you, will tend to the promotion of the best interests of the service." She would be paid $800 a year. Because Fanny had taught school before her marriage, she was no doubt qualified for the post. Again McGillycuddy circumvented federal rules about having no relatives employed in the Indian Service, although this time he was transparent in making the appointment.[15]

Final inspection of the schools was carried out in February 1881 by Superintendent of Schools F. E. McGillycuddy and resident missionary John Robinson. Each building at White Bird's camp on Clay Creek and at a location identified as the Orphan Camp on Wounded

---

[11]Brooks to McGillycuddy, August 6, 1880, RG 75, Series 2, Box 2, NARS, Kansas City, Missouri.

[12]Acting Indian Commissioner E. M. Marble to McGillycuddy, September 4, 1880, RG 75, Series 2, Box 2, NARS, Kansas City, Missouri.

[13]Marble to McGillycuddy, September 14, 1880, RG 75, Series 2, Box 2, NARS, Kansas City, Missouri.

[14]Marble to McGillycuddy, October 8, 1880, RG 75, Series 2, Box 2, NARS, Kansas City, Missouri.

[15]Marble to McGillycuddy, November 3, 1880, RG 75, Series 2, Box 4, NARS, Kansas City, Missouri.

Knee Creek measured twenty by thirty feet, with an addition of fifteen by thirty-six feet separated into three rooms. Each had six doors and nine windows and was deemed "well worth the $500.00 paid" for its construction.[16]

In March, Acting Commissioner Thomas M. Nichol wrote to McGillycuddy urging action regarding the appointment of additional teachers. He also requested details about the qualifications and competence of teacher Joseph Marshall, an Indian who had reported having no students during November, December, and January. "Wherever an Indian can do the work of a white Govt employe, the work and the pay should be given the Indian; but the educational interests of the Indians especially should not be allowed to suffer for the sake of helping along some worthy Indian who is not competent to instruct and train the pupils under his charge," Nichol wrote. He added, "At the same time every possible encouragement should be given an Indian who shows a disposition not only to help himself but to help his people."[17]

Once again the Indian Office urged construction of a boarding school on the reservation. Nichol said, "By no means should another season go by without the erection of a good boarding-school building, or the adaptation for that purpose of one of the buildings already erected."[18] To better equip the existing day schools, the Indian Office authorized purchase of desks in Chicago, to be delivered at Rosebud Landing along with other supplies and books. Bells and organs were approved, too, to be made available with annuity goods delivered for the next fiscal year.[19]

During the spring, teachers Joseph Marshall and Joseph Kocer were engaged in working as day laborers, so McGillycuddy was ordered to cut their teaching wages from $720 to $480 a year.[20] By December the Office of Indian Affairs notified the agent that it had no funding for

[16]F. E. McGillycuddy and John Robinson to Pine Ridge Agency, Dakota, February 22, 1881. Fanny McGillycuddy served as superintendent of schools at Pine Ridge until October 1883, when she resigned. She took at least one summer off as a vacation. RG 75, Series 6, Box 53 A and B, folder 1881–82, NARS, Kansas City, Missouri. Robinson would later transfer to a similar position on the Wind River Reservation in Wyoming, serving the Eastern Shoshones.

[17]Acting Commissioner Thomas M. Nichol to McGillycuddy, March 24, 1881, RG 75, Series 2, Box 4, NARS, Kansas City, Missouri.

[18]Ibid.

[19]Marble to McGillycuddy, April 11, 1881, RG 75, Series 2, Box 4, NARS, Kansas City, Missouri.

[20]Price to McGillycuddy, April 18 and 20, 1881, RG 75, Series 2, Box 4, NARS, Kansas City, Missouri.

additional teachers to serve at two new day schools just completed.[21] On April 28 McGillycuddy received authorization from Price to appoint Robert O. Pugh to fill one teaching vacancy, at a salary of $600 annually.[22]

Price obviously kept a close eye on the schools, likely because of the Indian Commission's position that through education the Indian children would be drawn from tribal practices toward "civilized" pursuits. On April 29 he instructed McGillycuddy, "I notice that the teachers of the Agency and Wounded Knee day schools render but three hours service per day. At least two hours should be added to this, and the exercises can be so varied as not to be irksome if industrial work is added to the curriculum. I do not see why this cannot be done in these schools and in the Medicine Creek school where there are both male and female teachers. Sewing, perhaps cooking, can be taught the girls, and gardening, or the use of tools, taught the boys. Their interest in gardening can be stimulated by giving them a share in the crops. At any rate manual labor in some form should occupy the place of importance in every Indian school."[23]

The Indian Commission's educational goal—to strip Indian children of their heritage—is evident in a June 26, 1882, letter to McGillycuddy from Price. "Use every practicable means," he wrote, "to prevent the returned Carlisle students from relapsing into Indian costume and customs, even to the extent of using Indian police force if that should be practicable *and advisable*."[24]

He continued: "The best way to prevent their relapse is to immediately provide them with occupation as herders, interpreters, assistant teachers, domestics, and in the various shops. They should be expected to continue without a break [in] the habits of civilized life learned at Carlisle, and to do this must have all the assistance which the agency can give. The girls especially need to be placed in families or in school. Perhaps they can be made assistant teachers in the day schools. It will be hardly possible for them to resist the influences of camp life."[25]

---

[21]Price to McGillycuddy, December 20, 1881, RG 75, Series 2, Box 5, NARS, Kansas City, Missouri.

[22]Price to McGillycuddy, April 28, 1882, RG 75, Series 2, Box 5, NARS, Kansas City, Missouri.

[23]Price to McGillycuddy, April 29, 1882, RG 75, Series 2, Box 5, NARS, Kansas City, Missouri.

[24]Price to McGillycuddy, June 26, 1882, RG 75, Series 2, Box 6, NARS, Kansas City, Missouri (emphasis in original).

[25]Ibid.

The commissioner added a statement suggesting that in going to Carlisle, the Indian children had willingly sought the opportunity to leave their families and traditions behind, which was not the case. "All these students should be made to understand that they are in honor bound to repay the Govt. for the expenditure made on their education by a manly course after leaving the school, that this is a debt which they owe, and on the payment of which the Government has a right to insist."[26]

Less than a month later, Price instructed McGillycuddy to choose another twenty-seven children to attend classes at Carlisle. At least thirteen of them needed to be girls, aged ten to fourteen, and the remainder, boys between the ages of twelve and sixteen. "They should be selected on account of intelligence, ability, good character, and in many instances, their relationship to leading men of the tribe. But the qualification which must be insisted on, above all others, is *absolutely sound health*," Price said.[27] Further, the children chosen to report to Carlisle in the fall of 1882 would be expected to remain there for five years. "Experience has shown," Price wrote, "that a three years' course is not long enough to fortify the students sufficiently against the surroundings which they must encounter on their return to their homes."[28]

Although many chiefs and headmen allowed—and in some cases encouraged—their children to attend the schools on the reservation and at Carlisle, Red Cloud strongly resisted attempts to force children from his band to attend school. McGillycuddy reported the absence of some children at the schools during the fall of 1883, which prompted the commissioner to point out the provisions of the 1868 and 1876 treaties with the Sioux, which provided for the distribution of cattle and oxen to families whose children were in school. Price told McGillycuddy to call the chiefs together and let them know that if they failed to send the children to school, their rations would be withheld.[29]

"You will . . . call your Indians together and explain to them fully that this is one of the provisions of the agreement signed by American

---

[26]Ibid.

[27]Price to McGillycuddy, July 19, 1882, RG 75, Series 2, Box 6, NARS, Kansas City, Missouri (emphasis in original).

[28]Price to McGillycuddy, August 3, 1882, RG 75, Series 2, Box 6, NARS, Kansas City, Missouri.

[29]Price to McGillycuddy, July 27 and November 6, 1883, RG 75, Series 2, Box 6, NARS, Kansas City, Missouri.

Horse, Red Cloud, High Wolf and others; that schools are established solely for the benefit of their children, and that if they are wise they will send their children regularly; but if they are foolish and do not do what is right by their children then the Gov't. proposes, for their children's sake, to keep its part of the agreement and withhold rations," Price wrote. "You will of course give due notice of your intention, and execute these instructions with great care and discrimination, and withhold rations only from such as have no good reason for refusal or neglect to send their children to school."[30]

In 1884, construction began on a boarding school at Pine Ridge. The eighty-by-forty-foot, two-story building had a one-story addition measuring twenty-four by twenty-eight feet. Built by contractor Elmer J. Sweet, it was ready for operation during the fall school session.[31] Additional day schools were authorized in 1884 on Big White Clay Creek, Wounded Knee Creek, Porcupine Creek, and Medicine Root Creek.[32]

That fall Robert O. Pugh, the Porcupine Creek teacher, wrote to McGillycuddy urging him to punish several Indians for failure to send their children to school. They included "Prairie Dog, one Daughter; Bad Knee, one Daughter; Yellow Shirt, two Daughters; Kills the Bear, one Son; Hollow Wood, one Daughter; Fond of Himself, one Daughter; Walks Under Ground, one Son, [and] Eagle Horse, one Daughter."[33]

This conflict over children not attending school originated with Red Cloud. It grew from a minor disagreement between the chief and McGillycuddy into a full-scale feud. It would permeate the men's relationship and eventually lead to a change of administration at Pine Ridge, but that was years in the making.

---

[30]Price to McGillycuddy, November 6, 1883, RG 75, Series 2, Box 6, NARS, Kansas City, Missouri.

[31]Correspondence related to construction of this boarding school can be found in Bureau of Indian Affairs, Records, RG 75, Series 2, Box 7, January 2, 1884; May 15, 1884; and June 11, 1884, NARS, Kansas City, Missouri.

[32]Acting Commissioner E. L. Stevens to McGillycuddy, June 19, 1884, RG 75, Series 2, Box 7, NARS, Kansas City, Missouri.

[33]Robert O. Pugh to McGillycuddy, September 27, 1884, RG 75, Series 2, Box 7, NARS, Kansas City, Missouri.

15
Red Cloud

THE VAST ACREAGE OF the Pine Ridge reservation was not large enough to prevent friction between Red Cloud, the old chief of the Lakotas, who had bested the frontier army in his fight for the Powder River country in 1866–68, and Valentine T. McGillycuddy, the stubborn agent who was determined to implement the policy of the U.S. Indian Bureau and pull the Indians along the road to assimilation.

It took only weeks after McGillycuddy became agent at Pine Ridge in March 1879 for Red Cloud to raise his first objections. The two sparred over the development of schools and establishment of an Indian police force and wrangled about the issuance of rations. At times they had an almost amicable relationship, but those instances were fleeting. More often they squared off like two prize fighters, each backed by loyal followers.

Red Cloud had support from Spotted Tail until that chief's death; from trader J. W. Dear, who often wrote to Washington on behalf of the Oglala headman; and eventually from the agency physician, Fordyce Grinnell. McGillycuddy's backers generally included George Sword, his captain of the Indian police, Young Man Afraid Of His Horses, trader George F. Blanchard, and of course his brother, Frank Stewart. The two men's positions were understandably reflective of their cultures. Red Cloud had set aside his war weapons and settled at the first agency named for him, on the White River near Camp Robinson, but even after agreeing to the Fort Laramie Treaty of 1868 he remained fiercely loyal to his tribal traditions.

McGillycuddy liked many of the Indians on the reservation and truly respected men such as Sword who helped him implement his policies. He supported those who began to abandon their traditions of hunting and gathering and who started farming and raising stock as a way to support their families.

As on other reservations, the Office of Indian Affairs authorized the construction of a house for Red Cloud. But in September 1879, C. V. Curry raised concerns about the original plans, saying that the "building of a house for Red Cloud on so large a scale as originally designed is unnecessary and ill-advised."

"The shell of a four-room house has been erected on the place selected by him, and I think if that be finished it will be amply sufficient," Curry wrote to Indian Commissioner Hayt. "The importance of the chiefs will disappear very rapidly in the near future," Curry said, "and I should not consider it wise to give them much outward signs of distinction as the building of houses implies, larger than those of the agents, and in fact better than any within two or three hundred miles. The plans had better be modified accordingly."[1]

The first year that McGillycuddy served as Pine Ridge agent involved a seesaw exchange with Red Cloud, but no exceptional conflict arose. By the fall of 1880, however, their animosity had grown to such proportions that Acting Indian Commissioner E. M. Marble sent a thirty-nine-cent telegram to the agent: "Rumors have reached here that trouble exists between yourself and Chief Redcloud in regard to issue operations. Report all facts in regards thereto. Answer at once."[2]

Two days later, on September 18, McGillycuddy replied, "Everything serene here. Red Cloud deposed by majority of Indians on account of false charges brought against me in Washington. . . . I shall always inform office if trouble is apprehended."[3]

Although McGillycuddy purchased a team of horses for Red Cloud's use in the fall of 1880, by the spring of 1881 the two were at odds again after McGillycuddy ordered a census of tribal members that Red Cloud attempted to block. The chief sent runners across the reservation ordering the headmen and tribal members "to stop the count." On March 6,

[1]Curry to Hayt, September 4, 1879, NARS 724, pp. 375–76, Kansas City, Missouri.

[2]Telegram, Marble to McGillycuddy, Pine Ridge, via Fort Robinson, Nebraska, September 16, 1880, received at Fort Robinson, September 16, 11:30 A.M., RG 75, Series 11, Box 722, NARS, Kansas City, Missouri.

[3]McGillycuddy to Commissioner of Indian Affairs, September 18, 1880, RG 75, Series 4, Box 35, Letterbook vol. 1, p. 441, NARS, Kansas City, Missouri.

Red Cloud's House, Pine Ridge Agency, date unknown.
Red Cloud's was one of the most prominent houses on the reservation
and for many years was the only two-story private residence.
Nebraska State Historical Society, RG2063 PH 31 4.

McGillycuddy reported to the commissioner of Indian affairs that the effort to halt the census had been unsuccessful, with the exception of Red Cloud and the twenty-seven families in his own band.[4]

Determined to make an accurate count, McGillycuddy ordered that rations be withheld from the Red Cloud band members until after they allowed the census to be completed. Previous policy of the Indian Bureau to permit such behavior from tribal members "has had much to do with the present arrogant bearing of many of these relics of barbarism recognized as chiefs," McGillycuddy wrote. His words make it clear that he had his own personal standard for the way tribesmen would be treated; he often exhibited condescension toward them, particularly Red Cloud.[5] McGillycuddy's attitude toward the Indians mirrored that of his superiors in the Indian Service at the time. Their policies were designed to expunge Indian culture and assimilate the natives into mainstream society.

---

[4]McGillycuddy to Commissioner of Indian Affairs, March 6, 1881, RG 75, Series 4, Box 35, Letterbook vol. 2, NARS, Kansas City, Missouri.
[5]Ibid.

Days later the agent reported to his superiors that Red Cloud had "concluded that he made a mistake" and allowed himself and those who lived near him to be counted. But the wounds existed and would only deepen as the two men's enmity grew over the next year.

During the summer of 1881, petitions and letters flew between Pine Ridge and the Office of Indian Affairs. On June 2, McGillycuddy informed Commissioner of Indian Affairs Hiram Price that the reason for distrust "among the Indians at this agency is that Ex-chief Red Cloud recently forwarded to your office a letter making rant" against the agent. McGillycuddy reported that the "leading chiefs and head men" wanted to examine that letter—which reportedly had their names signed to it—because they said they had not participated in the writing of it. Among those so concerned were Little Wound, Blue Horse, Red Dog, Little Big Man, High Wolf, Suit Braid, Slow Bull, Yellow Hair, Black War Bonnet, Brave Bear, White Bird, George Sword, No Flesh, Black Bear, Three Stars, Three Bears, and Old Man Afraid Of His Horses.[6]

This discontent and other issues led Price to request that Red Cloud and Young Man Afraid Of His Horses, both from the Pine Ridge Agency, and Spotted Tail, from the Rosebud Agency, visit Washington, D.C., in August 1881. They would travel with interpreter John A. Williamson, of the Yankton Agency.[7] The headmen selected for the trip agreed to make the journey east and asked that McGillycuddy be allowed to accompany them.

"You are our Agent and I do not wish to go unless you accompany us," Young Man Afraid told McGillycuddy. "Red Cloud and some of our Chiefs went to see the Great Father last season without you and they got us all into trouble." Showing his allegiance to the agent, the headman added, "Red Cloud got under the influence of bad white men and talked about there being stealing here. We have had two inspections out here that . . . made us more trouble and that talk keeps up. If we go alone now I fear it will be the same[,] as Red Cloud has not a strong heart."[8]

Young Man Afraid said that if the Indians went without McGillycuddy, he believed Red Cloud, Spotted Tail, and "the bad white men would make us trouble again."[9]

[6]McGillycuddy to Price, June 2, 1881, RG 75, Series 4, Box 35, Letterbook vol. 2, NARS, Kansas City, Missouri.

[7]Price to McGillycuddy, July 14, 1881, RG 75, Series 2, Box 5, NARS, Kansas City, Missouri.

[8]McGillycuddy to Commissioner of Indian Affairs, July 20, 1881, RG 75, Series 4, Box 35, vol. 2, NARS, Kansas City, Missouri.

[9]Ibid.

"The Great Father says he gives us agents to take care of us, and speak for us, and arrange our business. If, he means what he says, then when we go to him on business we should have our agent with us. I ask you to write to him what I say," Young Man Afraid instructed McGillycuddy.

Surprisingly Red Cloud also appeared to want McGillycuddy with the Lakota delegation. He alluded to trouble for the tribesmen when they were in the capital the previous year. "When the Great Father gives us an agent he says he is a good man and is to care for us and manage our business. When Indians go to see the Great Father, the agent should go with them to prevent trouble. There has been much womans talk at Washington and here, and it makes trouble for our people. If we go to Washington, I want you, our agent, to go with us and have this talk stopped. I see no use in going unless you go with us."[10]

In spite of this appeal, there was already discontent between Red Cloud and McGillycuddy over various issues, and it is at least questionable whether the chief was as supportive of the agent as this message, written by McGillycuddy, would indicate.

The doctor himself said, "If it is allowable for me as agent for these people to make any suggestions, I would certainly for various reasons consider it to the interest of the service for me to accompany them, whatever the business may be that calls them to Washington." He also paid off on what was no doubt a promise to a loyal employee, writing to request that George Sword be allowed to accompany the delegation to Washington.[11] It is possible that McGillycuddy anticipated the denial of his request to accompany the headmen to Washington and wanted Sword there in his stead, knowing of the captain's fealty.

It took only four days to receive a response from Price, the commissioner of Indian affairs: "Your request as to George Sword is approved." McGillycuddy, however, was not allowed to make the trip, because of the expense and "the necessity for your personal supervision of affairs at the Agency."[12]

Late in 1881, McGillycuddy presented an American flag to Red Cloud, perhaps an indication that the Office of Indian Affairs believed the difficulties at Pine Ridge had been assuaged. But the most contentious year on record between the agent and the chief was yet to come.[13]

---

[10]Ibid.

[11]Ibid.

[12]Ibid.

[13]Department of the Interior, Office of Indian Affairs, to McGillycuddy, December 29, 1881, RG 75, Series 2, Box 5, NARS, Kansas City, Missouri.

Annuities were distributed in the spring of 1882 without incident. McGillycuddy reported to Commissioner Price, "The quality was good & the supply ample."[14] He set aside some books, shoes, and clothing for use in the schools, giving those supplies to Captain Sword, who would issue and use them as needed. "I thought best to do this for the reason that long after the general issue takes place Indians come to me for work having no clothing suitable to work in and no money to purchase the same with," McGillycuddy said.[15] He thought it was illogical to distribute a "whole years supply of clothing" at one time to people who were not inclined to care for such an amount.[16]

In his 1882 general report to the commissioner, McGillycuddy outlined some of the issues that marked the Pine Ridge administration. When he had taken over in 1879, he said, the "entire management and council of the agency and Indians" was in the hands of Red Cloud and eight of his subordinate chiefs. If, at the time, an Indian attempted to assist the agent and the government by joining the police or engaging in labor, Red Cloud and his subordinates would remark, "That man is working against our good old Indian ways. He is becoming a white man." That attitude meant "the poor Indian and his family would be deprived of his annuities by the chiefs," McGillycuddy said.[17]

By better controlling the goods provided as annuities under the treaties negotiated with the tribe, the agent believed he could wrest control from Red Cloud and his most loyal followers. Further, early in his administration, McGillycuddy said, the chiefs often sold many of the annuities given to their bands "to white men generally squawmen [white men who married Indian women] who would take them . . . into Nebraska and Colorado to sell."[18] McGillycuddy abhorred that practice and consistently strove to halt it. His predecessor, James Irwin, he said, had allowed it to take place "simply for the sake of peace."[19]

To break up this system, McGillycuddy had informed the Indians as early as the fall of 1879 "that they could draw [annuity goods] independently of their chiefs if they desired." This change in distribution

[14]McGillycuddy to Price, March 17, 1882, RG 75, Series 4, Box 35, Letterbook vol. 3, 1882, pp. 137–43, NARS, Kansas City, Missouri.
[15]Ibid.
[16]Ibid.
[17]Ibid.
[18]Ibid.
[19]Ibid.

divided the nine original bands into twenty-one, took power from Red Cloud, and, according to McGillycuddy, "resulted in my becoming the everlasting enemy of Red Cloud and his chiefs and squawmen and my being twice investigated by the Dept. and brought before the Dakota grand jury on charges trumped up by the individuals of having stolen flannel, brass kettles and corn. The younger members of the tribe sustained me however which finally brought around the deposing of Red Cloud and the permanent weakening of the tribal system."[20]

In spite of his optimism, McGillycuddy that summer would face yet another challenge from Red Cloud. At the end of March, the agent removed Cloud Shield from the police force for "counciling" with Red Cloud and causing desertion in the police force.[21] McGillycuddy fully anticipated that Red Cloud would respond, and indeed, the agent's distribution of annuities to the Indian police for later dispersal came under scrutiny as Red Cloud leveled charges that McGillycuddy had improperly handed out the goods. The chief accused the agent of favoring some Indians with more than their entitlement and even converting goods for his personal gain.

"Ex Chief Red Cloud is holding his usual Spring councils with the intention of [securing] if possible the removal of the present agent and it is natural to expect that your office will soon receive one of his letters containing the usual . . . charges," McGillycuddy wrote to Price. Those allegations by Red Cloud would include claims "that the agent has held back some of the annuities, is pushing the Indians too hard . . . [that Red Cloud] can not control his young men and unless there is a change made in the agent, there will be an outbreak and bloodshed."[22]

There was a simple reason for the allotment of annuities to the Indian police, McGillycuddy said. He cited his earlier letter, "in which I explained that I had turned over some of the clothing to the police for safe keeping so that when Indians apply for work at the agency I will be able to cover their nakedness and not have them as samples of Indian civilization performing labor . . . in a pair of moccasins and a breech-clout." He handled the distribution of clothing for schoolchildren in the same way.[23]

---

[20]Ibid.
[21]McGillycuddy to Price, March 32 [*sic*], 1882, RG 75, Series 4, Box 35, Letterbook vol. 3, 1882, p. 164, NARS, Kansas City, Missouri.
[22]McGillycuddy to Price, April 5, 1882, RG 75, Series 4, Box 35, Letterbook vol. 3, 1882, NARS, Kansas City, Missouri.
[23]Ibid.

McGillycuddy acknowledged that he might have agitated people by "pushing those Indians too rapidly towards civilization." But he defended his methods, saying that he did so in order to reverse the practices of prior agents at both the Spotted Tail and Red Cloud Agencies, who had "acted merely as chief clerks and the . . . chiefs as agents."[24]

"It has been my practice at this agency to act as agent for all of the Indians paying particular attention to the younger members and I insisted that the present state of progression among these people will [demonstrate] the fact that I have not misjudged my duty."[25]

In this report, as in others he sent to the Indian Bureau, McGillycuddy again dismissed Red Cloud as ineffective. Although he admitted that Red Cloud "would not hesitate for a moment" to encourage young men in the tribe to take aggressive action, he said, "Our experience of six years among these people shows me that his day for making serious trouble is passed." Even so, McGillycuddy acknowledged, "Red Cloud has been the enemy of the Govt and civilization since he became the leader in the Fort Phil Kearney [*sic*] massacre in 1868 [*sic*] and will be until he dies."[26]

"With an Indian of his [background], the end justifies the means," McGillycuddy said, adding, "To be eternally harassed by this old man is getting to be somewhat monotonous."[27]

He suggested—perhaps facetiously—that if the commissioner had "any misgivings of the situation at this agency it might be perhaps well to send an inspector this way when convenient, but at the same time caution that official not to come under the impression that the safety of the U.S. Govt. depends on placating Red Cloud and catering and putting him to such an exile as to inflate the Indians with the idea that 'he is a bigger man than the agent.'"[28]

Just two days later McGillycuddy ripped off another letter to the commissioner concerning the recent "statement of charges" against him by Red Cloud. He added sarcastically that if he were judged guilty of all of them, he would face "capital punishment."[29]

---

[24]Ibid.

[25]Ibid.

[26]Ibid. This reference is to the attack involving Captain William J. Fetterman on December 21, 1866, near Fort Philip Kearny, north of the present town of Buffalo, Wyoming.

[27]Ibid.

[28]Ibid.

[29]McGillycuddy to Price, April 7, 1882, RG 75, Series 4, Box 35, Letterbook vol. 3, 1882, p. 199, NARS, Kansas City, Missouri.

Whether the agent could continue with advances at Pine Ridge "will much depend on the amount of support furnished Red Cloud by the Dept. paying attention to trumped up charges of this kind," he said.[30]

In June 1882, Price sustained McGillycuddy's action in arresting and confining to the guardhouse Walking Elk, a Sioux from the Yankton Agency who had attended the Sun Dance that month. There he was involved in "counciling with Red Cloud and a few other 'Sore-heads' with the end in view of getting rid of the agent, the police and the missionaries."[31]

"It was well, that you promptly gave him to understand that he and his followers could not come upon your reservation and take the management of officers out of your hands," Price wrote. "His arrest and confinement in the guard house until he promised to leave your reservation and never return, was the proper course to pursue."[32]

The animosity between Red Cloud and McGillycuddy that festered all summer eventually reached boiling point. On Sunday, August 13, chiefs Red Cloud, American Horse, and Red Shirt and another forty or so Indians gathered just off the reservation in northern Nebraska for a "council or feast" at the ranch of Louis Jangrau, or Shangrau.[33] Also present were William J. Godfrey, a Coloradan who was reportedly a friend of Secretary of the Interior Henry M. Teller's, and Yellow Hair, a Lakota known to be loyal to Red Cloud. Shangrau acted as interpreter. During the gathering these men prepared a letter for the secretary of the interior that was "practically one of threats, to the effect that if I was not removed by the Government inside of sixty days, they, the

---

[30]Ibid.

[31]Price to McGillycuddy, August 4, 1882, RG 75, Series 2, NARS, Kansas City, Missouri.

[32]Ibid.

[33]Although some contemporary records, including records and documents kept by McGillycuddy, referred to this man as Louis Jangrau, most historians and writers of other contemporary documents spelled his surname Shangrau. With no conclusive evidence of the correct spelling, I have opted to use Shangrau, which conforms with references by noted historians such as James Olson, in *Red Cloud and the Sioux Problem*, Robert Larson, in *Red Cloud*, and Richard E. Jensen, editor of *The Indian Interviews of Eli S. Ricker*, as well as correspondence from Nebraska State Historical Society senior historian James E. Potter. A John Jangrau signed the 1883 agreement with the Sioux tribes. Ricker interviewed both a John Shangrau and a Peter Shangrau, but their relationship, if any, to Louis Shangrau is unclear. During a congressional inquiry conducted in 1885 by William S. Holman, one man questioned was identified as Lewis Shangran, who is certainly the same man McGillycuddy identified as Louis Jangrau.

Indians, would remove me by force," McGillycuddy wrote later.[34] The agent notified Commissioner Price that "Red Cloud wrote department and commanding officer Ft. Robinson on Sunday, that unless I ~~was~~ am removed by October 1st he will break out details by mail."[35]

"Mixed up in the affair and one of the principal movers," McGillycuddy wrote, was Woman's Dress, an enlisted Indian scout attached to Fort Robinson. Because of his scout status, Woman's Dress was "presumed to assist in preserving law and order in place of violating the same," said McGillycuddy, who arrested and disarmed him the following day, holding him in confinement into September.[36]

Red Cloud acted as well, threatening freighters who were preparing to drive their wagons to Thatcher, Nebraska, to transport large quantities of bacon and other supplies to the reservation. Fearing that their lives and the lives of their horses were in danger if they handled the goods, the freighters refused to move. McGillycuddy countered by cutting off the distribution of rations. "As we had then about 600,000 pounds of freight including bacon at Thatcher, I saw that decisive action was necessary to prevent a blockade and danger to supplies, so immediately instructed the storekeeper to suspend the issue of coffee, sugar and bacon, as these articles of food account essentials," he said.[37]

When McGillycuddy sent a message to Price on August 15, he said, "It depends on your department whether I am to be agent, or chief clerk for Red Cloud."[38] Price immediately responded: "You will be sustained by this office as agent against the claims of Red Cloud."[39]

On the seventeenth McGillycuddy entered a long statement in the agency letterbook. Although a portion of it now is illegible, it is clear that he wanted a record of the situation at Pine Ridge. Although many tribesmen supported the agent and opposed Red Cloud, another faction of tribesmen and non-Indians wanted, according to McGillycuddy, to "overthrow the discipline and the power of the police at this agency. Their primary object being to get rid of me as agent." Once they had him out of the way, the agent said, they would "be able to

---

[34]McGillycuddy to Major W. J. Pollock, U.S. Indian inspector, September 16, 1882, RG 75, Series 4, Box 35, vol. 3, 1882, pp. 455–69, NARS, Kansas City, Missouri.

[35]Telegram, McGillycuddy to Price, August 20, 1882, RG 75, Series 4, Box 35, vol. 3, 1882, pp. 394–404, NARS, Kansas City, Missouri (strikeout in original).

[36]Ibid. Woman's Dress, a brother of Keeps The Battle, had first served with the Indian scouts before holding a position with the Indian police at Pine Ridge.

[37]Ibid.

[38]McGillycuddy to Pollock, September 16, 1882.

[39]Telegram, Price to McGillycuddy, August 15, 1881, RG 75, Series 4, NARS, Kansas City, Missouri.

help themselves to rations at the commissary and have the good, old time again where a white man could have two or three concubines, bring whiskey here in sufficient quantities and not have Indian Police to interfere with their *incorporated* rights in the tribe."[40]

"Red Cloud is but a tool in the hands of the others, but at the same time perhaps a dangerous one, having the prestige of an old chief, who to the disgrace of the government, has been allowed to manage agents in the past," McGillycuddy wrote. The agent's own actions were perceived as "interfering with perhaps a sovereign right of his, by not leaving his dominion and . . . returning like a whipped cur to the government I represent."[41]

Clearly McGillycuddy believed Red Cloud had become more aggressive in his attitude toward the agent after the return of Sitting Bull and other Northern Sioux who had surrendered at Fort Buford in 1881, ending their exile in Canada, where they had fled following the Great Sioux Wars.

Price, monitoring the situation at Pine Ridge from his office in Washington, fired off a telegram on August 18, ordering McGillycuddy to send "facts immediately" concerning several reports filtering to the capital "that Red Cloud is organizing a large force of warriors for hostile purposes."[42] General Crook, through his assistant adjutant general, requested similar information.

Despite the tension at Pine Ridge, McGillycuddy asserted control, sending horseback riders to all the villages within fifty miles of the agency and calling the chiefs and principal Indians to gather at the agency council room.[43] Feeling confident in his position as the result of the message from Price that he "would be sustained," McGillycuddy "advertised the council to the effect that on account of the action taken by Red Cloud threatening to set the law of the government at defiance, which was simply rebellion, we were assembled to discuss the question of 'troops or no troops.'"[44] The chiefs and principal Indians assembled at the council room on August 19.[45]

---

[40]McGillycuddy to [first part illegible so unknown to whom it was written, likely Price], August 17, 1882, RG 75, Series 4, Box 35, Letterbook vol. 3, 1882, NARS, Kansas City, Missouri (emphasis in original).

[41]Ibid.

[42]Telegram, Price to McGillycuddy, August 17, 1882, RG 75, Series 4, Box 35, vol. 3, 1882, NARS, Kansas City, Missouri.

[43]Telegram, McGillycuddy to Price, August 20, 1882.

[44]Ibid.

[45]Ibid.

Sioux Indian police on horseback in front of
Pine Ridge Agency buildings, August 9, 1882. Two weeks later
the police backed McGillycuddy in one of his most volatile disputes
with Red Cloud. *National Archives, image 519143.*

The contentious statements being bandied about by Red Cloud and
a recent disturbance at the agency raised the question, McGillycuddy
said, of "whether the law abiding and peaceable Indians will like the
matter in their own hands and fuell [*sic*] farther trouble or if it will be
necessary to call for troops for the protection of life and property."[46]

Just the threat of calling federal troops to the reservation may have
put a damper on the Indians. There had been no soldiers at Pine Ridge
since McGillycuddy had formed the Indian police force and assumed
full authority for law and order on the reservation three years earlier.

Man Who Carried The Sword (George Sword), the effective and
respected captain of the police, was the first to address his fellow
Lakotas at McGillycuddy's August council. He told them, "We can
manage our own affairs without the help of his soldiers. We do not
want soldiers." Noting that McGillycuddy's management had already
been investigated, Sword said, "The Great Father put this agent here
and has had him inspected. If things had been found wrong he would
have taken him away. I have kept close watch of things here and have
seen nothing wrong."

[46]Interpreter's report, Pine Ridge Agency, Dakota, August [18], 1882, RG 75, Series 4, Box 35,
vol. 3, 1882, pp. 380–91, NARS, Kansas City, Missouri.

Sword said that both McGillycuddy and the police worked "against things that are wrong." He urged his fellow tribesmen to "write to the Great Father and tell him that as Indians of his who have done so well for the past few years, [we] do not want trouble now." He admonished anyone present who had an intention of causing trouble, saying that he would "stand by the Great Father and agent in keeping the peace. I am here with the Police to keep the peace and I will do so."[47]

Backed by this burly policeman, McGillycuddy refused to extend his hand to American Horse when that chief took his turn at addressing the council. "You have refused to shake hands with me. I don't know what for," American Horse said. "I simply wanted to explain the present trouble."

To that McGillycuddy retorted: "This is no place to explain. You should have sent your explanations to the Great Father with the letter you signed threatening to make trouble for me at the Agency. When this thing is all settled, I shall refuse to have any thing to do with you."

American Horse apparently had no response, for the next recorded speech was that of Red Dog, who rambled long and tediously about the need for sawmills, hogs, sheep, and chickens. When he finally sat down, Yellow Hair—no friend of McGillycuddy's but on his side that day—rose and said to Red Dog, "You talk too much." He then went into his own lengthy statement, telling the others that the agent had given them "good advice," and "I want to see this trouble stopped right off."

Young Man Afraid Of His Horses, one of the more moderate and progressive leaders in the tribe, took his turn to speak by recalling the Lakotas' proud past and urging cooperation with the agent. "My old father has always obeyed the Great Father and I wish to follow his footsteps," he said. "Let us settle the present trouble and hear no more of it."

No Flesh, too, supported McGillycuddy: "If you have complaint to make against the agent make it, but do not threaten trouble. . . . This agent has issued us wagons and helped me. I have no hard feelings against General Crook or his soldiers but I do not want to see them here, this summer. I hope we will have no trouble here. We have police that ought to be sufficient to stop all trouble. Let us settle the trouble quickly."[48]

---

[47]Ibid.
[48]Ibid.

One after another, the headmen expressed their views.

Fast Thunder: "The Great Father sent our agent here to set things straight. What has he done that we should cause trouble[?] I can see nothing wrong with him."

Low Dog: "My relations are here and I want to bring them and the agent closer together. Where there is an agent and his family at an agency together it is right to pull all together. In doing so we can do good. I came here from the North for protection and want to live here. I was a prisoner with the soldiers and got good advice from them and want to live up to it."

Little Chief, a Northern Cheyenne: "My friends, I am here from the Indian Territory south. I asked three different times of the Great Father and General Crook to be allowed to come here with my people. . . . The Great Spirit gave us this land. He made me a relative of the Sioux and asked me to live in peace with them. . . . The Indians don't want trouble and are willing to lay their guns to one side. . . . The Great Spirit made us Indians. The Great Father asks to be like white men and we want to do so and live."

White Bird: "We have had our choice between civil and military agents. We wanted a civil agent and the Great Father gave us one. We had an old agent. You old chiefs used to council . . . with him. You promised not to trouble this agent. He made us a police force here. We used to lose horses. We lose none now." Expressing support for McGillycuddy's policies, White Bird noted that the Lakotas had cows, guns to kill the beef cattle issued to them, churches, and schoolhouses. "I have tried with others to trace the source of the present troubles but cannot find it," he said. "Let us have this back talk stopped and settle these differences at once and live peaceably again."

Wolf Ears noted Red Cloud's status in the tribe and urged him to come to the council to settle his differences with McGillycuddy: "Let us have a feast and talk this matter over and settle it."

Little Wound, who had come to the council from his home on Medicine Root Creek without knowing why it had been called, nevertheless said he wanted "to send for Red Cloud and ask him in council what the trouble between him and the agent is. He might give me some light on the matter." Little Wound admitted that the present situation existed in part because Red Cloud, with the support of whites and mixed-blood men living off the reservation in Nebraska, had engaged in a letter-writing campaign. Although he did not support

McGillycuddy overtly, Little Wound added, "If I knew that our agent was stealing our annuity goods, I would tell him to pack his trust and go. The way I look at this thing is this. There are plenty of white men watching this agent and if he was stealing he would have been caught before this and taken away."

There might have been speculation that northern Indians would move onto the reservation and cause an uprising, but Little Wound discounted that possibility. "There are no Indians north and no danger of trouble. They will stay at their agencies."

Blue Horse: "My friends, there is nothing for people to fear here. There will be no trouble and if there should be it would be so small that Captain Sword with his 50 police can take care of it. Red Cloud, you are a fool. I tell you so four times. You must stop making trouble. If you do not, we must have our police do so for you."[49]

Blue Horse's statement, the last in the formal council, is noteworthy for his telling Red Cloud that he was a fool "four times." The number four is sacred among the Lakotas, making this leader's apparently simple statement symbolic and important beyond its face value.

At the conclusion of the session, at least thirty-one of the chiefs, headmen, and other Indians present formally petitioned the government, saying, "We do not require the presence of troops here. We agree to settle the trouble with the aid of the [Indian] Police."[50]

The council had not been entirely a session of speeches; it had been broken by attempts to communicate with Red Cloud and draw him from his village to the agency itself. McGillycuddy gave his version of the day in a letter to Hiram Price written on August 20, which included copies of the speeches. "Early yesterday morning," McGillycuddy wrote, "I summoned the Chiefs and Police and instructed them to go to Red Clouds village and get definite answers from him and force a settlement, as he had refused to attend the council. At about 2 oclk PM the chiefs and police returned with an evasive answer from Red Cloud, who also denied that he had made any threats."[51]

[49] Ibid.

[50] Letter sent by Little Wound, Young Man Afraid Of His Horses, No Flesh, Blue Horse, White Face, White Bird, Two Lance, and many more, signed by interpreter Frank White and witnessed by W. Dear and William Foster, Pine Ridge Agency, Dakota Territory, August 18, 1882, RG 75, Series 4, Box 35, vol. 3, pp. 392–93, NARS, Kansas City, Missouri.

[51] Telegram, McGillycuddy to Price, August 20, 1882.

McGillycuddy learned from Captain Sword that Red Cloud had "assembled his Young men and that they were under arms at his village." He told Price: "At the same time the usual accompaniments of Indian racket, in the way of Indians skipping around naked with bad hearts [seeking to make trouble] etc began to appear."[52]

About three in the afternoon, McGillycuddy received notice from Price's office to "arrest Red Cloud and hold him a prisoner until further orders." The agent instructed the chiefs that Red Cloud needed to turn himself in at the council, and they sent an emissary to his village, about a mile away. The messenger soon returned "with the sarcastic reply from Red Cloud that *he was glad to hear from you and hoped you were well,* but with the information that he felt tired and would not come," McGillycuddy wrote to Price.[53]

Again telling the Lakota leaders that Red Cloud needed to report to the agency, McGillycuddy warned that he would "send force and bring him." Yellow Hair then stepped up and volunteered to go to Red Cloud, saying, "I will bring him."

As Yellow Hair departed, McGillycuddy took up his field glasses and scanned Red Cloud's camp. There he "noticed such excitement[.] Indians were flying around in all directions gathering their ponies, Squaws were leaving and bucks coming in, so that things looked like the old business times of 1876 when the army had to handle Red Cloud for his insolence and hostility. To render the old codger 'nothing ventured, nothing won' and to be prepared for trouble I immediately closed the shops and traders stores, put the fifty policemen under arms and opened up fifty surplus rifles and distributed arms to friendly Indians and employees."

Watching the camp, McGillycuddy saw "Indians skipping in and out and carriages skipping out with the freighters[,] traders," and other people, who set a course south, "evidently preferring the State of Nebraska to Red Clouds *domain.* The only regret was that we were without a camera to take instantaneous pictures, as the scene was such a *moving* one."[54]

Yellow Hair eventually returned and reported that Red Cloud was coming in. When he failed to show up, McGillycuddy again addressed the chiefs, asking them what they intended to do. The leaders withdrew,

---

[52]Ibid.

[53]Ibid. (emphasis in original).

[54]Ibid. (emphasis in original).

discussed the issue among themselves, and consulted with the Indian police. Then they told the agent, "Father, send Yellow Hair with these words to Red Cloud, tell him that we make the third and last call, that to prevent bloodshed, if he does not come at once we will ask our agent to call for troops, we will turn our Young Men and police in with the troops and disarm and [disable] Red Cloud." Although the chiefs believed Red Cloud would come in without bloodshed, they stood ready to force the issue, to the point of violence if necessary. "We have sworn to stand by the Great Father and the agent," they said, "and we will do so."

Again Yellow Hair rode to Red Cloud's camp. While he was gone, Old Man Afraid Of His Horses rose, and with dignity the seventy-year-old chief pledged support to McGillycuddy. "I am an old man, my fighting days are over," he said. "I am no longer brave. My son has taken my place. He is the white man's friend. I have been a great chief and have fought the white man. I never expect to fight again, but this is my agency." If needed, he said, he would again "help our Great Father."

This time Red Cloud complied with the directive of his fellow Lakotas. He eventually reached the agency and entered the council room, where he laid aside his arms. McGillycuddy read the arrest warrant that had been sent by Price and "then informed the Police Chief and Indians that I should hold them responsible for his future conduct." Without fanfare, McGillycuddy dismissed the council. The Indians returned home, as did all but a detail of ten policemen.

Amazingly, the following day Captain Sword left to attend a religious convocation at the Yankton Agency, and McGillycuddy himself departed for Omaha. The agent apparently felt that the issue had been fully resolved, for he told Price, "Everything is serene and quiet at the Agency today—which is the sabbath. The church bell is ringing and the U.S. Flag still floats."[55]

Even so, McGillycuddy said he expected Price would soon have "charges against me, of inefficiency, foolhardiness, etc." He added, "I have been termed by one of your traders here, a fool and other names too offensive to put on paper. He informs the people that I am 'bucking' against his store, that he will use his *political* influence to prevent my reappointment. He is a little too [premature] as I have not yet applied."[56]

---

[55]Ibid.
[56]Ibid. (emphasis in original).

Showing unusual restraint, McGillycuddy said, "Only that it might appear too arbitrary, I would put him in the guard house for inciting disturbance." Although he hoped and believed he had forced the "performance of the civil law . . . without bloodshed and to your satisfaction," the agent made it clear that he did not expect this to be the last set-to with Red Cloud and his supporters. "There is a ring of white men in this region that is bound to force my resignation, dismissal, assassination, or an outbreak on Red Cloud," he wrote to Price. "This reserve is hardly large enough for both of us unless affairs take a change."

To further describe the scene at Pine Ridge, he added, "The cowardly demeanor and actions of some of our white people here, however, was too disgusting to even comment on. My only advice to them is, that considering the fact that there is no one forces them to live in the Indian country, and they should skip out." Most of those who fled, he said, had been "the last few days cultivating Red Clouds friendship."

Other employees and whites living on the reservation clearly had McGillycuddy's admiration, including trader George Blanchard, with his family of nine women and children, missionary John Robinson, and the agency workers. "I must report that they acted like men, with one or two exceptions."[57]

Two days later, agency employees prepared a document that they sent to Commissioner Price. "We believe that in these days of August the Agent has only done what was action necessary for the protection of the persons and property and what duty required of him as Agent," stated the petition. It was signed by agency trader Blanchard; interpreter Frank White; agency clerk Alder; McGillycuddy's brother, Frank Stewart; engineer R. O. Hoyt, a relative of Fanny's; and twenty other men at the agency. Responding to claims by Red Cloud and his supporters, the petitioners wrote, "The Agent is right and they are wrong. Even if the agent were wrong, only serious harm can come by permitting Indians to take law into their own *hands*."[58]

The same day the agency workers drew up their petition, chiefs

---

[57]Ibid. In a separate letter written to Price on August 20, 1882, McGillycuddy said, "Red Cloud and the hostiles completely squelched[.] He was forced to come to office yesterday & your warrant for his arrest read. He is now on parole the ~~Indian~~ chiefs & police responsible for his conduct. The civil authorities are thus sustained." RG 75, Series 6, Box 53 A and B, folder 1881–82, NARS, Kansas City, Missouri (strikeover in original).

[58]Agency employees George Blanchard, J. W. Alder, Frank Stewart, R. O. Hoyt, and twenty more to Price, August 22, 1882, RG 75, Series 4, Box 35, vol. 3, pp. 409–410, NARS, Kansas City, Missouri (emphasis in original).

Little Wound, Young Man Afraid Of His Horses, No Flesh, White Bird, Little Big Man, Three Stars, Blue Horse, and Charging Shield, along with three dozen other prominent Lakotas, also petitioned Price's office. They expressed their "unbounded desire to be at peace with all whites and the government." They said they were "thoroughly satisfied with the present agents management and treatment of us" and urged the commissioner to "sustain our agent."[59]

McGillycuddy left for Omaha but kept in contact with the agency by portable telegraph. Thus he learned that agency employees were attempting to undermine his authority at Pine Ridge. One was agency physician Fordyce Grinnell. McGillycuddy immediately informed his superiors, and Price wrote to Grinnell on August 22, "Reported here that you and the Trader defy the authority of the Agent and encourage Red Cloud to Create trouble."[60]

Although McGillycuddy had support—and possibly respect—from some of the Lakotas, he had strong enmity from the Red Cloud faction, which continued to demand that he be removed from office by mid-October. The allegation that the agent had inappropriately distributed rations and other annuities and converted government property to his own use remained under investigation by Special Inspector William J. Pollock, who arrived at Pine Ridge on August 31 and immediately wired Price: "Arrived this evening: Everything quiet: Red Cloud over whose house floats the American flag came with the Police and others out on the road to meet and welcome us—I will proceed slowly and report frequently."[61]

— • ◂ ▸ • —

By early September McGillycuddy was back at Pine Ridge, preparing responses to the charges leveled against him by Red Cloud and his associates. Writing to Pollock on September 15, the agent said that Red Cloud's animosity toward him likely went back to 1875, when he took part in the Newton-Jenney Expedition to the Black Hills. That

---

[59]Letter from chiefs written by interpreter Frank White, presumably to Indian Commissioner Price, August 22, 1882, RG 75, Series 4, Box 35, vol. 3, pp. 405–407, NARS, Kansas City, Missouri.

[60]Telegram, Price to Fordyce Grinnell, physician, Pine Ridge Agency, August 22, 1882, RG 75, Series 2, Box 6, NARS, Kansas City, Missouri.

[61]Telegram, Pollock to Secretary of the Interior, August 31, 1882, 7:55 P.M., RG 75, "Records of controversies, Pollock Inspection of Agency," August 31–October 4, 1882, NARS, Kansas City, Missouri.

was a precursor to actions that usurped the Black Hills and led the Lakotas to their present status on the Pine Ridge reservation.

"From the fact that Red Cloud has always accused the 'Great Father' of having stolen the Black Hills, I am held by him to be an accessory before the fact having measured the amount of country to be stolen," McGillycuddy wrote to Pollock.[62]

Adding fuel to the fire, McGillycuddy had served as a surgeon with the Second and Third U.S. Cavalries in 1876 and was with General Crook at Camp Robinson "on the evening of the day that Red Cloud and Red Leafs bands were disarmed and dismounted on Chadron Creek, and Red Cloud incarcerated in the Post Gaurd [*sic*] House. I presume my presence in the vicinity at that time, with the army associates me, in Red Clouds mind with his misfortune, as he naturally has no very strong affection for the U.S. troops."

McGillycuddy's time with the Fifth U.S. Cavalry as medical officer and guide in 1876 had also pitted him against Red Cloud and the Lakotas. So had his work as assistant post surgeon at Camp Robinson and as attending surgeon for the Indians in 1877, and his role in caring for Crazy Horse—a known rival of Red Cloud's—in September that year. "I attended [Crazy Horse] until his death," McGillycuddy wrote, "and from the fact that Red Cloud was very Jealous of Crazy Horses presence as a forthright chief, it is difficult to say [whether] he blamed me under the supposition that I tried to save the Indians leader & did not succeed in doing so."

Other factors that McGillycuddy said could have contributed to Red Cloud's hard-line position against him included reports in 1878 of a "severe epidemic" among the Lakotas, in which the Indians were said to be "dying by [the] hundreds and were about to stampede to the interior." When McGillycuddy, then under authority of the military, investigated, he found "no sick, dying, or dead Indians, and very soon discovered it to be a 'bull-dozing' operation on the part of Red Cloud and the squaw-men, to force issue of the provisions for their removal to the interior." When he so informed authorities, as well as Red Cloud and men he called "white Indians," he "incurred their everlasting displeasure."

Finally, McGillycuddy told Pollock that he administered the agency in a way to benefit both the Indians and the government but not to please white men living on Indian land. "With regret I have to

---

[62]McGillycuddy to Pollock, September 15, 1882, RG 75, Series 4, Box 35, vol. 3, 1882, pp. 441–69, NARS, Kansas City, Missouri.

acknowledge almost childlike simplicity, and gullibility, in supposing the Department was in earnest in giving the opinion that Chieftainship, and the Tribal structure should be broken up, as one of the first advances toward civilization." Although he personally supported this policy and felt he had been "somewhat successful" in implementing it, he said the effort had drawn Red Cloud's scorn.[63]

In a rare statement about his own personality, he admitted that he had not been "largely endowed with Christian virtues of meekness, humility, and forbearance, I have not where smitten on the one cheek, turned the other to Red Cloud." Instead, he resented it when Red Cloud spoke against him and did not press "the old man to my bosom," as he said Agent Irwin had done.

Given a chance to tell his side of the long-standing dispute, McGillycuddy outlined other issues for Pollock: One of Agent Irwin's former trusted employees, a friend of Red Cloud's, had begun disparaging McGillycuddy to the chief as early as July 4, 1879. In 1880, when Red Cloud went to Washington, D.C., he was paid to "bring charges against myself, and trader Cowgill, with the hope that we might be removed" and thus enable former agency employees to get their jobs back. This action took place, McGillycuddy said, when Red Cloud met with H. C. Dear, the former agency trader, at his room in the Merchants Hotel in Yankton. Once in Washington, John W. Dear told Red Cloud essentially the same thing, and subsequently the Oglala and Spotted Tail "brought charges against me of stealing." Investigations by Inspector McNeill in June 1880, by the Dakota grand jury in August of that year, and by Inspector Gardiner in September "were declared cases of malicious persecution," McGillycuddy said.[64]

His blood obviously boiling, McGillycuddy said that both Inspectors McNeill and Gardiner, along with the grand jury, "have been charged with having been bribed to make a white washing report." He used vile epithets related to Indian women, whom he called "squaws," men who slept with them ("squawhumpers"), and white men who married them ("squawmen"). He claimed that as "witnesses on behalf of the Government," their affidavits, with few exceptions, "I feel honest in stating, are about as reliable and truthful as ones procured from the inmates of a combined penitentiary and lunatic asylum."[65]

---

[63]This policy would draw criticism from scores of people in succeeding generations.
[64]McGillycuddy to Pollock, September 15, 1882.
[65]Ibid.

From his first days as agent at Pine Ridge, McGillycuddy said, white men living just off the reservation in northern Nebraska had influenced Red Cloud because they wanted to "live on Indians supplies and be arrayed in Indian clothing by trading with the Indians." Quickly McGillycuddy had stopped this illegal trade, which launched what he saw as a vendetta against him by Red Cloud. The vendetta had culminated in the most recent dispute, which had exploded on August 13 when Red Cloud sent a "bull-dozing letter of threats for my removal." The letter had pushed Indians on the reservation to the edge of a violent outbreak before the threat was "suppressed by the reliable Indians of this Agency," McGillycuddy wrote.[66]

"Thus has the affair gone on from month to month, and year to year, charges upon charges, councils upon councils, and investigation after investigation, for no sooner have amicable relations been established between Agent and Red Cloud and his immediate followers, [than] the disreputable white interference again courses, so that in reality, Red Cloud is not entirely to blame. He is an old man, still ambitious, but with mental powers fast retrograding toward childhoods condition, and therefore easily suppressed and controlled, for bad as well as for good."[67]

McGillycuddy went so far as to say that he had no "personal quarrel" with Red Cloud. "It is however naturally the antagonism between Red Cloud—who represents the old barbarous and non-progressive element of the tribe, and the agent, whose endeavor it has been to carry out the practical negotiations of the service, and make some progress in civilization."[68]

The agent summarily dismissed the disagreement, saying, "The whole history of the trouble at this agency can be summed up in the following. It is the result of criminal and unwarranted interference, and exercised influence on the part of one or two agency employees, one trader and his employees, squawmen and neighboring white men, and a deposed and dissatisfied head chief, who is mourning over and sighing for his lost power, which power is simply antagonism to civilization and progress of his people."[69]

The following day, September 16, McGillycuddy sent another letter

---

[66]Ibid.
[67]Ibid.
[68]Ibid.
[69]Ibid.

to Pollock. In it he again outlined the events of August 13 through August 20. He mentioned the initial meeting between Red Cloud, American Horse, Red Shirt, and others at Shangrau's ranch, Red Cloud's threats to the Indian freighters, McGillycuddy's suspension of rations, the commissioner's August 15 telegram that McGillycuddy would be "sustained," the subsequent Indian councils, the ultimatum sent to Red Cloud's village, and the headman's eventual response to the agent and placement under control of the other chiefs and headmen.

On Saturday, August 19, when McGillycuddy met with the chiefs, tension had boiled at Pine Ridge. Although the agent said the council room was filled with "friendly Indians," he also said trader Cowgill and others felt particularly threatened. When ordered by McGillycuddy to close his store, Cowgill "shipped out so rapidly with his family in a wagon that it was impossible to catch him to offer protection."[70]

When agency physician Grinnell frightened the women and children at the agency by telling them that if Red Cloud launched an attack, they "would not last fifteen minutes," McGillycuddy demanded that he "keep quiet."[71] Grinnell and Cowgill were soon at odds with McGillycuddy and circulated a petition opposing him. "Trader Cowgill held secret council with Red Cloud, promised to assist him to have me removed as agent, applying to me the term 'S   O   Bitch.'"

In his September letter to Pollock, McGillycuddy counterpunched, charging Grinnell, Cowgill, J. G. Edgar, Cowgill's clerk, and another man "with concocting and circulating a petition containing untruths, with inciting the Indians to disturbance and interfering with the peace and welfare of the agency."

On October 4, Pollock notified Secretary of the Interior H. M. Teller, "I shall suspend Agent McGillicuddy for established malfeasance in office at seven o'clock tomorrow evening unless meantime I am removed from office by you."[72]

Pollack did suspend McGillycuddy, but the edict did not stand. Despite all of Red Cloud's blustering, there was no substance to the charges against the agent. Admittedly, he had a short temper and a sometimes caustic personality, but he kept detailed, accurate records. The deadline for his removal came and went without any overt action by Red Cloud and his supporters.

---

[70] Ibid.

[71] Ibid.

[72] Telegram, Pollock to H. M. Teller, secretary of the interior, October 4, 1882, 8:10 A.M., RG 75, Series 4, NARS, Kansas City, Missouri.

By the end of the month, the agent sent in a routine report in which he reiterated everything he had been saying for months: "The Indian Department instructs an agent that he should do all he can to break up the tribal and chief system, yet if he attempts to do so through the annuity issue, a howl goes up from the Indian sympathizers that he is interfering with 'treaty rights.'"[73]

The practical system of issuing annuities needed changing, he stressed, because it bolstered and supported "the chiefs and the tribal system, both of which are strongly antagonistic to civilization and progress." The conundrum, McGillycuddy said, was that when individual Indians cut loose from the tribe and adopted white men's ways, they were told by the chiefs during annuity distributions, "You have worked against the good old Indian ways, you have worked against your chief, you have taken the part of the white man, you can have none of these things, they are for Indians."[74]

The Indian policemen had been greeted with such a response back in 1879, when they were denied annuities. That was the situation that had set McGillycuddy on his course to "make a change in the system" and that put him in direct conflict with Red Cloud.[75]

Further, early in McGillycuddy's work at Pine Ridge, he and Red Cloud had squared off over education when the chief wanted Father Meinrad McCarthy, a Catholic priest, to operate a school. McGillycuddy, aware that responsibility for Indian education at Pine Ridge lay with the Episcopal Church, booted Father McCarthy off the reserve. His action set up a stand-off that lasted four months, until Catholic superiors recalled their representative.[76]

In 1880 the agent had been the subject of a letter written by American Horse, demanding that McGillycuddy be removed from the reservation. "We ask and beg of you to take our present Agent from us and give us another in his place so our people can be at peace once more which will never be as long as he remains with us."[77]

Over the years, further efforts had been made to oust the agent. These efforts were punctuated by commissions and councils coming to Pine Ridge and other Sioux agencies, attempting to change conditions of previous treaties with the tribesmen.

---

[73]McGillycuddy, report, October 30, 1882, RG 75, Series 4, Box 35, Letterbook vol. 4, p. 35, NARS, Kansas City, Missouri.

[74]Ibid., 36–37.

[75]Ibid.

[76]Larson, *Red Cloud*, 229.

[77]Ibid., 230.

The escalating hostility between Red Cloud and McGillycuddy in August 1882 coincided with action by Richard Pettigrew, the Dakota territorial representative to Congress, who endorsed an amendment that would provide $5,000 to negotiate treaty modifications. That fall, as the investigations went on into McGillycuddy's administration, a congressionally funded commission came to Pine Ridge. Headed by former Dakota territorial governor Newton Edmunds, it sought agreement on a corridor that would allow access through the Great Sioux Reservation, linking the Missouri River with the Black Hills gold fields. Serving with Edmunds on the commission were Cleveland resident James H. Teller, brother of Secretary of the Interior Henry M. Teller, and Peter Shannon, who had served as chief justice of the Dakota Territorial Supreme Court.

The agreement the Edmunds Commission negotiated allowed for a land corridor across the Great Sioux Reservation, ceded Indian land north of the Cheyenne River and west of the 102nd meridian, and split the reservation into smaller reservations. It divided the land among individual Indian families, provided for support items such as oxen and cows, and established positions on the reservations for physicians, carpenters, millers, engineers, farmers, and blacksmiths. Representatives from the various agencies signed: Santee, Pine Ridge, Rosebud, Standing Rock, and Cheyenne River.[78]

Although initially proposed on August 7, 1882, and ultimately given that date in its written form, the Edmunds Commission's work was not finalized until months later. The commissioners arrived at Pine Ridge on October 22, landing in the middle of the tension that permeated the area following the confrontation between McGillycuddy and Red Cloud the previous August. When Red Cloud predictably refused to sign the document, the commission appealed to McGillycuddy for assistance, and he showed his force of will by convincing eighty-five men, many of them leaders of small bands, to sign the document. This action, along with similar responses at the other agencies, set up the possibility that thousands of acres of Lakota land would be opened to homesteading. Before it could be fully adopted, Indian reformers cried foul, pointing out that the provision in the 1868 Fort Laramie

[78]Agreement with the Sioux of Various Tribes, 1882–83, January 23, 1883.

Treaty requiring any such action to have approval of three-quarters of
the adult males in the tribe had not been followed.

Senator Henry Dawes of Massachusetts led the effort to block rati-
fication unless the full complement of names could be obtained. As
might be expected, the Lakotas at Pine Ridge, with Red Cloud in the
vanguard, strongly resisted such a takeover of their land. Reverend
Samuel D. Hinman, traveling with George Sword, undertook the task
of going from one village area to another in the quest for legitimate
signatures for the document. Before enough men could be located and
convinced to sign the Edmunds agreement, Dawes himself came to
Pine Ridge, creating an opportunity for Red Cloud again to protest
the effort to usurp tribal land and ultimately leading to the failure of
the Edmunds Commission.

These machinations did not bode well for McGillycuddy. He had
endorsed the Edmunds Commission's effort to approve its agreement
without obtaining the required signatures in the first place. In having Sword travel with Hinman, he had further sided with those who
would reduce reservation land through individual allocation. In this
whole course of action, Red Cloud gained stature when tribal leaders
stood with him in opposition to the Edmunds Commission. Even
men who had previously backed McGillycuddy now firmly supported
Red Cloud.

Surprisingly, although Dawes's role in this about-face worked
against McGillycuddy, the senator then and later was actually a strong
proponent of the way McGillycuddy managed Pine Ridge.[79]

In 1887 Dawes would succeed in his own effort to allocate Indian
land to individual tribal members. But not until 1889 would the Crook
Land Commission succeed in breaking up the Great Sioux Reservation into component parts—the major reservations of Cheyenne
River, Pine Ridge, Rosebud, and Standing Rock.

⸻ • ◆ • ⸻

The conflict between McGillycuddy and Red Cloud settled down after
those tumultuous weeks in the late summer of 1882, but it continued to
simmer throughout the agent's remaining years at Pine Ridge.

Government policies hindered incentives for Indians to become
self-sufficient. McGillycuddy wrote in 1883: "The subsistence and other

[79]Larson, *Red Cloud*, 236–42.

Sun Dance, Pine Ridge Indian Agency, June 1883.
The Lakotas held the dance over Agent McGillycuddy's objections.
Nebraska State Historical Society, RG 1910 PH 0 8.

supplies, allowed and furnished my Indians are ample, in fact more than sufficient. If not how is it that I can save $5,000 per year on the issue of supplies? What earthly reason or inducement can be advanced why an Indian should go to work and earn his own living by the sweat of his brow, when an indulgent government furnishes him more than he wants to eat and clothes him for nothing? Select 8,000 whites of the pauper class, or send 8,000 of the 'assisted emigrants' to this reservation, feed them as you do these Indians, and they would hold a caucus and vote to assassinate the first one of their number who attempted to become self-supporting."[80]

McGillycuddy's short personal acquaintance with Crazy Horse had earned him respect from many of the tribal members who had

[80]McGillycuddy to Commissioner of Indian Affairs, August 10, 1883, U.S. Congress, House, Exec. Doc. 1, 48th Cong., 1st Sess., 1884, pt. 5, 2:93, quoted in Paulson, "Allotment of Land in Severalty," 149.

pledged fealty to that war leader. The friendship between the doctor and Crazy Horse meant that "in the long years" the chief's supporters "gave me their support in offsetting the continued opposition of the reactionary chief, Red Cloud, in my efforts to civilize and control the 9,000 Indians of the Pine Ridge or Red Cloud reservation of 4,000 square miles of territory."[81]

At the end of March 1883, McGillycuddy reported to Indian Commissioner Hiram Price, "I have the honor to report that matters with the Indians are in a more harmonious condition at this agency than have been known for years." Red Cloud, he added, "has informed his adherents in council that hereafter he will work with the agent."[82] McGillycuddy attributed Red Cloud's "apparent reform" to information shared with him when he visited Washington and even to a change in attitude regarding McGillycuddy from trader Cowgill and others "under whose bad influence he was formerly."[83] By June McGillycuddy reported that at the Sun Dance held at Pine Ridge that year, Red Cloud had told the general council "that he had been watching the Pine Ridge agent for some time and had concluded that he is a good man and is not stealing and therefore has nothing to say against him."[84]

Reverting to his previous sarcasm, McGillycuddy said this would "arrest the danger of 'the outbreak' but I do not suppose it will have much effect on Govt. securities in Wall Street and I merely report it to show that affect of the absence of the perspicacious influence of a class of designing white men on these Indians." He added, "My treatment of these Indians has not altered one iota since this time last year and yet these people are more happy and cheerful than at any time since the Sioux war of 1876."[85]

---

[81]Brininstool, *Crazy Horse,* 43–48. By most other accounts, there were no more than eight thousand Sioux on the reservation.

[82]McGillycuddy to Price, March 27, 1883, RG 75, Series 4, Box 35, Letterbook vol. 4, p. 261, NARS, Kansas City, Missouri.

[83]Ibid.

[84]McGillycuddy to Price, June 26, 1883, RG 75, Series 4, Box 35, Letterbook vol. 4, pp. 384–85, NARS, Kansas City, Missouri.

[85]Ibid.

16

The Most Investigated Agent

COMPLAINTS ABOUT Indian agents in general, and those serving the Lakotas in particular, were not new. As the *New York Times* reported in 1875, "Chief Red Cloud always complained about all Indian agents." That year paleontologist Othniel Charles Marsh visited the region, requesting permission from Red Cloud and other Lakotas to travel into the Dakota Badlands and conduct research. Recognizing that the scientist could serve his own interests, Red Cloud "told Marsh that agent J. J. Saville and the contractors were furnishing poor supplies in insufficient quantities" for the tribesmen. The chief refused to allow Marsh to proceed with his expedition until he "promised to take the complaint directly to the president." Marsh not only pledged to do so but in "due time took the complaint directly to President [Ulysses S.] Grant and also to the newspapers."[1]

Among the charges of Indian agency fraud and corruption against Agent John Saville had been assertions that he was unfit for the job, that the Indian census count was too high, that the annuities issued "looked suspicious," that the Indians had inadequate clothing for winter weather, and that the pork, flour, beef, sugar, coffee, and tobacco were all of inferior quality or unfit for consumption.[2]

President Grant investigated the alleged "Indian ring," as Episcopal bishop Hare had previously done. In 1873 the Hare Commission had reported conditions virtually the opposite of what Marsh saw.

---

[1]*New York Times,* July 14, 1875, pp. 1–3; August 12, 1875, p. 5; and April 30, 1875, p. 2: quoted in Phillips, "Indian Ring in Dakota Territory," 354.
[2]Phillips, "Indian Ring," 355–56.

Hare's commission had endorsed Saville and Agent E. A. Howard at the Spotted Tail Agency, noting that the two conducted themselves with "energy and honesty."[3]

Although exonerated following Grant's investigation, both Secretary of the Interior Columbus Delano and Indian Commissioner E. P. Smith resigned. Saville was removed for "inefficiency" in 1876 although the investigation showed he had not been "dishonest." Howard was removed from Spotted Tail but later was appointed agent for the Poncas in Nebraska.[4]

During this period, few Indian agents escaped investigation, and charges were filed against most of the men working in the field. The two agents who followed Saville at Pine Ridge—James S. Hastings and James Irwin—escaped serious charges, but Valentine T. McGillycuddy, who held the agency position longer than any other man during the nineteenth century, underwent intense scrutiny. By his own account, McGillycuddy was "the most investigated man in the country." He was exonerated of all charges and in turn "accused nearly all who opposed him of being members of the Indian ring."[5]

Although considerable fraud was associated with the various agencies, courts did not convict and governmental commissions did not punish anyone, for lack of specific, irrefutable evidence of corruption within the Indian service.[6] Brigadier General George Crook stated the feeling of many: "If you will investigate all the Indian troubles, you will find that there is something wrong of this nature at the bottom of them, something relating to supplies, or else a tardy and broken faith on the part of the general government."[7]

Senator Henry Dawes, who would be forever linked with Indian affairs for his role in writing and gaining approval for the 1887 Dawes Act—which divided the Indian reservations and turned land over to individual tribal members—supported McGillycuddy and his work at Pine Ridge. In a letter written on August 5, 1884, and published two days later in the *Springfield (Missouri) Republican*, Dawes heartily endorsed the work at Pine Ridge. He wrote, "Agent McGillicuddy

[3] Ibid., 358.
[4] Ibid.
[5] Ibid., 366.
[6] Ibid., 366–67.
[7] Crook, *General George Crook*, 229.

administers the law, and assigns Red Cloud no other position and permits him to exercise no more power than any other Indian."[8]

When Red Cloud preferred charges against McGillycuddy in 1882, a full investigation followed, resulting in a report that "not only declared the charges false, but highly commended [McGillycuddy] for the work he was doing at that agency," Dawes wrote.[9]

Red Cloud, undaunted, found support in many quarters, not least from George Bland, the intrepid editor of *Council Fire,* a Washington, D.C., publication that was highly critical of the Indian Service. According to Dawes, Bland, urged on by Red Cloud, induced a third inspection of McGillycuddy's conduct at Pine Ridge. The final report exonerated McGillycuddy of any wrongdoing. It commended him for his efforts on behalf of the Federal Indian Service at Pine Ridge.[10]

In his lengthy letter to the *Springfield Republican,* Dawes said, "I will tell you briefly what is the trouble at Pine Ridge agency, and what has resulted from it. It is a question between the old and the new, between the power of the chiefs and the power of the law. Old chief Red Cloud and Dr. Bland are for the old order of things, when chiefs ruled and made themselves rich out of the Indians. . . . The struggle on the part of the chiefs to maintain their control has been going on among the Sioux at the Pine Ridge and Rosebud agencies for several years." He added: "The Indian Commission, interested in the question whether or not the chiefs should control the Indians as heretofore, hearing of the good work McGillicuddy was doing, made an independent investigation of the facts, and visited the agency. Their report to the Interior Department was in the highest degree commendatory of Agent McGillicuddy. Herbert Welsh, of Philadelphia, son of our late minister to England, John Welsh, and himself the agent of the Indian Rights Association, visited the agency last summer, and again investigated the doings of McGillicuddy, and came back with the highest praise of his administration. Reverend C. C. Painter, of Great Barrington, agent of an Indian Missionary Association, spent a good many weeks on the Sioux reservation, and brought back the

[8]"The Case of Mcgillicuddy [*sic*]: Senator Dawes Explains the Troubles at the Sioux Agencies," *Springfield (Missouri) Republican,* August 7, 1884; copy at Lee Library, Brigham Young University, Provo, Utah.
[9]Ibid.
[10]Ibid.

same report. Miss Alice Fletcher, who has perhaps done more for the Indian than any other woman in America, spent several weeks at this agency, and her testimony is to the same import. The Senate committee of which I was a member was at this agency last summer, and took much pains to satisfy itself of the truth in this matter. They were unanimously of the opinion that at no agency which they visited, or had any knowledge of, had so much been done for the advancement of wild Indians as at this place."

Through all these investigations, officials "had every opportunity to discover any lack of honesty in administration," Dawes wrote. "They heard every complaint and statement which Red Cloud desired to make. . . . They were satisfied of both the integrity and wisdom of Mr. McGillicuddy."

With the various investigations concluded, McGillycuddy was reappointed. Review of the charges against him took place before a Senate committee. "Bland himself, with Pollock," Dawes wrote, "made all the statements they desired to make to the members of that committee," who "unanimously recommended the confirmation of McGillicuddy, and the Senate confirmed him without a dissenting vote."[11]

＊＊＊

Supported by Nebraska Democrats and George Bland, Red Cloud made another trip to Washington, D.C., in the spring of 1885. He obtained an audience with President Grover Cleveland on March 18 and told him, "Our agent is a bad man. He steals from us, and abuses us, and he has sent all the good white men out of our country and put bad men in their places."[12]

Three weeks later, Indian Commissioner John Atkins called McGillycuddy to Washington. The agent made the trip in company with George Sword and Young Man Afraid Of His Horses. Cleveland took no direct action following McGillycuddy's appearance in the nation's capital but instead turned the ever-bubbling problem over to a partisan commission headed by Indiana Democratic congressman William S. Holman. Holman had been appointed on March 4, 1885, to chair a special committee to "inquire into the expenditure of public moneys in the Indian service." With two other Democrats

---

[11]Ibid.
[12]Larson, *Red Cloud*, 244.

and two Republicans, Holman gathered testimony from Indian agencies across the country. The committee also set out to investigate and resolve the ongoing feud between McGillycuddy and Red Cloud.[13]

Although the committee visited and questioned residents at various agencies, much of its work centered on Pine Ridge, where agency physician Fordyce Grinnell, school principal Robert O. Pugh, missionary John Robinson, and Louis Shangrau (whose name was given as Lewis Shangran in the official report) testified. By far the most extensive inquiry involved Red Cloud and Valentine McGillycuddy.[14]

Questioning began on the issue of schools, evolved to a discussion of the quality of land on Pine Ridge, and then moved to livestock issues and distribution of clothing annuities—two matters that would resurface later. Further examination revolved around employees, finances at the agency, and payroll. Eventually questions turned to relations between the agent and the Indians, particularly Red Cloud.

"State whether or not it has been your policy to weaken the power of the chiefs since you have been agent," the committee said. McGillycuddy responded, "It has been my policy and instructions that it was the duty of the agent in every way possible to break up the authority of the chiefs, and I have endeavored in every way possible to break up the authority of the chiefs where that authority tended to work against civilization." The agent added that when a chief encouraged the Indians to build a house, he would "sustain that chief as much as possible." But a chief "who has absolute power over his people has almost the absolute ownership of them," he said.

When asked if anyone at Pine Ridge held such sway, McGillycuddy named Red Cloud. Yet personally, he said, he recognized Red Cloud only as "chief of his immediate band of about 300 people; we acknowledge no head chief at all."

In further questioning, McGillycuddy said he did not expect Red Cloud to "go in and work" if given a new agent. Furthermore, the Lakotas had a strong attachment to the Black Hills and their current reservation, regardless of whether they could profitably farm in the area. Recurring rumors that the Lakotas, like other tribes, would be relocated to Indian Territory met strong resistance from the tribesmen.

---

[13]Ibid.; Olson, *Red Cloud*, 300–301.

[14]House of Representatives, Report no. 1076, 49th Cong., 1st sess. (hereafter referred to as "Report 1076").

Gathering of Lakotas at the Rosebud Agency to meet with members
of the Crook Commission, May 4, 1889. The meeting was held to
discuss a controversial effort to have the Sioux accept the
Sioux Bill of 1889, which ultimately divided the
Great Sioux Reservation into smaller reservations.
Nebraska State Historical Society,
John A. Anderson Collection, RG2969 PH 2 47 a.

"They won't listen to a removal to any other place," McGillycuddy
said. "Indians are like cats, they are attached to localities, and I do not
care if they are in a poor country they become attached to it and would
not exchange it for a good one."

Red Cloud responded to queries concerning schools, attendance by
children from his band, and agricultural development. Asked why he
had not engaged in farming, the venerable chief sagely told the committee, "I did not have but one breaking plow, and we loaned it from
one place to another."

Given a chance to respond to charges that livestock scales in use
on the reservation were improperly adjusted, McGillycuddy wrote in
a statement on September 24, 1885, that if the scales had been tam-
pered with, it had been done "for the express purpose of *putting up
a job* on the agent." Any such tampering would have been an effort
to allow other people, including Pollock, J. G. Edgar, the clerk in

Cowgill's store, and Red Cloud, to be placed "in supreme control of Pine Ridge."[15]

Again McGillycuddy recounted the events that had taken place at Pine Ridge in August 1882, noting once more that Red Cloud personified the old tribal ways. "Red Cloud is and always has been the embodiment and representative of that system, and has always been, and is now, antagonistic in every way to schools, civilization, and progress." Red Cloud, according to McGillycuddy—who never minced words—had recognition as chief over his immediate band and was supported by "a small ring of squawmen, sentimentalists, quasi-philanthropists, cranks, and so-called attorneys around the agency and East."

Those who lived near Red Cloud, McGillycuddy said, spent their time "dancing scalp and war dances, recounting their old deeds of rapine and murder, and deploring the degeneracy of the young men of some of the other bands for adopting the ways of the white man." While "two or three" men in Red Cloud's band engaged in farming, the remainder were "doing nothing but loafing, eating Government rations, and dancing."

In an interesting conclusion to his lengthy statement, McGilly-cuddy shifted to the third-person point of view in writing about himself: "If he is not the proper man for agent, recommend his removal, for the world is wide. He is still comparatively a young man, and time will vindicate him if he needs vindication."[16]

Holman's committee took no decisive action regarding McGilly-cuddy and Red Cloud. The final report, submitted to Congress on March 18, 1886, showed partisan division. There was no recommendation to break up the Great Sioux Reservation, yet Republicans wanted division of land among the tribesmen. Regarding McGillycuddy, the Democrats suggested that a good agent would have respect and confidence from the Indians under his administration, whereas the Republicans stressed the necessity for an agent to be firm in maintaining control.[17]

---

[15]Ibid., 37 (emphasis in original).
[16]Ibid., 39.
[17]Larson, *Red Cloud*, 246.

McGillycuddy weathered the early storm that blew up against his administration as Pine Ridge agent, but he would find that Red Cloud was a formidable adversary who had friends in high places and supporters with powerful influence. George Bland, likewise, had made it his mission to remove McGillycuddy from authority at Pine Ridge. In April 1886, Bland wrote to Little Wound, "[It] appears that you Indians can get nothing from the government except what McGillycuddy will let you have, and I told the Commissioner that he is down on you because you are a friend of Red Cloud."

Bland added, "I have not quit trying to get McGillycuddy turned out. I went to see the President about it yesterday. He wants a new Agent, but is waiting for the Commissioner to find a new one."[18]

After years of trying, McGillycuddy's foes finally managed to have him suspended a month later, on May 20, 1886. James Montgomery Bell, a captain in the Seventh Cavalry, took over as acting Indian agent at Pine Ridge.[19] On the same day, McGillycuddy was instructed to forward property accounts to the Bureau of Indian Affairs and deposit unused funds "to the credit of the United States in the nearest U.S. Depository." If there were "sufficient funds . . . applicable to the purpose," wrote the acting commissioner of Indian affairs, "you will pay your own salary and the salaries of your employees up to and including the day preceding that upon which you were relieved."[20]

This time there was no redemption. Politics had shifted in the Washington landscape, and McGillycuddy was out permanently. But he did not go quietly.

Valentine Trant O'Connell McGillycuddy's removal as Pine Ridge Indian agent came not because of any serious infraction on his part—although there were charges that he had inappropriately distributed work oxen and cattle and provided rations to three undeserving persons—but because he refused to remove his clerk to make way for a new appointee from a different political party. Democrat Grover

---

[18]George Bland to Little Chief, April 17, 1886, RG 75, Series 4, Box 53 A and B, vol. 4, p. 189, NARS, Kansas City, Missouri.

[19]James M. Bell to Assistant Adjutant General, Department of the Platte, Omaha, Nebraska, May 19, 1886, RG 75, Series 4, Box 53 A and B, vol. 4, p. 204, NARS, Kansas City, Missouri; Acting Commissioner, Office of Indian Affairs, to Bell, instructing him to "relieve Mr. V. T. McGillicuddy" from his position as agent at Pine Ridge Agency, May 20, 1886, RG 75, Series 2, Box 8, NARS, Kansas City, Missouri.

[20]Acting Indian Commissioner to McGillycuddy, May 20, 1886, RG 75, Series 2, Box 8, NARS, Kansas City, Missouri.

Cleveland had taken up residence in the White House, and as often happened with a change in political administration, government employees secure under former party leadership found themselves ousted with the new.[21]

McGillycuddy sealed his own fate when he sent an April 27, 1886, telegram to the commissioner of Indian affairs saying, "Justice to bondsmen and myself will prevent my placing your appointed Clerk Clark on duty. Please wire me what action Department will take in matter to enable me to properly govern my future movements." The same day he telegraphed Senator Dawes, making virtually the same statement to him.[22]

When McGillycuddy refused to replace his clerk, he was himself removed from his position. Responding to this action, he turned to well-placed friends, including Herbert Welsh, corresponding secretary of the Indian Rights Association in Philadelphia. Welsh answered him in a letter dated September 22: "I have already made a statement in your defense and repelling the charge of partisanship brought against *me* by further presentation of the facts. I believe that now is the moment for actions on your part which will force your enemies to so formulate their attacks that you may have a fair and sufficient opportunity to reply to them. I have stood by you to the best of my ability, knowing the efficiency and excellence of your administration at Pine Ridge so far as the general management of the agency was concerned, and believing you to be an honest and faithful servant of the Government."[23]

Throughout the fall Welsh corresponded routinely with McGillycuddy, presenting information he believed would support the former agent's assertion that he had engaged in no malfeasance of office. In one letter, dated November 2, Welsh said the doctor-agent had been subjected to "malignant persecution."[24]

In a statement made on October 15, 1886, McGillycuddy outlined the issues set forth against him, answering each charge in careful diction.

[21]"Dr. Valentine McGillycuddy, Part 2," *Black Hills Visitor* online magazine, January–February 1999 (www.blackhillsvisitor.com).

[22]Telegram, McGillycuddy to Commissioner of Indian Affairs, April 27, 1886, Valentine T. McGillycuddy Collection, Devereaux Library, South Dakota School of Mines and Technology (SDSMT), Rapid City.

[23]Herbert Welsh to McGillycuddy, September 22, 1886, McGillycuddy Collection, SDSMT.

[24]Welsh to McGillycuddy, November 2, 1886, McGillycuddy Collection, SDSMT.

He explained how the issuing of beef cattle took place on the reservation, the locations of the cattle range and issue pens, and how the chief herder could not be in two places at the same time. Other charges had been levied against McGillycuddy's administration regarding the issuing of rations to three Indians identified as Warrior, Gopher, and Volunteer, with the claim that they were unknown on the reservation. McGillycuddy gave identifying details about each. "Warrior," he said, "is a well known member of Kiyaksa band on second Medicine Root Creek under Chief Little Wound." Gopher, a member of the Loafer band, lived on "first Medicine Creek" and was the father of Chief American Horse. As for Volunteer, that was "the liberal interpretation of the name 'offers himself' or 'agrees to fight' I do not recollect what band he belongs to."[25]

During subsequent weeks, McGillycuddy prepared a collection of statements from men he had worked with at Pine Ridge, all attesting to his careful discharge of official duties. The statements, clearly written by McGillycuddy, were prepared for signature by herders who were responsible for the work oxen and other cattle, along with Captain George Sword and Lieutenants Standing Soldier and Fast Horse of the Indian police.[26]

A strong statement on McGillycuddy's behalf came in October 1887 from David Brown, the former chief herder at Pine Ridge. In an affidavit prepared in Sheridan County, Nebraska, and attested to by the clerk of the district court, Brown said he had worked as chief herder from April 1, 1885, until August 23, 1886. He called the statement by an inspector that 256 head of oxen had not been properly issued to the Indians "absurd." Instead, the oxen, "when received by the Agent, were inspected and branded with the Government brand under the supervision of an Army officer, thus precluding the possibility of loss to the Government or the Indians."

Brown went on to explain the general operations at Pine Ridge regarding the distribution of cattle and other annuity goods to the tribespeople. He said he had outlined such practices to officials after McGillycuddy's removal from office in May 1886, and he knew "that every head of oxen and cows for which Agent McGillycuddy was

---

[25]"Answers to Exceptions in Accounts of V. T. McGillycuddy, October 15, 1886," South Dakota State Historical Society (SDHS) Archives, Pierre.

[26]Statements dated November 1886 and November 23, 1886, SDHS Archives.

responsible up to the date on which he transferred all property to his successor, Major Bell, U.S.A. was properly accounted for." He further identified Gopher, Warrior, and Volunteer as tribal members. He said in the case of money needed to pay for telegrams, which was not forthcoming in time for payment of bills every month, McGillycuddy used "his private funds" to cover the costs, "trusting to providence and the Treasury Department that the Operator performing the services would allow the warrant."[27]

It took months, but eventually McGillycuddy's accounts were reconciled, no outstanding issues could be identified, and he was cleared of any inappropriate action while serving as agent at Pine Ridge. That did not return him to his former position, but it did keep him in the Black Hills and allowed him the opportunity for future work with the Indians of Pine Ridge.

Captain Bell, who replaced McGillycuddy in May 1886, was himself soon replaced by Hugh D. Gallagher, an Indiana Democrat appointed by President Cleveland. He would serve until October 1, 1890, when Daniel F. Royer took charge at Pine Ridge—at a time that would test even the ablest of men and that certainly overwhelmed the new agent.

"Valentine T. McGillycuddy of Red Cloud Agency doubted the willingness of western Sioux to change their lifestyle quickly or to accept family farming over time," one historian remarked. "Cynically, he reported that Indians under his administration lived a 'life of ease and nonproductiveness' on annuity issues under treaty terms. Pessimistically, he remarked that the 'Sioux Reserve is not much of a 'land in severalty region,' concluding, 'neither are the present inhabitants 'land in severalty people.'"[28]

Elaine Goodale Eastman, a poet, teacher, and reformer who married Charles Eastman, a physician who served the Sioux tribe from 1890 to 1903, was "critical of the ration system [which] forced the Indians to leave home or farm to come into the agency to collect rations." But significantly, "when she reached the western-most agency—Pine Ridge and the Oglalas—she came down unequivocally [*sic*] on the side of reform. She greatly praised Agent Valentine McGillicuddy [*sic*] who had organized an Indian police force and who, she believed, ran

---

[27]David Brown, Affidavit, October 7, 1887, Sheridan County, Nebraska, SDHS Archives.
[28]Hoover, "Sioux Agreement of 1889," 62.

the agency legally, fairly, efficiently, and firmly." In Eastman's eyes, McGillycuddy "had the support of the 'progressive' Indians—those willing to accept the white man's way in 'the church, the school, the plough.'" The so-called traditionals, "who clung tenaciously to Indian dances, dress and customs, rallied around old Chief Red Cloud in their defense of 'barbarism,'" to Eastman were "'malcontents,' 'chronic grumblers,' 'lazy Indians.'"[29] Eastman even endorsed McGillycuddy's belief that the beef rations should be cut. "The Indian is naturally a carnivorous animal," she wrote, "and it is civilizing to give him a greater proportion of vegetable food."[30]

At a conference held by Indian reformers at Lake Mohonk, New York, in October 1886, Eastman presented information about attendance at Indian day schools. "Pressure could be exerted to compel attendance," she asserted, mentioning McGillycuddy's "practice of withholding rations from families whose children did not attend."[31]

Years later McGillycuddy would write, "As I look back the Oglalas were very good people and meant well, I was young in those days, and I had to come down pretty hard on them at times, and some did not understand what I was trying to get at." But he meant it all for the best, he said. He and Red Cloud had quarreled, "but I expect that if I had been in his place I would have had less use for the agent than he had."[32]

---

[29]Goodale, "Red Cloud and His Agent," quoted in Alexander, "Finding Oneself," 20.
[30]Goodale, "Does Civilization Civilize?" quoted in Alexander, "Finding Oneself," 20.
[31]Ibid.
[32]McGillycuddy to Garnett, October 3, 1926, quoted in Clark, *Killing of Crazy Horse,* 120.

IV

PUBLIC SERVANT

Ghost Dance held at Wounded Knee, November 25, 1890.
This was one of the events that led up to the massacre
there just over a month later. G. Trager, photographer.
Nebraska State Historical Society, RG2845 PH 2 2.

17
Wounded Knee

FOR SOME MEN, removal from a position of authoritarian rule
such as the agent had administered for seven years might have
spelled the end of public service. Valentine McGillycuddy,
though, was not one to sit back and watch life go on around him.
After leaving Pine Ridge, he relocated to Rapid City, South Dakota,
where he became vice president of the Lakota Banking and Invest-
ment Company and of the Black Hills National Bank. He organized a
hydroelectric power company and supervised its development. Determined to remain in the Black Hills, he oversaw construction of a fine
two-story home on the slope of a hill at the southern edge of the
city. The house's white sandstone foundation was accented by an upper
story painted olive green.[1]

In spite of his removal as their agent, residents of the Pine Ridge
Agency regularly visited McGillycuddy and Fanny at their new home,
drinking coffee with the cookies, bread, and doughnuts Fanny served
them.[2] Through this contact McGillycuddy kept abreast of issues on
the reservation.

A letter from George Sword, his Indian police captain, on June 6,
1887, gave McGillycuddy insight into how things had changed in the
year since he was removed from office. "I have received your welcome
letter sometime ago," Sword wrote, "in which you said that we the
policemen ought to keep up in good terms one with another. It was
not my fault that we do not seem to get along. It is Standing Soldier &

---

[1]McGillycuddy, *McGillycuddy, Agent,* 255–56.
[2]Ibid., 256.

Fast Horse's doings & they take side with the ante-citizen [*sic*] parties," Sword wrote.[3]

The Indian council that had been established under McGillycuddy's tenure to resolve differences among tribal members was in danger of collapse. "This council is getting worse or out of the way & when I think that they do things out of the way or the way in which the agt will not appreciate, I stoped [*sic*] it and I do not take part in it & thereby the agent did not like their ways & stopped the whole thing," Sword wrote. In consequence, "Standing Soldier, Fast Horse, & Garnett & others have work against me. They are with Red Cloud now & the agent knows it."

Those once progressive men had taken a stand against Sword in an effort, he asserted, to remove him from his position of authority. "There is two divisions here now, and the officers of the police (except me) are with the Red Cloud party. . . . I did not wish to have anything to do with Standing Soldier & others who have been working against me."

Those who opposed Sword and the new agent, Hugh Gallagher, included Standing Soldier, Fast Horse, and Pumpkin Seed, all initial members of McGillycuddy's Indian police, as well as Indian leaders such as Young Man Afraid Of His Horses, Little Wound, American Horse, Yellow Hair, and, of course, Red Cloud. Also in the opposition party were the mixed-blood interpreter Billy Garnett and "hundreds more others with Red Clouds party," Sword wrote.

Sword's difficulty with the tribesmen likely arose from his continued support of Agent Gallagher. Some who had worked long and tirelessly to purge the reservation of McGillycuddy no doubt expected general operations to change with a new agent. According to Sword, that had not happened. "We have got a good agent now that is he is such as pretty near good as you. It pleases me to see how he runs this Agency."

The police captain also shared personal information. He said his wife was "now a good house keeper," and they had a "nice frame building nicely fixed up, walls paper all round & carpet." This move to adopt white ways and housing was further incentive for the Indians supporting Red Cloud to oppose Sword. "This is all for the present. My wife & self send our best wish to you & Mrs. McG."[4]

---

[3]George Sword to McGillycuddy, June 6, 1887, McGillycuddy Collection, SDSMT.
[4]Ibid.

Once ensconced in the city, McGillycuddy not only took to civic and business activities but also eventually became surgeon-general on the governor's staff for Dakota Territory, working closely with Governor Arthur C. Mellette.[5]

In 1888 the doctor expended considerable effort in an attempt to secure a position with the Indian Service, if not as commissioner of Indian affairs or an assistant, then as an inspector. To bolster his chances he contacted former supporters such as Herbert Welsh, Henry Dawes, and George Crook, all of whom gave him advice and some support. But it did not lead to a new position in the Office of Indian Affairs.[6]

———————— ·•‹•·• ————————

Within the next year, a sense of renewed optimism for the future came to the Lakotas at Pine Ridge and other reservations in the Dakotas. It arrived in the form of a message that the old order would be restored if people embraced the beliefs set forth by Wovoka, a Paiute. He introduced to native people a new religious dance as part of a messianic religion that would bring back the buffalo and freedom for Indians.

Tribesmen from across the West met with Wovoka, heard his prophecy, and began engaging in what became known as the Ghost Dance. The Paiute said he had been to heaven and seen God, who "told me to come back and tell my people they must be good, and love one another, and not fight, or steal, or lie. He gave me this dance to give to my people."[7]

Ethnologist James Mooney explained the Ghost Dance religion this way: "The great underlying principle of the Ghost dance doctrine is that the time will come when the whole Indian race, living and dead, will be reunited upon a regenerated earth, to live a life of aboriginal happiness, forever free from death, disease and misery."[8]

This was a concept that played into the beliefs of traditionalists like Red Cloud and, more so, Sitting Bull, who had fled to Canada following the battles of the Great Sioux War. Sitting Bull had resigned himself and his followers to life on the reservation when he surrendered his

---

[5]McGillycuddy, *McGillycuddy, Agent*, 255.
[6]Correspondence, McGillycuddy Collection, SDSMT.
[7]Mooney, *Ghost-Dance Religion*.
[8]Ibid., 19.

arms in 1881 at Fort Buford, in part because his people had little support and virtually no food to sustain themselves any longer in Canada.

McGillycuddy, admittedly on the edge of tribal politics, saw no great danger in allowing the Indians to dance. "I should let the dance continue," he said. "If the Seventh-Day Adventists prepare their ascension robes for the second coming of the Saviour, the U.S. Army is not put in motion to prevent them. Why should not the Indians have the same privilege?"[9]

But few other white people in the Dakotas embraced his position, and eventually the governor took action. He enlisted the doctor's assistance by appointing him a commander in the National Guard and charging him with the responsibility for investigating the situation, particularly at Pine Ridge.

An early telegram went out from an army captain to the agent at Pine Ridge on November 5. "Have Indians quit their ghost dancing[?]" asked the missive. A similar message went out under the signature of James Dahlman on November 24, addressed to the Chadron, Nebraska, newspaper.[10]

Across the region, Indian agents raised alarms. On November 23, some of them sent a note to Brigadier General John Rutter Brooke, army commander of the Department of the Platte. "As the agents appealed for Protection & Reported they had lost all control over their Indians it became necessary for the military under your orders to assume general control," said the letter.[11]

That same day, R. Williams, the U.S. assistant adjutant general, cautioned Brooke, "Do not allow your command to become mixed up with Indians friendly or otherwise. Hold them all at a Safe Distance from your command[.] Guard against suspicion or treachery." Williams noted that the Seventh Cavalry and additional troops from Omaha had been ordered into the field, and he instructed Brooke, "Order these and what available troops are not needed at other places to such points as you can use them Most effectively to control indians [*sic*] on Reservation or Elsewhere in case the[y] break away[.] if they

[9]"Dr. V. T. McGillycuddy on the Ghost Dance," no. 49 in Vestal, *New Sources in Indian History*, 89; Kutac, "He Saw Troopers Die," 52.

[10]Captain Wells to Pine Ridge Agent Royer, November 5, 1890, RG 75, Series 11, Box 722, folder November 1890, NARS, Kansas City, Missouri.

[11]Letter, unknown Indian agents to John Brooke, November 23, 1890, RG 75, Series 11, Box 722, folder November 1890, NARS, Kansas City, Missouri. This letter is unavailable in its full form, and no author is identified.

find they can't take you at disadvantage they may pretend submission." He added that the Indian leaders "should be arrested if favorable opportunity offers by command of Genl Miles."[12]

A day later, Lieutenant Colonel George Forsyth sent a telegram to Brooke indicating that nineteen officers and 270 men from Companies A, B, I, and K, Seventh Cavalry, had departed for Rushville, Nebraska, at 3:30 A.M., along with sixty-nine mules needed to draw wagons and thirty-five pack animals. The men had with them "thirty days rations and two hundred rounds carbine ammunition per man." They clearly had gone into the field prepared for a serious campaign.[13]

The tension was palpable throughout the Black Hills that late November. It led seventy citizens to petition McGillycuddy, then on duty with the South Dakota National Guard, to find guns to be distributed for "protection of Dakota City settlers."[14] Just two days earlier, on November 25, Indian rights advocate Herbert Welsh telegraphed McGillycuddy: "Give me your view on situation. Could I render any service here or with you[?]"[15]

McGillycuddy had already provided information about the Indian unrest at Pine Ridge to Governor Mellette. Now he received orders to go to Pine Ridge and assess the potential danger to settlers.[16] Governor Mellette appointed H. M. Day "Commander in Chief Black Hills," and the governor wrote to him on December 5 to note the killing of three Indians by white settlers and guardsmen. He cautiously added, "Be descreet in kiling [*sic*] the Indians. If I had the force I would furnish protection to the property of allyou [*sic*] people but as I have not the means to do this we must be content to protect the lives of our people; however, if you feel you [*sic*] forces are sufficient, you can properly repel any assault upon property by the Indians being careful, of course not to do anything which would preciptiate an attack ~~upon them~~ by them upon un-protected settlers. . . . I shall so send you 200 more guns."[17]

[12]Telegram, R. Williams, acting adjutant general, to Brooke, November 23, 1890, RG 75, Series 11, Box 722, folder November 1890, NARS, Kansas City, Missouri.

[13]Telegram, George Forsyth to Brooke, November 24, 1890, RG 75, Series 11, Box 722, folder November 1890, NARS, Kansas City, Missouri.

[14]Telegram to McGillycuddy signed "Republican," November 27, 1890, RG 75, Series 11, Box 722, folder November 1890, NARS, Kansas City, Missouri.

[15]Telegram, Herbert Welsh to McGillycuddy, November 25, 1890, RG 75, Series 11, Box 722, folder November 1890, NARS, Kansas City, Missouri.

[16]McGillycuddy, *McGillycuddy, Agent*, 258–59.

[17]Arthur C. Mellette to H. M. Day, December 5, 1890, SDHS Archives (strikeover in original).

Further December correspondence involved direction from the governor on where and how the citizen force was to protect itself in the event of an Indian uprising. Letters written later in the month reflected the position of the army about how the commanders would handle the escalating tension in the Dakotas.

On December 11, 1890, Emma C. Sickels, who had helped organize and taught at the boarding school at Pine Ridge when it opened in 1884 and had maintained her connections with the Lakotas, wrote to McGillycuddy from Pine Ridge Agency. She told him she had discussed the ongoing upheaval with tribal members. "I have learned that it is the opinion of those who have shown their opinion and deeds worthy of respect.—that if you were here this trouble would be settled effectively," she wrote. "As I came here because of my acquaintance with the people here, my connection with the press and the support of some very influential people, I am heartily interested in learning the ways and means. Would you kindly tell me whether you would take the place at the request of the progressives, honorable Indians?"[18] McGillycuddy's response to his former colleague is unknown.

In addition to contacting residents in the region and working with any Indian leaders he could meet, McGillycuddy fired off letters to influential people in Washington and elsewhere. In one response, written on December 22 and marked "Confidential," Third Cavalry Captain John Bourke, who had known McGillycuddy since their 1875 reconnaissance of the Blacks Hills with Newton and Jenney, wrote, "It is a pleasure to find in this Sahara of a job about the 'Indian outbreak,' an oasis of common sense such as is contained in your note to Herbert Welsh now going the rounds of the press."

Bourke added, "Had you been in charge at Pine Ridge there would have been no necessity for *murdering* Sitting Bull [who had been killed at the Standing Rock Agency a week earlier], or of firing one hostile shot. Of course, I can do nothing but keep my mouth shut and wait for better days when Govt officials may have more sense." Obviously not anticipating that the worst was yet to come at Pine Ridge, Bourke concluded the letter, "Hoping that Mrs. MacGillycuddy and you may pass a very merry Christmas."[19]

---

[18]Emma C. Sickels to McGillycuddy, December 11, 1890.

[19]John G. Bourke to McGillycuddy, December 22, 1890 (emphasis in original).

By late November McGillycuddy had reached the agency and found soldiers on the ground. Upon learning of their former agent's presence in the region, the Lakotas invited him to a council to discuss why troops had come into the area. The invitation came from Red Cloud and other chiefs.[20]

In his account of the events of late 1890 and early 1891, McGilly-cuddy wrote, "Red Cloud addressed the council, telling them that I was 'Little Beard' who had been their agent winters ago, when I was a boy, which he did not like, and also that I had come from the army which he did not like." Red Cloud said the two had quarreled a "great deal" and he believed McGillycuddy then wanted to show his power and authority. Responding, McGillycuddy told the assembled Indians he had been forceful "for their good." At that Red Cloud stated, "I see it now, and if we had in those days listened to him we would not have this trouble now."[21]

Red Cloud then told McGillycuddy, "Little Beard, we have not behaved half as badly as we did in your day, but you never sent for troops. . . . Can you not send these soldiers away, and if you will, we give you twenty-five of our young men you can take as hostages, and everything will be settled in one sleep."[22]

In her similar account of this meeting, Julia McGillycuddy said that Red Cloud told McGillycuddy, "The soldiers have stolen here in the night; it looks as though they were here to fight; we do not want to fight. We ask that you take these soldiers away and we promise that in one sleep after they are gone everything will be quiet. We will give you twenty-five of our young men as hostages until all is settled."[23]

The former agent told Red Cloud he no longer had authority to make any deal with the Indians. "I have no power here, I only repre-sent the Governor, but I will take your words to the soldier chief at the Agency."[24]

---

[20]Vestal, *New Sources*, 82–89, and McGillycuddy, *McGillycuddy, Agent*, 259–74, give McGil-lycuddy's version of events during late 1890 and early 1891 at Pine Ridge. Presumably, McGillycuddy provided both accounts, which are similar but have subtle word differences. Almost all accounts of McGillycuddy's role at Pine Ridge during this tumultuous time draw from these two sources. In most cases I rely on the document in Vestal, because it is the earlier publication.

[21]Vestal, *New Sources*, 82.

[22]Ibid., 83.

[23]McGillycuddy, *McGillycuddy, Agent*, 260.

[24]Vestal, *New Sources*, 83; McGillycuddy, *McGillycuddy, Agent*, 260.

When McGillycuddy reported to General Brooke, the commander, "in a very pompous manner," asked McGillycuddy, "Do you think that you could settle this matter?" The former agent confidently replied, "Yes, I think so. Take the troops over the Nebraska line, and trouble will end."

When Brooke suggested that McGillycuddy had a misguided opinion of his influence with the Lakotas, the doctor stood his ground. He told the commander he had spent ten years among the people at Pine Ridge. "They have my confidence, and vice versa. It is now November, a cold Winter is coming; this is not the time Indians go on the warpath."[25]

McGillycuddy, never one to back down from a fight, pressed on. With troops on the ground during "a religious excitement," he predicted to Brooke, "you are going to have the biggest racket you ever had on your hands." At this Brooke "went up in the air." McGillycuddy said that had he not had authority from the governor of South Dakota, he surely would have been "removed from the reservation."[26]

Later, according to Julia's reporting, Red Cloud spoke with military leaders about McGillycuddy, saying, "That is Wasicu Wakan. Seven winters he was our agent; I did not want him then; he came from the army; he was only a boy. There was bad feeling between us; but when he went away four winters ago, he said: 'Some day you will say that my way was best for the Indian.' I will tell him now that he spoke the truth. If we had listened to him, we would not now be having this trouble. We did much worse things when he was our Father, but he never sent for soldiers. We settled our troubles among ourselves. We want you to take the soldiers away. We will give no trouble to anyone."[27]

During the council Little Wound said, "Porcupine has come to us with this story [of the Ghost Dance and forthcoming messiah]. Whether it is true or not I do not know, but it is the same story the white missionaries have told us—that the Messiah will come again. I gathered my people together and told them 'If it is a good thing we should have it. If it is not a good thing it will fall to the earth of itself.' Therefore learn the signs and the dances, that if the Messiah comes in the spring he will not pass us by."[28]

---

[25]Vestal, *New Sources*, 83.
[26]Ibid., 84.
[27]McGillycuddy, *McGillycuddy, Agent*, 260.
[28]Vestal, *New Sources*, 89.

The presence of troops gave some Indians reason to believe the prophecy would come to pass. As Little Wound told McGillycuddy, "If the Messiah is *not* coming, and by his coming will again make us a strong people and enable us to hold our own in this land give[n] us as a home by the Great Spirit, and the white man is not afraid of that, *why* have the white soldiers been brought here to stop the dance?"[29]

Later McGillycuddy told Brooke that Little Wound's statement was meaningful, for he believed "they will dance through the winter. The green grass comes, with it no Messiah, and the thing ends."[30] He added, "Were I still agent here. I should let the dance continue. The coming of the troops has frightened the Indians. Winter is here—a time when they do not go on the warpath if it is possible to avoid it."[31] Proving that he knew the sentiment on the reservation, McGillycuddy added, "If the troops remain, trouble is sure to come—not through the old warriors, but through the men too young to have felt the power of the white man in the Sitting Bull campaign."[32]

As December arrived and the Indians gathered in the valley along White Clay Creek, Red Cloud asked McGillycuddy to come to their camp. Brooke denied the request, saying he would send his own representative. Meantime, the army brought in howitzers and Hotchkiss guns, along with additional troops. All requests by the Pine Ridge Indians to talk with their former agent were denied.

Farther north, tension escalated to outright violence as an effort to arrest Sitting Bull went sour at Standing Rock on December 15, leaving the venerable leader dead. This pushed some Miniconjous, including Big Foot and his band, to flee toward the Dakota Badlands. The Oglalas continued massing at Pine Ridge, in part because of directives by the army that they come in. Regular army troops and members of both the Dakota and Nebraska National Guards also infiltrated the region. Brigadier General Leonard Wright Colby, commanding the Nebraska National Guard, positioned guardsmen south of the reservation for more than a hundred miles to both east and west, attempting to allay the fears of Nebraskans. Communication among the military

---

[29]Ibid.; McGillycuddy, *McGillycuddy, Agent*, 261 (emphasis in original).

[30]Vestal, *New Sources*, 89. In *McGillycuddy, Agent*, 261, Julia McGillycuddy wrote that "when the spring came and the Messiah did not appear, matters would adjust themselves."

[31]McGillycuddy, *McGillycuddy, Agent*, 261.

[32]Ibid., 262.

branches was aided by the use of three heliograph stations, and of course messengers also relayed information.[33]

Major Samuel M. Whitside, commanding a column of the Seventh Cavalry, intercepted the Indians with Big Foot near Porcupine Butte on December 28 and accompanied them to a camp on Wounded Knee Creek. This site, some fifteen miles east of Pine Ridge Agency, became the final camp for many of the 350 men, women, and children with Big Foot. Whitside's command, reinforced during the night, was taken over by Colonel James W. Forsyth, who decided on December 29 to disarm the Indians.

That day the troops, with their Hotchkiss guns, were in place around Big Foot's camp, which had a white flag clearly flying. When soldiers entered the camp and began a search of the Indian men, confiscating weapons, Yellow Bird told the Indians: "My children, don't be frightened—the Great Spirit—is with you—your ghost shirts will protect you from the white man's bullets."[34] But as the search proceeded, soldiers found a gun held under the blanket of one Indian. A shot rang out, setting off a melee and leading to the tragedy known as the Wounded Knee Massacre, in which hundreds of Indian men, women, and children died, along with dozens of troopers. Some soldiers fell to an Indian counterattack, but many were struck by bullets fired by their own comrades.

In the aftermath of Wounded Knee, injured tribesmen were taken to Pine Ridge for treatment. There, according to Julia McGillycuddy, the former agent and surgeon did what he could to tend their injuries. McGillycuddy had not been present when the firing began at Wounded Knee; he had returned to Rapid City to confer with officials there. On January 3, 1891, he climbed aboard an open wagon equipped with three seats and, along with three other doctors, including surgeon John Vance Lauderdale, a major in the army medical department, set out from the Commercial House in Rushville, Nebraska, for Pine Ridge. As the wagon bounced along under sunny skies on a "cool and delightful" day, McGillycuddy sat beside Lauderdale, who wrote to his wife that McGillycuddy was "a very intelligent ex-physician."[35]

Many of the injured Indians had been taken to the Episcopal church

[33]Colby, *Sioux Indian War of 1890–'91*, 154.
[34]McGillycuddy, *McGillycuddy, Agent*, 258.
[35]J. V. Lauderdale to his wife, Joe, January 3, 1891, quoted in Green, *After Wounded Knee*, 47.

Soldiers on the field at Wounded Knee after the tragic events
there on December 29, 1890. G. Trager, photographer.
Nebraska State Historical Society, RG2845 PH 13 5.

at Pine Ridge, where the doctors found and treated them as they lay
on blankets placed on the floor.[36]

McGillycuddy almost certainly raised questions and spit out concerns about conditions on the reservation. Pine Ridge Agent Daniel
Royer, who had been appointed to his position only on October 1,
sent a telegram on January 6 to his superiors at the Office of Indian
Affairs. "Dr. McGillycuddy is at this agency," he wrote, "severely crit-
icizing the Interior dept and especially yourself he is doing me dirt in
the hope of getting me removed he told me yesterday he was fighting
your dept & would continue to do so his presence here is injurious to
the service."[37]

When a special Indian agent came to investigate, McGillycuddy, in
his customary direct manner, "opened up on the Indian Office by wire
through the Governor, and insisted on an immediate investigation."
With his usual sarcasm, he said that the charge against him, if true,
"should warrant my being led out and shot." As he no doubt expected,

[36]Ibid., 50, 51.
[37]Telegram, Daniel Royer to Commissioner of Indian Affairs, January 6, 1891, McLaughlin
   Papers, Roll 35, Doc. no. 1891-509, Special Case no. 188, Denver Public Library.

he "heard nothing more about it." Royer's contacting Washington officials to deal with McGillycuddy, whom he saw as a troublemaker, could be contrasted with McGillycuddy's own tactics in similar situations. Whereas Royer wrote asking that something be done, McGillycuddy would have booted the pot stirrer off the reservation and dealt with the consequences himself.[38]

As it turned out, Royer himself was removed almost simultaneously with his statement of concern about McGillycuddy. The less experienced man had presided over the most violent episode in Pine Ridge history and subsequently earned the sobriquet "Man Who Was Afraid of Indians."[39] He and McGillycuddy would later fling additional barbs at each other, with little effect on their respective careers.

By mid-January, all hostile tribal members had surrendered, ending the tension that had prevailed across the region for the two months before the attack at Wounded Knee. During the escalating hostility and outright attack at Wounded Knee, Young Man Afraid Of His Horses had been away in Wyoming. Upon his return, he inquired of McGillycuddy, "Is there nothing that can be done, Wasicu Wakan, to prevent the whites from having another outbreak and bringing so much trouble to the Indians?"[40]

Later, residents in Rapid City asked McGillycuddy who had been responsible for Wounded Knee. His response, wrote Julia, was, "Whoever fired the first shot. After that, nothing short of the Almighty could have stopped the killing."[41]

McGillycuddy had more to say on the matter. In a letter to General Colby, commander of the Nebraska National Guard, written on January 15, 1891, he said the blame for events at Wounded Knee went back "to a combination of causes gradually cumulative" that dated to the inauguration of the nation's "faulty Indian policy."[42] He was referring to Indian Bureau decisions. This reflects a change in attitude, because while he was the Pine Ridge agent he supported federal policies.

---

[38]Vestal, *New Sources*, 84.

[39]The reference to Royer's sobriquet comes from Green, *After Wounded Knee*, 24; Mooney, *Ghost-Dance Religion*, 824. Lauderdale, in a letter dated January 7, 1891, noted, "We have just heard that Agent Royer has been removed and that an Army Officer is to be placed in charge of the agency. Thank the Lord for this move." Quoted in Green, *After Wounded Knee*, 61. On January 11, 1891, General Nelson Miles appointed Captain Francis Edwin Pierce as Pine Ridge agent.

[40]McGillycuddy, *McGillycuddy, Agent*, 273.

[41]Ibid.

[42]McGillycuddy to Colby, January 15, 1891, quoted in Colby, *Sioux Indian War*, 176.

Broken promises and failed treaties, together with shortages of annuities and scant meat supplies, were contributing factors, the former agent charged, as were poor management practices at the agencies. He particularly criticized the work of the Pine Ridge agents who had succeeded him. Although his old friend George Sword had earlier expressed support for Agent Gallagher, McGillycuddy had his own critical opinion of the man's ability as an agent. Gallagher, McGillycuddy said, was "totally ignorant of Indians and their peculiarities; a gentleman with not a qualification in his make-up calculated to fit him for the position of agent at one of the largest and most difficult agencies in the service to manage; a man selected solely as a reward for political service."[43]

McGillycuddy boasted of his own relations with the tribesmen, noting that he "managed this agency without the presence of a soldier on the reservation" for seven years. "And in those times the Indians were naturally much wilder than they are to-day."

Acknowledging that occasionally there were "exciting times" at Pine Ridge, McGillycuddy said that generally he had governed with Indian assistance. "We believed in placing confidence in the Indians; in establishing, as far as possible, a home rule government on the reservation," he told Colby. "We established local courts presided over by the Indians with Indian juries; in fact we believed in having the Indians assist in working out their own salvation."

Under his administration, he said, the "progressive and orderly element" of people on the reservation became loyal allies. After McGillycuddy's departure, Gallagher had removed from a role of influence anyone who had worked with McGillycuddy. "The progressive chiefs, such as Young-Man-Afraid, Little Wound and White Bird, were ignored, and the back of the element of order and progress was alienated from the agent and the Government, and in the place of this strong backing that had maintained order for seven years, was substituted Red Cloud and other non-progressive chiefs, sustainers of the ancient tribal system," McGillycuddy told Colby.

When Agent Gallagher was removed and replaced by Royer, a political appointee who was unprepared for the rapidly developing situation at Pine Ridge, the move "unwittingly threw the balance of power at Pine Ridge against the government." This turn of events,

---

[43]Olson, *Red Cloud*, 325, citing Mooney, *Ghost-Dance Religion*, 833.

when combined with the appeal of those who believed the Ghost Dance would restore their culture, "resulted in a most dismal failure," McGillycuddy said.[44]

The Ghost Dance, he claimed, had been no real threat to settlers in the Dakotas or in Nebraska. In fact he believed "too much attention has been paid to it," and it was a "symptom" of a "deep-rooted, long existing difficulty." Comparing it to a dread disease, he claimed that the effort to squelch the Ghost Dance was about as effective as treating the eruption of smallpox sores without treating the disease itself.[45]

Disarming the Lakotas "is neither advisable, nor practicable," McGillycuddy wrote. "You will succeed in disarming and keeping disarmed the friendly Indians because you can, and you will not so succeed with the mob element because you cannot."[46]

Again he boasted of his relations with the Lakotas, which, although tense more than once during his seven-year term as agent, had resulted in no overt violence between the two cultures. "If I were again to be an Indian Agent, and had my choice, I would take charge of 10,000 armed Sioux in preference to a like number of disarmed ones; and furthermore agree to handle that number, or the whole Sioux nation, without a white soldier."[47]

Clearly, McGillycuddy retained supreme confidence in his ability to manage the tribe and believed wholeheartedly that the absence of soldiers during his tenure had helped maintain peace in the volatile region. He had only to point to the situation he had diffused in August 1882 to make his case. That year, when Red Cloud threatened violence, the mere possibility of bringing federal troops onto the reservation was enough to turn progressive Indian leaders into proponents of home rule.

At Wounded Knee he believed the army had overplayed its hand. Surprisingly, he supported the rights of the Indians to their own beliefs, a break with his previous formal endorsement of federal Indian policy.

---

[44]Olson, *Red Cloud*, 179.
[45]Ibid., 180.
[46]Ibid.
[47]Ibid.

18

Full Circle

THE YEARS AFTER McGillycuddy left Pine Ridge could have been restful ones, but his wife, Fanny, increasingly needed his attention. She had gained weight and suffered from frequent headaches. One morning as she left home to attend church, she suffered a stroke, which left her permanently disabled. Her once neat handwriting deteriorated significantly. She now spoke with slurred diction, although Valentine could understand her wishes. With his constant care, she recovered slowly, until she could walk without assistance and once again drive the phaeton the couple used for transportation.

For a time following her stroke in 1888, Fanny returned to stay with her mother, but her separation from the doctor was difficult for her. "I guess you have got home by this time," she wrote him on July 8. "I thought of you and wondered how you would be and what you were doing. The birds, the plants, the cat and the dogs are all well." Her recovery was progressing, she told him. She could "ride without getting lame," and "all but my hand and foot [are] getting the action in them." Writing of a friend who had also had a stroke, she told of his condition, noted that her watch battery had given out, and lamented, "I can't spell easy words I know. I don't know what is the meaning of it."[1]

A week later she seemed particularly to miss her "petty," the endearment she used for McGillycuddy. She told him that when friends had brought her the mail, which included only newspapers, she had thought, "You know papers are not mail," but when they later brought a letter from McGillycuddy, she was overjoyed. "They brought me

[1]Fanny McGillycuddy to Valentine McGillycuddy, July 8, 1888, McGillycuddy Collection, SDSMT.

one letter from my petty. Nothing is equal to it. I am tired my petty. I want to come home." Although begging to be allowed to return home, Fanny admitted, "I cannot walk yet." She closed with, "Good night my love my life."[2]

On July 23 she wrote another letter, which showed her anguish over her failing health: "Oh if I can only be well again." She signed it "from your petty Fanny."[3]

Since his removal as Pine Ridge agent, McGillycuddy had unsuccessfully appealed for a new opportunity to be involved in the Indian Service. In April 1891 he was elected president of the board of trustees of the School of Mines in Rapid City. The school was struggling with budgets and enrollments, partly because area residents "felt practical training served more purpose than a college degree."[4] Two years later McGillycuddy resigned as board president to become dean of the school, even though there was some talk about whether it should remain open at all; in 1894 the School of Mines had only forty-two students. The previous year, because of an extremely tight budget, the only equipment purchased was a typewriter and a camera to be used for fieldwork. As dean, McGillycuddy acquired an extensive collection of tin ore samples for the school's museum. The board also authorized $50 to fund improvements that would alter the "somewhat bleak and barren appearance of the School of Mines."[5] While serving as dean, McGillycuddy engaged in two seemingly disparate jobs: examining mines and teaching classes.

Active in politics, he took part in letter-writing campaigns to support his favorite candidates, served as mayor of Rapid City in 1897, and cared for Fanny. But after another stroke, she died that year. Bereft over her death and disheartened with politics, McGillycuddy decided to leave the Black Hills, where he had worked and lived for half his life.[6]

---

[2]Fanny McGillycuddy to Valentine McGillycuddy, July 17, 1888, McGillycuddy Collection, SDSMT.

[3]Fanny McGillycuddy to Valentine McGillycuddy, July 23, 1888, McGillycuddy Collection, SDSMT.

[4]Stymiest, *Centennial*, 16–19.

[5]Ibid.

[6]After Fanny's death, McGillycuddy arranged for some buffalo she had raised from calves to be sent to the Smithsonian Institution, where they became the nucleus of the herd at the National Zoo.

Relocating to San Francisco, he became a medical inspector for the Mutual Life Insurance Company of New York.[7] Although most of his work involved inspections on the West Coast, he also had responsibility for accounts in the Great Plains and occasionally returned to the Black Hills. Once, he ran into his old friend Calamity Jane. He later struck up a relationship with Julia Blanchard, a young woman whose father had served as the storekeeper at Pine Ridge. McGillycuddy had once referred to her as "the little blonde daughter of the trader."

Julia, born in 1870, the daughter of George F. and Marie Louise Holbrook Blanchard,[8] had first seen Valentine McGillycuddy when she was a child at her father's store. To the girl, he became "in short time a figure of heroic mold," the *Oakland Tribune* reported years later, upon the publication of her book about his life. "In her estimate, his autocratic rule over all that he surveyed was tempered with benevolence. She found justification for the fact that his word was law and his authority absolute over not only the Indians on the reservation, but over all others with whom he came in contact."[9]

"She saw much of McGillycuddy and his first wife Fannie [*sic*], and little that went on at the agency escaped her notice, with chiefs and sub-chiefs coming in accompanied by their followers for rations and to trade at her father's store, or when summoned by the agent for council on one or more of the myriad disturbing subjects that constantly were uppermost," the *Oakland Tribune* reported.[10] In the preface to her book, Julia wrote that before she was "old enough to know better," she once asked Fanny "if she thought the Doctor would marry me when she died."[11]

With her sisters, Mamie, Belle, Maud, and Mollie, Julia received her early education at Pine Ridge, learning at the hand of governess Harty Abbott, a graduate of Vassar. While instructing the girls, Abbott became a part of the Blanchard family. Eventually she married an employee in Blanchard's store and moved to Nebraska.[12]

Of necessity, Blanchard was involved in the politics of the reservation, and his daughter became aware of "everything that was common knowledge, besides a bit now and then not known generally."

---

[7]McGillycuddy, *McGillycuddy, Agent,* 274.
[8]Records of the Bureau of the Census, 1880, RG 29, Roll 746, NARS, Washington, D.C.
[9]"On a Sioux Reservation," *Oakland Tribune,* April 6, 1941.
[10]Ibid.
[11]McGillycuddy, *McGillycuddy Agent,* vii.
[12]Ibid.

Through conversations of her father's that she overheard, "she knew of the often recurring threats of outbreaks against white authority. She soon learned that McGillycuddy was peculiarly adroit in preventing all these threatened outbreaks from materializing, through the medium of the Indian police service he had organized, armed, uniformed, and trained."[13]

At eight o'clock in the evening on Tuesday, October 10, 1899, at St. Paul's Church in Fayetteville, Arkansas, Valentine T. McGillycuddy married Julia Blanchard. A daughter was born to the couple on November 11, 1905, and they named her Valentine.[14] Now living in California, McGillycuddy regaled his new family with stories of the early days in the Black Hills and the friends he had made there. In later years Julia would take these stories and others and craft them into the first biography of her husband, *McGillycuddy, Agent,* later reprinted as *Blood on the Moon,* both of which gave detailed information about the agent's early life but were decidedly sympathetic accounts.

The old days weren't left entirely behind them. When Buffalo Bill Cody brought his Wild West show to California, the family visited its Indian camp. Some of the Indians traveling with Cody who had known McGillycuddy during his years as agent at Pine Ridge also visited the Hotel Fairmont, where the McGillycuddys lived in a suite of rooms.[15]

During World War I, McGillycuddy, then nearing seventy, requested an appointment as a surgeon or reconnaissance officer with the War Department. He was turned down because of his age.[16] But he did not give up in his effort to serve the country. In 1917 he wrote to William Garnett, "We are at war now, and I notice that there is talk of raising several regiments of Indian Cavalry[.] [D]o you think, if in case the Government needed Indian soldiers, I would have any influence in getting the young men to enlist, in case I came to the agency for that purpose[?]"[17]

---

[13]Ibid.

[14]E-mail, Dale Gianturco to Candy Moulton, September 8, 2008. The Blanchard family had relocated to Fayetteville, Arkansas, where they became prominent members of the community, as evidenced by many newspaper reports in the *Fayetteville Democrat.* Following their marriage, Julia and Valentine McGillycuddy routinely visited the Blanchards in Arkansas.

[15]Ibid.

[16]McGillycuddy, *McGillycuddy, Agent,* 277.

[17]McGillycuddy to "Friend Garnett," June 7, 1917.

The following year, when a worldwide influenza epidemic killed thousands, McGillycuddy visited Dr. W. C. Billings, chief surgeon of the Public Health Service of the Pacific Coast in San Francisco, and again presented his services as a doctor. Three days later he was offered a position at the quicksilver mines in New Idria in San Benito County, southeast of present San Jose, where the influenza had broken out. Although McGillycuddy had no experience with influenza, he packed a black medical case and boarded a southbound train for his duty station, where he had four nurses to assist him.

Expecting to treat the symptoms of men suffering from influenza, McGillycuddy arrived at the mine to find that other issues were in play. Some union organizers and workers were trying to force the mines to close; troops had been called in to quell any disturbance. When the mine manager learned of McGillycuddy's past experience not only as a doctor but also in mining, he gave him full authority. With both troops and miners suffering from influenza, McGillycuddy asserted firm control. He established a tent hospital and quickly filled forty cots with patients. Then he closed three saloons and ordered members of the Industrial Workers of the World out of the mines.

Whether his remedies had any efficacy or not, the doctor treated the sick men with aconite—the dried root of the monkshood plant—belladonna, and other remedies. These were the same medicines he gave himself when he felt ill with the flu.[18]

As Julia McGillycuddy wrote, in three weeks the epidemic ran its course; the patients either died or recovered. From the mining operation, McGillycuddy went to an oil camp farther south. There he slept in a cold schoolroom and suffered from his own high fever, which he did not reveal to anyone around him.[19] He served in other districts until November, when he returned briefly to San Francisco before receiving orders to travel to Utah, where mining camps were reeling from the influenza outbreak. Although the doctor took out his buffalo coat, sealskin cap, and gloves—garments he had used years before to endure harsh winters in the Dakotas—he left them behind in California when he set out for Utah.[20]

Bells pealed and people hugged both friends and strangers at the train

---

[18]McGillycuddy, *McGillycuddy, Agent*, 280.
[19]Ibid.
[20]Ibid., 281.

station as McGillycuddy waited for his train to Utah. It was chaotic at eleven o'clock on the morning of November 11, 1918. The armistice had been signed, ending World War I and making the day he departed for his medical mission one he would always remember. Once in Utah he proceeded into the Wasatch Mountains and quickly regretted leaving his buffalo coat in California. But he found a heavy coat, some blankets, and a pair of galoshes to keep his feet dry. He was in Utah caring for ill coal miners until after Christmas, when he returned to San Francisco, believing the epidemic had run its course. He resigned from the Public Health Service and resumed his former job.[21]

Less than four months later, his superior from the Public Health Service contacted McGillycuddy and told him that the influenza epidemic had struck Alaska. "Asked how long it would take him to prepare for a trip to the Aleutian Islands, he replied two hours," according to a later article in the *Oakland Tribune*.[22]

Although it might have taken him more than two hours actually to prepare for the trip north, McGillycuddy was soon aboard the U.S. cruiser *Marblehead*. It put in at the port in Seattle for food, medical supplies, and fuel before continuing to Unalaska, in the Aleutian Islands. Using a Coast Guard steamer, the *Unalga*, and a forty-foot gas launch, the *Attoo*, McGillycuddy, by then considered an influenza expert, went to Cape Constantine as the head of a company of twenty-five naval and civilian physicians and trained nurses. There the group found that influenza had already killed many residents.[23] A man from Wood River told the doctor that inland villages had been hard hit by the epidemic, so using the *Attoo*, the medical team struck out toward the village of Igarochauk. The horror and extent of the epidemic were everywhere in the village. The team found many of its residents dead and dogs gone mad from near starvation.

Undaunted, McGillycuddy provided what aid he could. At one igloo he found a dog feeding on a dead man. The husky, feral from hunger, attacked the doctor as he entered the room, sinking its fangs into his left hand. Although seventy by then and frail in appearance, McGillycuddy was still strong. He closed his hand on the dog's jaw and hung on until a naval officer with him could shoot and kill the

---

[21]Ibid., 283–84.
[22]"Liked the Red Man," *Oakland Tribune*, June 11, 1939.
[23]*Fayetteville (Arkansas) Democrat*, July 12, 1919.

canine. Evidence of the attack would stay with him, though; he "bore the teeth marks to his death."[24]

After bandaging his hand, McGillycuddy continued upriver to the next village, which had not been so badly affected by the virulent influenza strain. In Port Haiden, however, there were many more victims, whom the doctor and his companions found and buried.[25]

This work in the native villages must have been among the most difficult McGillycuddy had ever endured, for he "found entire villages wiped out by the plague. In one, a single human—a small boy—lived."[26]

In early July 1919, McGillycuddy returned to California from Alaska.[27] Soon he was granted a license to practice medicine and approved as a member of the California Medical Society. But his years of active medical practice were effectively behind him. His career as a doctor had spanned fifty years, from before he was twenty and treated prostitutes and inmates at a mental institution through a final few weeks of service among the natives of Alaska who suffered in the worldwide influenza epidemic. In between those events, he had cared for frostbitten surveyors working on the Northern Boundary Survey, soldiers fighting in the last battles of the Northern Plains Indian wars, and Lakota warriors, women, children, and chiefs, including the incomparable Crazy Horse and his wife, Black Shawl Woman.

Once again back in California, McGillycuddy became involved in a land development company, Los Verjels Land and Water Company, for which he served as president. The company had seven thousand acres of land with "ample water rights" near Bangor, in the Oroville citrus belt, an area that was particularly well suited for the production of olives, oranges, grapefruits, lemons, figs, English walnuts, and other tree products.[28]

In 1924 McGillycuddy corresponded with former interpreter William Garnett and supported Garnett's request for a pension. In a letter to Edward S. Stewart on April 4, 1924, he made it clear that he was

---

[24]Ibid.

[25]McGillycuddy, *McGillycuddy, Agent,* 287.

[26]*Oakland Tribune,* "Liked the Red Man."

[27]*Fayetteville (Arkansas) Democrat,* July 12, 1919.

[28]Undated letter written by McGillycuddy for Los Verjels Land and Water Company, copy at Fort Robinson Museum Archives.

well connected throughout the West when he wrote, "I am taking the matter up with the Senators of California-Montana-North and South Dakota-Wyoming and Nebraska by personal letter with copy of enclosed statement. Also with Garnetts [*sic*] relatives in Washington, to swing in Virginia influence. I presume that you will care for Colorado."[29]

In 1926 he wrote to Garnett, "They are going to have the fiftieth year anniversary on the Little Bighorn on June 25th, of the Custer fight, and want me to come over. I am not going. I would meet too many Ghosts of my old comrades who were in the campaign of 1876, and too many of the 'sole survivors' who were not there in 1876."[30] He added, "I often feel like making a visit to the old agency, and running over the old ground, but I guess that I would regret it, every thing changed, the old time ones, whites and Indians gone, I wish that the old days could come back."[31]

With decades between his days as Pine Ridge agent and his semi-retirement in California, he told Garnett, "I saw the coming of the changes, and the crowding in of the white man, and it was my duty to prepare the younger Indians for the day coming when they would have to meet the white man at his own game, many of the Indians did not understand me, particularly the older ones, but the young men stood by me, and I never forget it." He said, "You, Billy I shall always remember as the best interpreter we ever had."[32]

"I would like to have got around to Pine Ridge," the doctor told Garnett, "but the same as you I am getting old and it is a long ride, and it would have been lonesome, for nearly all of my old acquaintances are gone, and all that remains is their ghosts that come back to me in my dreams." He admitted, "I suppose I made some mistakes as agent, for I was young, but I did what I at the time thought was best."[33]

And he recalled the man he once considered his nemesis. "If I had been Red Cloud, raised as he was, I expect that I would have tried to raise the devil with the agent."[34]

---

[29]Clark, *Killing of Crazy Horse*, 111–12.
[30]McGillycuddy to Garnett, May 8, 1926, quoted in Clark, *Killing of Crazy Horse*, 117.
[31]McGillycuddy to Garnett, October 3, 1926, quoted in Clark, *Killing of Crazy Horse*, 119.
[32]Ibid., quoted in Clark, *Killing of Crazy Horse*, 120.
[33]McGillycuddy to Garnett, September 30, 1927, quoted in Clark, *Killing of Crazy Horse*, 127.
[34]Ibid., quoted in Clark, *Killing of Crazy Horse*, 128.

Valentine T. McGillycuddy, who had experienced the Northern Plains Indian wars and the great San Francisco earthquake in 1906, lived to see his daughter attend college, earn a degree in architecture, tour Europe, and marry Elio Gianturco, whom she met at the University of California–Berkeley. The couple had three children, daughter Adriana, born in May 1939; son Delio (Dale), born in 1940; and daughter Manuela, born on February 14, 1945—the day that would have been her grandfather's ninety-sixth birthday. But none of Valentine McGillycuddy Gianturco's children ever knew their grandfather. He died on June 6, 1939, just a month after the birth of his eldest granddaughter.[35]

Nor did McGillycuddy see the publication of his wife's book, *McGillycuddy, Agent,* which took place two years after his death.

Knowing that the doctor's love for the Black Hills had never diminished, even though he lived nearly the last four decades of his life far from their rugged beauty, Julia Blanchard McGillycuddy and the doctor's nephew, Trant McGillycuddy, who then lived in Rapid City, South Dakota, arranged for a funeral to be held in November 1939 and for the doctor's cremated remains to be buried on Harney Peak. The ashes were placed in a brass box, and through the cooperation of Black Hills National Forest Supervisor E. A. Snow, of Custer, a crypt was made in a "gigantic boulder at the foot of a new stone fire lookout." The box was placed there in October 1940, bringing McGillycuddy full circle to the place where he had first stood in 1875 as a member of the Walter P. Jenney expedition exploring the Black Hills.

His second wife, Julia, much younger than he, lived until 1950, when she died in Washington, D.C. Their daughter, Valentine McGillycuddy Gianturco, lived in Washington, D.C., and died there on July 16, 1987. Her ashes were scattered in San Francisco Bay, near the city of her birth.[36]

---

[35]E-mail, Dale Gianturco to Candy Moulton, September 8, 2008 (see www.gianturco.it/Gens_Gianturco/Genealogia.html).

[36]Ibid.

Bibliography

ARCHIVAL RESOURCES

Adjutant General's Office. War Department. Records. RG 393. National Archives and Records Service, Washington, D.C.

Agreement with the Sioux of Various Tribes, 1882–1883, January 23, 1883. Digital copy at *www.sioux.org/agreement_of_1883*.

Brennan, John R. Papers. South Dakota State Historical Resource Center, Pierre.

Brown, David. Affidavit, October 7, 1887, Sheridan County, Nebraska. South Dakota State Historical Society Archives, Pierre.

Bureau of Indian Affairs. Records. RG 75. National Archives and Records Service, Washington, D.C.

———. Records of Pine Ridge Agency. RG 75. National Archives and Records Service, Central Plains Region, Kansas City, Missouri.

Camp, Walter M. Papers. Brigham Young University, Provo, Utah.

———. Papers. Denver Public Library, Denver, Colorado.

———. Papers. Lilly Library, University of Indiana, Bloomington.

———. Papers. Fort Robinson Museum, Crawford, Nebraska.

Chase, G. J. (*sic;* should be F.). "The Battle of Slim Buttes," January 26, 1914. Denver Public Library, Denver, Colorado.

Ellison, Robert Spurrier. Papers. Denver Public Library, Denver, Colorado.

Field Notes of Boundary Surveys, 1875. National Archives and Records Service, Washington, D.C. Copy at South Dakota State Historical Resource Center, Pierre.

Fort Robinson General Records. Crawford, Nebraska.

Gianturco, Delio. Papers. Private collection, Falls Church, Virginia.

McGillycuddy, Fanny. Diary, April 11, 1877–October 31, 1878. South Dakota State Historical Resource Center, Pierre.

McGillycuddy, Valentine T. Affidavit, March 2, 1929, sworn in Alameda County, California.

————. Collection. Devereaux Library, South Dakota School of Mines and Technology, Rapid City.

————. "Diary Kept While a Member of the Yellowstone and Big Horn Expedition, May 26–December 13, 1876." Special Library Collections, Harold B. Lee Library, Brigham Young University, Provo, Utah. Transcript at Nebraska State Historical Society, Fort Robinson, Nebraska.

————. Diary, 1879, Pine Ridge Agency. South Dakota State Historical Resource Center, Pierre.

————. Papers. Fort Robinson Museum, Crawford, Nebraska.

————. Papers, 1879–1924. South Dakota State Historical Resource Center, Pierre.

McLaughlin Papers. Denver Public Library.

Mellette, A. C. Papers. South Dakota State Historical Society Archives, Pierre.

Mills, Anson. "Battle of Slim Buttes," January 24, 1941. Walter Camp documents in Robert Spurrier Ellison Papers, Denver Public Library.

Orders and Circulars of the Black Hills Expedition. RG 393. National Archives and Records Service, Washington, D.C.

Ricker, Eli S. Papers. Nebraska State Historical Society, Lincoln.

Stanton, Daniel. Papers. Private collection, Rapid City, South Dakota.

GOVERNMENT DOCUMENTS

Nebraska Legislative Resolution, February 5, 1875. Copy at Fort Robinson Museum, Crawford, Nebraska.

Treaty, 1868, Fort Laramie, Wyoming Territory.

U.S. Commissioner of Indian Affairs. Annual Reports. Washington, D.C.: Interior Department, 1877–1886.

U.S. Congress. House. 48th Cong., 1st sess., Executive Doc. 1, 1884.

U.S. Congress. House. 49th Cong., 1st sess., Report no. 1076.

BOOKS AND ARTICLES

Alexander, Ruth Ann. "Finding Oneself through a Cause: Elaine Goodale Eastman and Indian Reform in the 1880s." *South Dakota History* 22, no. 1 (1992): 56–94.

Behrens, Jo Lea Wetherilt. "In Defense of 'Poor Lo': National Indian Defense Association and *Council Fire's* Advocacy for Sioux Land Rights." *South Dakota History* 24, no. 3 (1994): 153–73.

Bettelyoun, Susan Bordeaux, and Josephine Waggoner. *With My Own Eyes: A Lakota Woman Tells Her People's History.* Lincoln: University of Nebraska Press, 1998.

Bourke, John G. *On the Border with Crook.* New York: Charles Scribner's Sons, 1891. Reprint, Lincoln: University of Nebraska Press, 1971.

Brady, W. M. *The McGillycuddy Papers.* London: Green and Company, 1889.

Bray, Kingsley. *Crazy Horse: A Lakota Life.* Norman: University of Oklahoma Press, 2006.

Brininstool, E. A. "Chief Crazy Horse: His Career and Death," *Nebraska History* 12, no. 1 (1929): 4–78.

———. *Crazy Horse: The Invincible Ogallalla Sioux Chief.* Los Angeles: Wetzel Publishing, 1949.

Brown, Dee. *Bury My Heart at Wounded Knee: An Indian History of the American West.* New York: Holt, Rinehart and Winston, 1971.

Brown, Larry. *The Hog Ranches of Wyoming: Liquor, Lust, and Lies under Sagebrush Skies.* Glendo, Wyo.: High Plains Press, 1995.

Buecker, Thomas R. "'Can You Send Us Immediate Relief?' Army Expeditions to the Northern Black Hills, 1876–1878." *South Dakota History* 25, no. 2 (1995): 95–115.

———. *Fort Robinson and the American West, 1874–1899.* Norman: University of Oklahoma Press, 1999.

———, and R. Eli Paul, eds. *The Crazy Horse Surrender Ledger.* Lincoln: Nebraska State Historical Society, 1994.

Camp, Walter Mason. *Custer and Company: Walter Camp's Notes on the Custer Fight.* Edited by Bruce Liddic and Paul Harbaugh. Lincoln: University of Nebraska Press, 1998.

Campbell, Archibald, and Captain W. J. Twining. *Reports upon the Survey of the Boundary between the Territory of the United States and the Possessions of Great Britain from the Lake of the Woods to the Summit of the Rocky Mountain: Authorized by an Act of Congress Approved March 19, 1872.* United States Northern Boundary Commission, U.S. Department of State. Washington, D.C.: Government Printing Office, 1878.

Clark, Robert A., ed. *The Killing of Chief Crazy Horse: Three Eyewitness Views by the Indian, Chief He Dog, the Indian-White, William Garnett, the White Doctor, Valentine McGillycuddy, with commentary by Carroll Friswold.* Glendale, Calif.: Arthur H. Clark, 1976. Reprint, Lincoln: University of Nebraska Press, 1988.

Colby, Brigadier General L. W. *The Sioux Indian War of 1890–'91.* Transactions and Reports of the Nebraska State Historical Society, vol. 3. Fremont, Neb.: Hammond Brothers, Printers, 1892.

Coleman, William S. *Voices of Wounded Knee.* Lincoln: University of Nebraska Press, 2000.

Crook, George. *General George Crook: His Autobiography.* Norman: University of Oklahoma Press, 1946.

DeBarthe, Joe. *The Life and Adventures of Frank Grouard*. Edited by Edgar I. Stewart. Norman: University of Oklahoma Press, 1958.

DeMallie, Raymond J., ed. *Handbook of North American Indians*, vol. 13, *Plains*. 2 vols. Washington, D.C.: Smithsonian Institution, 2001.

Dodge, Richard Irving. *The Black Hills: A Minute Description of the Routes, Scenery, Soil, Climate, Timber, Gold, Geology, Zoology, Etc. With an Accurate Map, Four Sectional Drawings, and Ten Plates from Photographs, Taken on the Spot*. New York: James Miller, 1875. Reprint, Gretna, La.: Pelican Publishing, 1998.

———. *The Plains of North America and Their Inhabitants*. New York: G. P. Putnam's Sons, 1877. Reprint, Newark: University of Delaware Press, 1989.

Donovan, James. *A Terrible Glory: Custer and the Little Bighorn—The Last Great Battle of the American West*. New York: Little, Brown, 2008.

Doyle, Susan Badger. *Journeys to the Land of Gold*. 2 vols. Helena: Montana Historical Society Press, 2000.

Dunlop, Richard. "Fighting Doctors of the Frontier." *Westerners Brand Book* 20, no. 11 (1964): 81–88. Chicago: Corral of Westerners.

Erisman, Fred, and Patricia L. Erisman. "Letters from the Field: John Sylvanus Loud and the Pine Ridge Campaign of 1890–1891." *South Dakota History* 26, no. 1 (1996): 24–45.

Finerty, John. *War-Path and Bivouac, or, The Conquest of the Sioux: A Narrative of Stirring Personal Experiences and Adventures in the Big Horn and Yellowstone Expedition of 1876, and in the Campaign on the British Border, in 1879*. Chicago: Donohue Brothers, 1890. Reprint, Norman: University of Oklahoma Press, 1961. Digital copy at http://digital.library.wisc.edu/1711 .dl/history.Finerty.

Frost, Lawrence A. *Some Observations on the Yellowstone Expedition of 1873*. Glendale, Calif.: Arthur H. Clark, 1981.

Goodale, Elaine, "Does Civilization Civilize?" *Southern Workman*, December 1885.

———. "Red Cloud and His Agent." *Southern Workman*, April 1886.

Gray, John S. *Centennial Campaign: The Sioux War of 1876*. Fort Collins, Colo.: Old Army Press, 1976.

———. "A Triple Play: John S. Gray Pegs Out Off-Base Myths from John Richard to California Joe to Lonesome Charley Reynolds." *Westerners Brand Book* 26, no. 3 (1969): 17–18. Chicago: Corral of Westerners.

Green, Jerry. *After Wounded Knee*. East Lansing: Michigan State University, 1996.

Greene, First Lieutenant F. V. "Report, June 30, 1876." Chapter 3 in Archibald Campbell and Captain W. J. Twining, *Reports upon the Survey of the*

Boundary between the Territory of the United States and the Possessions of Great Britain. . . . Washington, D.C.: Government Printing Office, 1878.

Greene, Jerome A. *Nez Perce Summer 1877: The U.S. Army and the Nee-Me-Poo Crisis.* Missoula: Montana Historical Society, 2000.

————. *Slim Buttes: An Episode of the Great Sioux War.* Norman: University of Oklahoma Press, 1982.

Grinnell, George B. *The Fighting Cheyennes.* 2nd edition. Norman: University of Oklahoma Press, 1956.

Hammer, Kenneth, ed. *Custer in '76: Walter Camp's Notes on the Custer Fight.* Provo, Utah: Brigham Young University Press, 1976. Reprint, Norman: University of Oklahoma Press, 1990.

Hanson, Margaret Brock. *Frank Grouard, Army Scout.* Mayoworth, Wyo.: Privately published by Margaret Brock, 1983.

Hardorff, Richard G. *The Death of Crazy Horse: A Tragic Episode in Lakota History.* Glendale, Calif.: Arthur H. Clark, 1998. Reprint, Lincoln: University of Nebraska Press, 2001.

Hassrick, Royal B. *The Sioux: Life and Customs of a Warrior Society.* Norman: University of Oklahoma Press, 1964.

Hebard, Grace Raymond, and E. A. Brininstool. *The Bozeman Trail.* Cleveland: Arthur H. Clark, 1922. Reprint, Lincoln: University of Nebraska Press, 1990.

Hedren, Paul L. *Fort Laramie and the Great Sioux War.* Norman: University of Oklahoma Press, 1998. Original published under the title *Fort Laramie in 1876: Chronicle of a Frontier Post at War.* Lincoln: University of Nebraska Press, 1988.

————. *Traveler's Guide to the Great Sioux War: The Battlefields, Forts, and Related Sites of American's Greatest Indian War.* Helena: Montana Historical Society Press, 1996.

————. *With Crook in the Black Hills: Stanley J. Morrow's 1876 Photographic Legacy.* Boulder, Colo.: Pruett, 1985.

Heitman, Francis B. *Historical Register and Dictionary of the United States Army, 1789–1903,* vol. 1. Washington, D.C.: Government Printing Office, 1903.

Hinman, Eleanor H. "Oglala Sources on the Life of Crazy Horse." *Nebraska History,* Spring 1976, 31.

Hoover, Herbert T. "The Sioux Agreement of 1889 and Its Aftermath." *South Dakota History* 19, no. 1 (1989): 56–94.

Hulston, Nancy J. "Federal Children: Indian Education and the Red Cloud–McGillycuddy Conflict." *South Dakota History* 25, no. 2 (1995): 81–94.

Hutton, Paul Andrew, ed. *The Custer Reader.* Lincoln: University of Nebraska Press, 1992.

Hyde, George E. *Red Cloud's Folk: A History of the Oglala Sioux Indians.* Norman: University of Oklahoma Press, 1937.

——. *A Sioux Chronicle.* Norman: University of Oklahoma Press, 1956.

——. *Spotted Tail's Folk: A History of the Brulé Sioux.* Norman: University of Oklahoma Press, 1961.

Jackson, Donald. *Custer's Gold: The United States Cavalry Expedition of 1874.* New York: Bobbs-Merrill, 1934. Reprint, Lincoln: University of Nebraska Press, 1972.

Jenney, W. P. *U.S. Geological and Geographical Survey of the Black Hills.* Washington, D.C.: Government Printing Office, 1875.

Jensen, Richard E. *The Indian Interviews of Eli S. Ricker, 1903–1919,* vol. 1. Lincoln: University of Nebraska Press, 2005.

——. "Introduction." In *From Fort Laramie to Wounded Knee: In the West that Was.* by Charles W. Allen. Lincoln: University of Nebraska Press, 1997.

——. *The Settler and Soldier Interviews of Eli S. Ricker, 1903–1919.* Lincoln: University of Nebraska Press, 2005.

Johnson, Barry C. "Reno as Escort Commander." *Westerners Brand Book* 29, no. 7 (1972): 53–55. Chicago: Corral of Westerners.

Josephy, Alvin. *The Nez Perce Indians and the Opening of the Northwest.* New Haven, Conn.: Yale University Press, 1965. Reprint, New York: Houghton Mifflin, 1997.

Kappler, Charles J., comp. and ed. *Indian Affairs: Laws and Treaties.* 2 vols. Washington, D.C.: Government Printing Office, 1904.

Kime, Wayne R., ed. *The Black Hills Journals of Colonel Richard Irving Dodge.* Norman: University of Oklahoma Press, 1996.

King, Charles. *Campaigning with Crook.* Norman: University of Oklahoma Press, 1964.

Kutac, C. "He Saw Troopers Die; He Saw Indians Die; He Was Valentine McGillycuddy, Who Understood Hurt." *Frontier Times,* May 1980, pp. 18, 19, 50–52.

Larson, Robert W. *Gall: Lakota War Chief.* Norman: University of Oklahoma Press, 2007.

——. *Red Cloud: Warrior-Statesman of the Lakota Sioux.* Norman: University of Oklahoma Press, 1997.

Lee, Lucy W. "Recollections." *Nebraska History* 12, no. 1 (1929): 52.

Lemley, H. R. "The Passing of Crazy Horse." *Journal of the Military Service Institute of the United States* 54 (1914). www.arlingtoncemetery.net/hrlemly.htm

——. *Vanishing Victory: Custer's Final March.* El Segundo, Calif.: Upton and Sons, 2004.

Lindmier, Thomas. *Drybone: A History of Fort Fetterman, Wyoming.* Glendo, Wyo.: High Plains Press, 2002.

Lubetkin, John. *Jay Cooke's Gamble.* Norman: University of Oklahoma Press, 2006.

Ludlow, William. *Report of a Reconnaissance of the Black Hills of Dakota, Made in the Summer of 1874.* Washington, D.C.: Government Printing Office, 1875.

Mansfield, J. B., ed. *History of the Great Lakes,* vol. 1. Chicago: J. H. Beers, 1899. Reprint, Halton Hills, Ontario, Canada: Maritime History of the Great Lakes, 2003. Digital copy at http://www.halinet .on.ca/GreatLakes/Documents/HGL/.

Marshall, Joseph M. III. *The Journey of Crazy Horse: A Lakota History.* New York: Viking, 2004.

McDermott, John D. *A Guide to the Indian Wars of the West.* Lincoln: University of Nebraska Press, 1998.

McGillycuddy, Julia B. *McGillycuddy, Agent.* Stanford, Calif.: Stanford University Press, 1941. Reprinted under the title *Blood on the Moon.* Lincoln: University of Nebraska Press, 1990.

McGillycuddy, V. T. "First Survey of the Black Hills." *Motor Travel,* September 1928. Copy at Devereaux Library, South Dakota School of Mines and Technology, Rapid City, Valentine T. McGillycuddy Collection, Box 2.

McLaird, James D. *Calamity Jane: The Woman and the Legend.* Norman: University of Oklahoma Press, 2005.

———, and Lesta V. Turchen. "Exploring the Black Hills, 1855–1875: Reports of the Government Expeditions. Colonel William Ludlow and the Custer Expedition, 1874." *South Dakota History* 4, no. 3 (1974): 403–38.

Miller, Don. "Pine Ridge Standoff." *Real West* 24, no. 178 (1981): 10–13, 52.

Milner, Joe E., and Earle R. Forrest. *California Joe: Noted Scout and Indian Fighter.* Caldwell, Idaho: Caxton Printers, 1935.

Monnett, John H. *Tell Them We Are Going Home: The Odyssey of the Northern Cheyennes.* Norman: University of Oklahoma Press, 2001.

Mooney, James L. *The Ghost-Dance Religion and the Sioux Outbreak of 1890.* Fourteenth Annual Report of the Bureau of Ethnology, Part 2. Washington, D.C.: Government Printing Office, 1896. Reprint, Chicago: University of Chicago Press, 1965.

Moquin, Wayne, with Charles Van Doren, eds. *Great Documents in American Indian History.* New York: Praeger, 1973.

Moulton, Candy. *Chief Joseph: Guardian of the People.* New York: Forge Books, 2005.

———. "Jerry Keenan Keen on Luther Kelly." *Wild West,* December 2007, pp. 14–16.

————. *Roadside History of Wyoming.* Missoula, Mont.: Mountain Press, 1995.

Nebraska State Historical Society. *Transactions and Reports,* vol. 4. Lincoln: State Journal Company, Printers, 1892.

Newton, Henry, and W. P. Jenney. *Report on the Geology and Resources of the Black Hills of Dakota, with Atlas.* Geographical and Geological Survey of the Rocky Mountain Region, U.S. Department of the Interior. Washington, D.C.: Government Printing Office, 1880.

Niehardt, John G. *Black Elk Speaks.* New York: Morrow, 1932. Reprint, Lincoln: University of Nebraska Press, 1961. Reprint, New York: Pocket Books, 1975.

Olson, James. *Red Cloud and the Sioux Problem.* Lincoln: University of Nebraska Press, 1965.

Paul, R. Eli, ed. *Autobiography of Red Cloud, War Leader of the Oglalas.* Helena: Montana Historical Society Press, 1997.

————. *The Nebraska Indian Wars Reader 1865–1877.* Lincoln: University of Nebraska Press, 1998.

Paulson, Howard W. "The Allotment of Land in Severalty to the Dakota Indians before the Dawes Act." *South Dakota History* 1, no. 2 (1971).

Phillips, George H. "The Indian Ring in Dakota Territory, 1870–1890." *South Dakota History* 2, no. 4 (1972): 345–76.

Prucha, Francis P. *American Indian Policy in Crisis.* Norman: University of Oklahoma Press, 1976.

————. *Documents of United States Indian Policy.* 3rd edition. Lincoln: University of Nebraska Press, 2000.

Rees, Tony. *Arc of the Medicine Line.* Lincoln: University of Nebraska Press, 2007.

Robinson, Charles M. III. *The Diaries of John Gregory Bourke,* vol. 1, *November 20, 1872–July 28, 1876.* Denton: University of North Texas Press, 2003.

————. *General Crook and the Western Frontier.* Norman: University of Oklahoma Press, 2001.

Sandoz, Mari. *Crazy Horse: The Strange Man of the Oglalas.* New York: A. A. Knopf, 1942. Reprint, Lincoln: University of Nebraska Press, 1992.

Schell, Herbert S. *History of South Dakota.* Lincoln: University of Nebraska Press, 1975.

Schubert, Frank N. *Outpost of the Sioux Wars: A History of Fort Robinson.* Lincoln: University of Nebraska Press, 1995.

Shaefer, Jack. *Heroes without Glory: Some Good Men of the Old West.* Boston: Houghton Mifflin, 1965.

Smith, Shannon. *Give Me Eighty Men: Women and the Myth of the Fetterman Fight.* Lincoln: University of Nebraska Press, 2008.

Spring, Agnes Wright. "Dr. McGillycuddy's Diary." *Westerner's Brand Book* 9 (1953): 277–307. Denver: Corral of Westerners.

Stewart, Edgar I. *Custer's Luck*. Norman: University of Oklahoma Press, 1980.

Stymiest, Ruth Anne. *Centennial: An Illustrated History 1885–1985*. Rapid City: South Dakota School of Mines and Technology, 1985.

Thrapp, Dan. *Encyclopedia of Frontier Biography*, vols. 1–3. Glendale, Calif.: Arthur H. Clark, 1988.

———. *Encyclopedia of Frontier Biography*, vol. 4, *Supplement*. Spokane, Wash.: Arthur H. Clark, 1994.

Turchen, Lesta Van Der Wert, and James D. McLaird. *The Black Hills Expedition of 1875*. Mitchell, S.D.: Wesleyan University Press, 1975.

Utley, Robert M. *Cavalier in Buckskin: George Armstrong Custer and the Western Military Frontier*. Norman: University of Oklahoma, 1988.

———. *The Indian Frontier 1846–1890*. Revised edition. Albuquerque: University of New Mexico Press, 2003.

———. *The Lance and the Shield: The Life and Times of Sitting Bull*. New York: Henry Holt, 1993.

———. *The Last Days of the Sioux Nation*. New Haven, Conn.: Yale University Press, 1963.

———. "The Little Big Horn." In *The Custer Reader*, edited by P. A. Hutton, pp. 239–56. Lincoln: University of Nebraska Press, 1992.

Vaughn, J. W. *The Battle of Platte Bridge*. Norman: University of Oklahoma Press, 1963.

———. *With Crook at the Rosebud*. Harrisburg, Pa.: Stackpole, 1956. Reprint, Lincoln: University of Nebraska Press, 1988.

Vestal, Stanley. *New Sources of Indian History, 1850–1891: The Ghost Dance—The Prairie Sioux; a Miscellany*. Norman: University of Oklahoma Press, 1934.

Watson, Elmo Scott. "Crazy Horse, Fighting Chief of the Sioux." *Crawford (Nebraska) Tribune*, September 4, 1934.

Worster, Donald. *A River Running West: The Life of John Wesley Powell*. New York: Oxford University Press, 2001.

Index